ARCHAEOLOGY
An Introduction

The Arch of Hadrian, Athens, with the temple of Jupiter (Olympeion) beyond, which Hadrian completed in the early second century AD, demonstrating his informed enthusiasm for ancient Greek culture and architecture. The engraving was made in the late eighteenth century by Stuart and Revett (vol. III, Ch. III, pl. I).

ARCHAEOLOGY
An Introduction

The History, Principles and Methods of Modern Archaeology

Kevin Greene

B.T. Batsford Ltd London

First published 1983

© Kevin Greene, 1983

ISBN 0 7134 3645 X (cased)
      0 7134 3646 8 (limp)

Filmset by Servis Filmsetting Ltd,
Manchester
Printed in Great Britain by
The Anchor Press Ltd,
Tiptree, Essex
for the Publishers
Batsford Academic and Educational
a division of B.T. Batsford Ltd
4 Fitzhardinge Street, London W1H 0AH

Contents

List of Illustrations

ACKNOWLEDGEMENTS

I have received help from a large number of individuals and institutions in Britain and abroad, particularly in obtaining illustrations. They include Prof. L. Alcock; Bodleian Library, Oxford; Prof. R. Braidwood; British Film Institute; British Museum; Cowen Library, Dept. of Archaeology, University of Newcastle upon Tyne; Charles Daniels; Dr R. Dennel; Deutsche Staatsbibliothek, Berlin; Dr P. Echlin; Dr J. Évin; Prof. K. Flannery; Dr R. Funk; Hancock Museum, University of Newcastle upon Tyne; Dr E. Harris; Dr I. Hodder; Prof. F. Hole; Library, University of Newcastle upon Tyne; Prof. J. Michels; Museum of Antiquities, University of Newcastle upon Tyne; National Museum, Copenhagen; National Portrait Gallery, London; Pitt Rivers Museum, Oxford; Prof. C. Renfrew; Dr W. Rodwell; Römisch-Germanisches Museum, Cologne; Salisbury and South Wiltshire Museum; Dr M. Schvoerer; Dr I. Scollar; Dr A. Sherratt; Smithsonian Institute, Washington; Society of Antiquaries, London; Dr D. Tarling; Rheinisches Landesmuseum, Trier; and D.R. Wilson, Committee for Aerial Photography, University of Cambridge.

Most of the diagrams have been adapted or designed and drawn by Ian Munro of the Audio Visual Centre, University of Newcastle upon Tyne, whilst prints of many other illustrations were prepared by the Centre's photographic section or the Library Photographic Service of Newcastle University. Several students and colleagues have read and commented on all or parts of my text, notably David Boyson, Joanna Rowley, and Dr John Chapman; I am particularly grateful to Caroleen McClure, librarian to the John Cowen Library of the Department of Archaeology, for not only critically reading the text but providing much general assistance in bibliographical matters. My wife Julia has helped me considerably with proof-reading and indexing.

Further gratitude may be extended to the less definable influences absorbed during my archaeological education and research at University College, Cardiff, from 1966–73, and subsequently to my colleagues and students in the Departments of Adult Education and Archaeology here in the University of Newcastle upon Tyne.

Kevin Greene
Newcastle upon Tyne, March 1982

NOTE ON REFERENCES

References to publications made in the text are given in author/year form (e.g. Evans 1860) and are listed in alphabetical order by authors' names in the consolidated bibliography at the end of the book. At the end of each chapter is a guide to further reading, including some basic works relating to the particular themes of the individual chapters; these are also included in the consolidated bibliography. A few very general books are listed below.

BACKGROUND READING

This book cannot provide any kind of general outline of the various prehistoric and historical periods to which it occasionally refers, nor can it always fully explain each technical term the first time it is mentioned. Two very recent books should solve most of these problems – *The Cambridge Encyclopedia of Archaeology*, edited by Andrew Sherratt (1980), and Sara Champion's *Dictionary of Terms and Techniques in Archaeology*, 1980. The third edition of Grahame Clark's *World Prehistory* (1977) is comprehensive and in fact covers many early historical periods as well as prehistory. Also highly informative are a number of collections of archaeological articles from *Scientific American*, notably *Avenues to Antiquity*, 1976. The periodical *Antiquity* contains short articles on a wide range of archaeological sites, theories, and current issues, as well as an entertaining editorial by Prof. Glyn Daniel.

Preface

Much of our knowledge of archaeology or any other subject is based upon assumptions which are often far from secure, but are rarely discussed. Theories are produced by scholars; they may be gradually modified by long discussion and criticism, dramatically overthrown by a single new idea or piece of evidence, or simply go out of fashion for no particularly obvious reason. To people not directly involved, the vision of a subject suddenly reversing its ideas is disconcerting, especially if they have gone through a traditional education based upon the learning of 'facts' which lead to 'right' answers. There is a natural tendency either to reject new ideas, or to embrace them enthusiastically, for reasons that are often emotional rather than intellectual. A more sinister reaction is to jump at revolutionary new theories from outside the academic world, which today often seem to involve extra-terrestrial influences upon mankind, and dismiss academic 'experts' as reactionary snobs unwilling to consider anything new, especially if it is proposed by anyone outside their ivory towers.

It is my contention that there is another way of looking at the shifting body of archaeological evidence, particularly in the last quarter of the twentieth century when changes in thinking are accelerating at a previously unparalleled rate. The most sensible approach is not simply to try and keep up with the latest opinions, but to understand how they have been arrived at. It takes a certain amount of courage to accept that there are no 'true' answers, and that all interpretations are based upon assumptions of greater or lesser probability, not certainty. I believe that the result is a much more stimulating approach to archaeology; instead of having to decide whether a new interpretation is 'right', the reader can analyse it quite simply – how did the archaeologist reach his conclusion? what

kind of evidence was involved? what are the assumptions upon which it is based? The later chapters of this book are an attempt to explain the sources of information from which the assumptions and interpretations are derived, by showing how the basic evidence is recovered and studied.

However, I also feel that the workings of archaeology today are more easily understood in a historical context. Hindsight illuminates the links between early writers and the development of their thinking; it also shows how influences from other disciplines – natural history, geology, anthropology, philosophy, and political theory – entered archaeology and contributed to the body of basic assumptions upon which their interpretations of the past were based. The essential stages in the development of modern archaeology have taken many centuries to complete, but throughout this time two factors have been consistently important, and retain their significance for the present and future. The first is the imaginative thinking of a long succession of individuals who have not shrunk from standing back from accepted opinions and procedures, and reassessing their value; the second is the immense contribution made by other fields of learning which have shed new and often unexpected light on the remains of the past, from which yet more – and better informed – interpretations can be formulated.

This book is aimed at beginners in archaeology or non-specialists with a passing aquaintance of the subject derived perhaps from television programmes or general reading; the contents are of course selective, and no two archaeologists would ever make the same selection. I have been guided by those aspects of the subject which I personally find interesting and useful, and by questions which have frequently been raised by students during Adult Education classes on various archaeological periods. More recently, I have had the difficult task of teaching a course entitled 'Introduction to Archaeology' to first-year students in the University of Newcastle upon Tyne, whose ranks include not only honours archaeology students, but Arts and Science students taking it as part of a more general degree, and subsidiary students from other honours department such as History and Geography, or (more rarely) less obviously related subjects ranging from Psychology to Music. It is certainly true that you cannot please all of the people all of the time; this book is ultimately derived from what I felt this mix of students *ought* to know about archaeology, modified by what they could be expected to understand or tolerate. I often wondered during the last few years why so few writers had attempted to write simple general introductions to archaeology since the 1960s – now I know the answer. If this book helps to guide sixth-formers/undergraduates/adult students/general readers through the inner workings of the subject, which has suffered from an 'information explosion' along with most other academic disciplines in recent decades, it will have achieved its purpose.

The book has been influenced more or less directly by a number of individuals: Prof. R.J.C. Atkinson, and his Department of Archaeology in University College, Cardiff; Prof. Glyn Daniel, and his historical studies of archaeology, to which my debt will be apparent throughout this book; Graham Webster, archaeology's leading 'adult educator'; and Prof. George Jobey, sympathetic colleague and fellow first-year teacher here in Newcastle upon Tyne, where the Department of Archaeology has provided much support in this venture.

1 The Idea of the Past

The assumptions which early antiquaries made about the past and the concepts within which they framed their writings can seem pitifully naïve today. When in the early nineteenth century Danish scholars first organized prehistoric objects into three successive 'Ages' (Stone, Bronze and Iron), they were content to set these Ages into a time-span which began in 4004 BC – the date of the creation of the Earth calculated from the Book of Genesis by seventeenth-century theologians. The much longer time scale demanded by geology and evolution did not break through the biblical scheme until the 1860s. However, such major reorientations did not end in the nineteenth century; the dating of prehistoric man has undergone two major revisions since the Second World War, first as the radiocarbon dating technique was introduced and accepted, and later as further research demanded a revision and recalibration of its results. Some of today's most convincing interpretations of the past will undoubtedly require comparable re-examination as more sites are excavated, dating techniques are improved, and new ideas are devised. The lesson to be learned from the history of archaeology is clear; we can only work within the limitations of the best available assumptions, and these are liable to unpredictable changes. Little can be gained from treating older research as simply redundant and sometimes humorous; we can learn a great deal of value by examining the way in which early antiquaries and archaeologists tackled the formidable problem of making sense of man's past without most of the libraries, museums, travel and technical facilities which are available today. From this point of view, a study of their work will result in admiration, not amusement.

THE AWARENESS OF MAN'S ORIGINS

An interest in origins must be an early aspect of human consciousness. Even amongst the most primitive peoples, the phenomenon of death naturally gives rise to reflections on afterlife or rebirth, and can be detected by archaeologists in the form of special attention to burial rites as early as the Old Stone Age (Leakey & Lewin 1977, 125–8). Most societies develop sophisticated mythologies to explain their origins, which often contain a notion of change, frequently in the form of a decline from some former Golden Age rather than advance from a more primitive state. In association with religion, the whole environment may be fitted into an orderly system in which major natural features may be the work of gods, whilst artificial mounds, abandoned occupation sites and ancient objects can be associated with deities, fairies, ancestors or other denizens of the world of mythology. Traces of such explanations abound in surviving folklore; an awareness of the physical remains of the past and attempts to explain them thus seem to be fairly basic human characteristics, and are the origins of the present disciplines of archaeology and history. However, the development of any kind of archaeological thinking similar to our own belongs to very recent centuries.

Collections of ancient curios and works of art were not uncommon in the Ancient World, from Babylon in the sixth century BC, through the civilizations of Greece and Rome, and more sporadically through the medieval period to the Renaissance. In the first century AD, Roman poetry and Chinese tradition contained ideas about the successive importance of stone, bronze and iron, 1800 years before the Three-Age System was proposed; but these ideas were not applied to the past in any historical sense. Greek travellers wrote accounts of peoples whose life-styles were obviously more primitive than their own, but more out of curiosity than in an attempt to understand the development of their own societies. It is difficult now for us to appreciate fully the basic problem which confronted historians or philosophers in literate societies right up to the eighteenth century; they could follow their societies back as far as written records existed, but before that lay a complete void, full of unverifiable traditions which merged into a mythological and religious world of ancestors, gods, and some form of creation. Most conspicuously lacking was any concept of the *depth* of time. Up until the mid-nineteenth century, historians saw no difficulty in compressing the period before written records into the biblical timescale which began in 4004 BC – indeed, the propositions of geology and evolution which demanded an almost unimaginable length of time were fiercely contested. Even today, the depth of archaeological and geological time is underestimated in the contemporary mythological world of the cinema and cartoons. An array of long-extinct monsters confronted a physically evolved but still grunting Raquel Welch in the film *One Million Years BC* (fig. 1), and no cartoon-strip prehistoric man is complete without his club, animal skin, stone wheel and pet dinosaur.

This basic problem for historians and antiquarians did not really change from the Greek and Roman period until the eighteenth century and later. The only possible basis for the study of sites and artefacts was to link them with past peoples and events known from documents, or virtually to dismiss them into the unknown void. Samuel Johnson stated: 'All that is really known of the ancient state of Britain is contained in a few pages. . . . We can know no more than what old writers have told us.' Historians of the middle ages like Geoffrey of Monmouth (died *c.* 1155) filled out early periods with fantastic tales of mythological and real figures like Brutus the Trojan, King Arthur, and Julius Caesar. The only real difference between Geoffrey and the 'enlightened' historians of the eighteenth century was in the quantity of

mythology which might be accepted; the later writers tended to associate earthworks with Romans or Danes rather than Trojans or Druids. The ability to give depth to prehistory was still absent, although a greater understanding of the ways of life of the Ancient Britons described by Julius Caesar and their forebears could be gained from reports of the various 'savages' encountered in Africa and the Americas, whilst ancient European artefacts could be compared with those still in use in primitive societies.

PREHISTORY AND HISTORY

Archaeologists today tend to be divided into two categories – prehistorians or historical archaeologists. The division is neither particularly real nor helpful, but simply distinguishes those whose work involves the study of people or places within periods during which written records were made from those concerned with any period before the use of such documents. Their methods are much the same, but whereas the historical archaeologist usually has a basic framework of dates and some general idea of the life and society of a particular period into which to fit his findings, the prehistorian has to create some kind of framework from his artefacts and sites alone. There is a considerable overlap between their ideas and interests, and many of today's better scholars happily cross the boundaries between the two kinds of archaeology. In the past, however, there was a distinct difference between the ancient historian, classicist, or biblical scholar who set out to locate physical traces on the ground of the familiar events and civilizations described in his literature, and the historian, natural scientist, or plain collector who tried to make sense of the totally undocumented tools, pots, graves and dwellings which obviously stretched back into times before the earliest surviving written records. If such a 'prehistorian' believed in the biblical Creation in 4004 BC, at least there was an upper time limit to the age of any of these items. But if he did not, the possibilities were endless, and at first sight insoluble. Which of the different sites and objects were in use at the same time, and how many years elapsed between

those which looked primitive and those which seemed more advanced? Did technical improvements represent the gradual series of inventions of a single people, or did innovations mark the arrival of successive waves of conquerors with superior skills? Even today questions like these cannot always be answered – once more we are forced to admire those individuals who first seriously attempted to organise and measure the dark void before the written word, without any of the theoretical, technical, or scientific knowledge which is available to every archaeologist today. Their work established the antiquity of man.

THE ANTIQUITY OF MAN

The Society of Antiquaries of London was founded in 1717, and from 1770 published an impressive periodical, *Archaeologia*, whose style and format have changed little up to the present day. In 1800 it included a minor item of which the full significance was not to emerge for sixty years – a letter from **John Frere**, of Norfolk, drawing the members' attention to observations which he made in a clay pit at Hoxne, Suffolk. He reported the finding of flint weapons at a depth of twelve feet in a layer of gravel *overlain* by a bed of sand containing bones of extinct animals and, remarkably, shells and remains of marine creatures, '. . . which may be conjectured to have been once the bottom, or at least the shore, of the sea'. Frere was conscious of the implications of this: 'It may be conjectured that the different strata were formed by inundations happening at distant periods. . . .

1 In *One Million Years BC* (Hammer Films Ltd, 1968), Raquel Welch was surrounded by dinosaurs, volcanoes and equally ferocious savages. Current research suggests that the successful development of humans at this date relied on increasingly sophisticated language and craftsmanship, together with social co-operation rather than conflict (e.g. Leakey & Lewin 1977, 207–37). Only the film industry includes long-extinct creatures amongst the influences on early hominid development. *National Film Archive*

The situation in which these weapons were found may tempt us to refer them to a very remote period indeed; even beyond that of the present world . . .' (1800, 205). References to the biblical Creation and Flood are conspicuous by their absence: cracks were appearing in the foundations of the assumptions of centuries.

Frere's letter attracted little attention, but finds of human bones and artefacts associated with extinct animals were noted with growing frequency in Europe in the early nineteenth century – and were as often explained away by theologians as accidental. In addition geologists were beginning to be divided by the heretical idea that gravel layers and sedimentary rocks were formed slowly over a considerable period of time by the same processes of erosion and deposition by weather and water which were observable in the modern world, rather than by the catastrophic floods of the Book of Genesis. The new ideas of the antiquaries and geologists gradually converged, until the biblical edifice was finally toppled soon after the middle of the nineteenth century.

By the time of Frere's death in 1807 a key figure was already becoming interested in archaeology in France: **Boucher de Perthes** (fig. 2) spent many years studying the gravel quarries of northern France, and was a strong advocate of two ideas. First, he was impressed by the great depth of fine and coarse deposits of sediments, and felt that they were far too varied to result from biblical floods, although he did not explicitly reject the authority of the Old Testament. Second, he fought hard to convince contemporaries that the various axes and other flint tools which he had collected were in fact made by man, and could be recognized by their artificial shaping (fig. 3). It was an uphill struggle – he commented that 'at the very mention of the words "axe" and "diluvium", I observe a smile on the face of those to whom I speak. It is the workmen who help me, not the geologists.' His two interests came together in the fact that he was able to prove that these tools actually came from within the ancient gravel beds, and that man had existed before what he described as 'the cataclysm that gave our country its present configuration'; man was

2 Jacques Boucher de Perthes, portrayed by Grèvedon in 1831. Boucher de Perthes, it seems, was not a pleasant man; the adjectives 'silly' and 'bombastic' have been used to describe him. He had inherited many of his ideas about artefacts and their stratification from Casimir Picard, who had published notes on them from the 1830s, and whose main findings were taken over by Perthes without acknowledgement in one of his own books in 1847. 'Few people took his book seriously; of those who had met him, none' (Evans, 1956, 282). Despite his vanity, Perthes' central idea of the great age of man-made artefacts in the gravels of northern France was fully supported by independent observations in 1859. *Print: Society of Antiquaries, London*

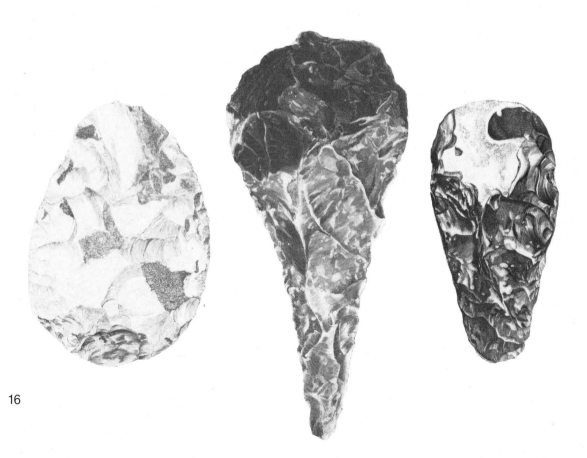

therefore also contemporary with a wide range of extinct animals. The Creation in 4004 BC was unthinkable, of course; Boucher de Perthes did not abandon the Flood, however, but suggested that it must have preceded the 'gradual' cataclysm whose results he observed. 'Let us not bargain over the duration of ages; let us believe that the days of the creation, those days that began before our sun, were the days of God, the interminable days of the world. Let us remember, finally, that for this eternal God a thousand centuries are no more than one second. . . .' Not only was the Earth now very ancient, but man too was being drawn back into a void of seemingly immeasurable depth.

Not all geologists treated Boucher de Perthes' work with disbelief and amusement. An English geologist, Joseph Prestwich, organized a visit to meet him and see the celebrated gravel pits together with an authority on ancient implements, John Evans (fig. 4). On 1 May 1859 they were rewarded with the opportunity of seeing a flint axe still firmly embedded in an ancient gravel bed, and any remaining doubts were fully removed. Before May was out, Prestwich read an account of their observations to the Royal Society, and a summary appeared in print in 1860. At this point, the wheel turned full circle, as Prestwich referred back to John Frere's letter published in 1800, and pointed out that his observations were in complete agreement with the new findings from France.

3 Flint implements from the Somme valley, published by John Evans soon after his visit to the sites in northern France where they were found. 'That they really are implements fashioned by the hand of man, a single glance at a collection of them placed side by side . . . would, I think, be sufficient to convince even the most sceptical. There is a uniformity of shape, a correctness of outline, and a sharpness about the cutting edges and points, which cannot be due to anything but design' (Evans 1860, 288). The 'hand axe' (centre) is c. 17cm long. *Evans 1860, pl. 15, facing p. 291*

Catastrophists and Fluvialists

In some ways, the recognition of the truth of the finding of flint axes in association with bones of extinct animals created greater problems for geologists and historians – how long ago did these men and animals live? Prestwich's own words reveal the predicament:

The author does not, however, consider that the facts, as they at present stand, of necessity carry back Man in past time more than they bring forward the great extinct Mammals towards our own time, the evidence having reference only to relative and not to absolute time; and he is of the opinion that many of the later geological changes may have been sudden or of shorter duration than generally considered. In fact, from the evidence here exhibited . . . the author sees no reason against the conclusion that this period of Man and the extinct Mammals . . . was brought to a sudden end by a temporary inundation of the land (Prestwich 1860, 58).

Thus in the 1860s, despite the passing from belief of the Creation in 4004 BC and the Great Flood of the Bible, the idea of sudden 'catastrophes' causing the formation of geological deposits had still not departed. But against these 'catastrophists', a rival school of thought was gaining ground. In the 1830s Sir Charles Lyell (1777–1875) had published a series of books entitled *Principles of Geology* which firmly asserted that the great depths of gravel, sand and clay deposits could only have been created by the same processes which could be seen in operation in present times; great floods were not admissible to this 'fluvialist' way of thinking. It must not be forgotten that more and more exposures of such deposits were becoming available to geologists as canals, railway cuttings, and quarries were required to support the growth of the Industrial Revolution at this time. Thus, a side effect of economic development influenced the science of geology, and 'fluvialist' geology in its turn held great implications for the interpretation of early human tools and weapons. If the levels observed by Frere and Boucher de Perthes were really laid down by the slow processes of erosion by wind and water, and gradually deposited by rivers and oceans, an immense length of time must be involved. It could not be measured, but,

unlike mysterious catastrophic floods, it could be sensed and visualized. During this period, finds of human bones as well as stone tools were being found in early geological deposits with growing frequency in many parts of Europe. From the Neander Valley in Germany came a skeleton which was initially dismissed as that of a deformed modern man, but eventually gave its name to a familiar stage of hominid development – Neanderthal Man. In 1863, Lyell finally brought the 'new' geology and archaeology together in his book *The Geological Evidences of the Antiquity of Man*.

This new appreciation of the depth of time was not only limited to geology and archaeology. Perhaps the most famous scientific development of the nineteenth century – Darwin's theory of evolution put forward in *The Origin of Species by Means of Natural Selection* (1859) – demanded exactly the same kind of thinking. Science then was not divided up into such small specialized compartments as it is today, and Darwin would have been well aware of the implications of the geological thinking, which had been developing since the late eighteenth century. Both he and the geologists demanded the acceptance of the same concept – that the present surface of the Earth, and the

plants and animals (including Man) which inhabited it were the results of an immense period of very gradual changes. The slow development and remarkably recent acceptance of any clear concept of the 'Antiquity of Man' has been described here to illustrate the way in which progress could only be made by gradually changing whatever general explanations prevailed at the time, and the resistance that was usually offered to any new ideas. A steady confident approach was needed by individuals who could look at new evidence in a scientific manner and think out its implications, rather than simply knocking it into whatever shape fitted least offensively into the existing framework of ideas; this attitude is just as necessary today as it ever has been in the past.

The antiquity of man was the most important single idea which had to be established before archaeology could develop into its modern form, but it was far from being the only or even the first field of study. Archaeology is still essentially concerned with sites and objects – the physical remains of past human activity – and the growth of interest in these, sheds further light upon the basic principles which underlie the work of modern archaeologists. Considerable progress in setting these tangible remains into some meaningful context had been made since the sixteenth century, with the help of such pursuits as travel, the collecting of curios, and the anthropological information which filtered back to Europe after the discovery of the New World around AD 1500.

Speculation about the past was not uncommon in the Ancient World, particularly amongst the Greeks and Romans. Anthropology (rather than archaeology) was prominent in Greece, where intense interest in their own society and political system probably led men such as Poseidonius and Herodotus to travel amongst primitive 'barbarian' (i.e. non-Greek speaking) peoples like the heavy drinking, head-hunting Celts; their observations of institutions, customs, and general way of life can still earn the respect of twentieth century anthropologists. These travellers may have felt that an understanding of other peoples would give

4 John Evans (1823–1908) combined a busy life in the paper industry with interests in geology and the collection and study of ancient coins and artefacts. In 1859 he visited the gravel pits in northern France where Boucher de Perthes claimed to find flint axes in deep deposits together with bones of extinct animals; Evans, and geologist Joseph Prestwich, were convinced of the authenticity of the finds and rapidly published papers which led to their widespread acceptance. This photograph demonstrates his continuing involvement in archaeology thirty years later, excavating a Roman burial at Youngsbury, Ware, in Hertfordshire. Evans' son Arthur revealed the Minoan civilization of Crete through his excavations at Knossos from 1899.
Photo: Society of Antiquaries, London

greater insight into their own society, but on a more practical level, their observations were useful to other travellers, for Greek culture and commerce embraced the whole Mediterranean as well as parts of its barbarian hinterland. These studies were paralleled by advances in anatomy, astronomy, and biology, to the extent that an idea of evolution was emerging, and a concept of human development from more primitive stages. It was to be another two thousand years before these concepts were taken up again during the Renaissance and advanced to a stage where the basis for true archaeological research could exist.

With few exceptions, Roman writers were content either to ignore barbarian cultures, or simply to re-hash the observations made by earlier Greek investigators. A notable exception was Tacitus, who wrote an interesting account of the Germans in the late first century AD (trans. Mattingly 1948). However, it was not scientific curiosity which motivated his description of the simple life and virtues of these barbarians, but a desire to contrast them with the corruption of Roman society. It is an early example of the 'Noble Savage' myth, and did much to popularise it down to the present. Unlike his predecessors, Tacitus made no attempt to gather first-hand information by travelling amongst the Germans, but embellished and updated Greek writings through conversations with senior army officers and civil servants from his social circle who had held appointments in the Rhine provinces on the borders of the Roman Empire. His book could have formed a basis for comparative study of the origins of Roman society, but merely served as an occasion to grind his favourite political and philosophical axes.

Some features of modern archaeology did exist in the Roman world, however. Collections of Greek sculpture and vases were popular, various stages of architectural development were appreciated, and tourist visits to ancient monuments had already become common – but it was only respectable to look back to earlier Rome or Greece. The Emperor Hadrian (AD 117–138) is a good example of a traveller and collector (fig. 5): in the course of his tours of the

5 Hadrian, Roman Emperor AD 117–138, broke a long tradition by sporting a beard and curly fringe in contrast to the severely clean-shaven and straight-haired portraits of his predecessors. His appearance and reflective expression are obviously intended to place him amongst philosophers rather than generals, and contributed to his nick-name 'Graeculus' – 'Greekling'. *Vatican Museum, Rome*

Empire, he visited ancient Greek shrines, and restored or completed Greek buildings; in Italy, he designed a country villa inland from Rome at Tivoli which housed a library and a collection of Greek sculpture, and incorporated gardens and lakes reminiscent of places he had visited in Egypt and Greece. He changed a century-old fashion by sporting curly hair and a beard in the Greek manner which contrasted sharply with the severely clean-shaven and short-haired appearance of his predecessors. Later in the century, Marcus Aurelius (AD 161–180) was portrayed in Greek philosopher's robes, and wrote introspective meditations as well as performing the military functions of his position.

This kind of self-conscious antiquarianism was completely lacking in the depth and originality of early Greek research, and was unlikely to have led to any scientific inquiry into matters relating to archaeology. It was in any case swept away by the political and economic chaos of the third and fourth centuries AD, after which the western half of the Roman Empire gradually disintegrated and passed under the control of the descendants of Tacitus' Germans – tribes from northern and eastern Europe who invaded and settled in the old Imperial lands in the fifth and sixth centuries. The remaining Roman culture of these areas and the surviving eastern Roman Empire had meanwhile become largely Christian, and philosophical speculation was replaced by rigid Biblical doctrine.

MEDIEVAL ATTITUDES TO ANTIQUITY

An understanding of Christian theologians' attitudes gives considerable insight into the lack of significant progress in archaeological thinking before the nineteenth century, when as we have seen, it coincided with revolutionary developments in geology and biology which forced a new scientific view of Man upon the Christian world. For most of its history, Christianity has been founded on total belief in the Bible; to doubt its word not only offended God, but also the political organization of Church and State which enforced its acceptance. Thus, independent thinking was discouraged by both intellectual and social circumstances, and new ideas were likely to be treated as heresy. In particular, archaeological speculation was hampered by the existence of a full account of the creation of the World and Man and the subsequent populating of known lands in the Old Testament, whose later books were linked to the familiar cultures of Egypt, Palestine and the Roman Empire. Some aspects of antiquarianism can be

found in the medieval church which are superficially similar to those of Romans like Hadrian, but on closer inspection are usually found to be motivated by religion: 'tourism' to ancient shrines was common, as was collecting – principally of relics of saints and martyrs, and manuscripts. Many travellers combined both purposes, for collections of relics enhanced the status of churches as centres for pilgrimage themselves, and better ecclesiastical reference libraries similarly improved the reputation of monastic centres of learning. Such libraries would contain the works of some of the more acceptable pagan Latin and Greek authors, as well as theological works, and an educated churchman could have gained a fair knowledge of the Classical world and its culture through these. A medieval bishop of Winchester made a purely aesthetic collection of Roman antiquities in the twelfth century, which included at least one shipload of marble sculptures from Rome itself, presumably as a result of visits to Italy and the reading of Roman authors such as Pliny and Vitruvius on art and architecture. Many medieval kings and nobles acquired a similar education in religious centres, and the Frankish Emperor Charlemagne (d. AD 814) was so conscious of inheriting the political authority of the old Roman Empire that he modelled his palace at Aachen (Aix-la-Chapelle) on late Roman imperial buildings in Ravenna in northern Italy, and inspired a royal court full of Latin learning and art in contrast to his barbarian Germanic origins.

In the Byzantine Empire, classical culture fared better, as 'Roman' rule lasted until the fifteenth century AD, although it was very much a Greek Christian culture which emerged from the ruins of the former Roman Empire. Perhaps its most significant role was played in its final years, when it was largely ruled by Italian states, before falling to the Turks in 1453. The connections with Italy, followed by the flight of many scholars to Western Europe after its conquest, are inextricably bound up in the great intellectual resurgence of the West which began in Italy in the fourteenth century, the Renaissance. Scholars, artists, and architects turned to pre-Christian Greek and Roman sources for

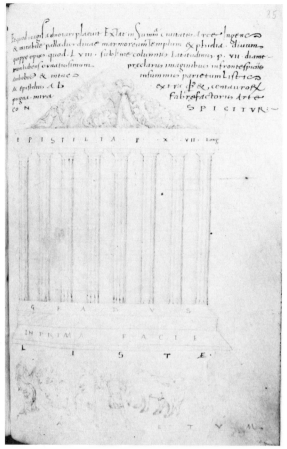

6 A drawing of the Parthenon, Athens, by Cyriac of Ancona, early fourteenth century AD. Cyriac is a particularly early example of a scholar who studied the past by fieldwork and travel as well as through documents. *Deutsche Staatsbibliothek, Berlin, DDR*

archaeologist – the active recording and study of physical remains of the past, whether sites or objects, through fieldwork. In addition, as a historical archaeologist, Cyriac carried out his researches with the help of a full knowledge of the literary and historical background of the culture which he investigated. The missing element was of course excavation, but the idea of *adding* to the information which could be gained from surface inspection by the dissection of buried remains lay far in the future.

The Renaissance atmosphere of discovery and speculation gradually spread to the rest of Europe, including areas in the north whose connection with the Classical World had been either brief (like Britain) or non-existent (like much of Germany and Scandinavia). The same spirit of enquiry was thus also directed towards the non-Classical past of these countries, and the first steps towards the methods of prehistoric archaeology began to be taken, frequently by individuals whose means did not permit them to travel widely in southern Europe. Thus it will become evident that most of the advances towards scientific archaeology occurred in the North, and that these methods and ideas fostered on the fringes of the Classical World were applied much later to sites in Italy, Greece and the Near East, where for economic and political reasons the conditions for scholarship had been unhelpful since the Renaissance.

The Renaissance atmosphere of science and thought became closely bound up with the many voyages of discovery which began shortly before AD 1500 and continued into the sixteenth century. The New World was revealed, with a number of societies at different levels of savagery or civilization, and the world was finally proved to be a sphere, justifying the revival of the ancient Greek view by Renaissance astronomers; both discoveries conflicted with the authority of the Bible. The psychological effect was potentially dramatic, but few dared to state the logical conclusions; if peoples unknown to the Bible could exist in other parts of the globe who had not simply spread out from the Garden of Eden over a flat continent, they were obviously not related to the creation story surrounding Adam. If this could be true of the New

largely forgotten information and ideas, and new inspiration. The Renaissance attitude to the examination of the past resembled that of the Romans, and involved travel, the study of buildings, and the collection of works of art and manuscripts. One scholar with this outlook appeared at the very outset, well before the fall of Constantinople. **Cyriac of Ancona** was born in 1391, and spent twenty-five years of the early fifteenth century in Greece, visiting sites and libraries for himself, and publishing commentaries on his observations (fig. 6). He embodied some of the principal components of a modern

World, then why should races of men similarly unrelated to Adam not have existed in the Old World before the Creation described in the Bible? One writer voiced these doubts in print – Isaac de la Peyrere, a French protestant, who proposed that Adam was simply the 'father of the Jews, not of all men' in a theological book published in 1655. His views were founded upon knowledge of the ancient civilizations of the Near East, and the newly discovered inhabitants of various parts of the world; he even proposed that what most people still called 'thunderbolts' were in fact stone implements used by the men who preceded Adam. Peyrere was forced to recant by the Inquisition, and his book was publicly burnt in Paris. Many must have sympathized with his views, but they were quite beyond proof until, as we have seen, the developments of geology and biology in the nineteenth century enabled archaeologists like Boucher de Perthes to substantiate them by careful observation and fieldwork.

Peyrere's thinking was ahead of its time, but the Renaissance interest in pagan classical literature and New World discoveries combined to create an atmosphere in which more basic archaeological work became acceptable. After all, Herodotus and Tacitus had written about primitive peoples on the fringes of the known (Greek and Roman) world, and the latter included Germany and Britain, which were both now caught up in the new scholarship. In addition, information from the Americas became increasingly available in the seventeenth century. The precedent of the ancient authors made it respectable to turn to the study of the primitive state of Europe. In the 1670s, John Shefferius (a Swedish professor of law) published a study of Lapland, inspired by Tacitus' *Germania*; in the rest of Europe primitive peoples like the Lapps were not readily available for study, so it is not surprising to find that the outcome of this way of thinking in other countries was the examination and description of archaeological remains. As has already been observed, such a study was more complicated in northern Europe than in countries around the Mediterranean, with its abundance of documented Classical sites. Prehistoric earthworks, tombs, and artefacts had to be classified and explained *without* any direct historical evidence.

ARCHAEOLOGY IN THE 'AGE OF REASON'

The aims and concepts of research into the past which followed the diffusion of Renaissance thinking into Northern Europe may be illustrated by the work of a series of antiquarians who engaged in active field archaeology in Britain between the early sixteenth and mid-eighteenth centuries – Leland, Camden, Aubrey, and Stukeley. Before the sixteenth century, historical writers occasionally included references to monuments, with little purpose other than to display sheer wonder, or to add circumstantial detail to some actual or invented episode in their works. Stonehenge is even recognizably illustrated in one fourteenth-century manuscript – but only to show Merlin building it. The advent of the new Tudor dynasty led to an increased national consciousness, from which more reasoned attempts to examine the continuity of Britain from Roman times resulted. The fanciful speculation which had formerly attributed the founding of Britain to unlikely or imaginary individuals and tribes (such as Brutus the Trojan or Phoenicians) was replaced by a greater reliance on references contained in the Classical sources, a study of languages, and comparative analogies from the New World. This was the atmosphere in which systematic attention was first paid to field monuments.

John Leland (1503–1552)

Leland was educated in London, Cambridge, Oxford, and Paris, and under Henry VIII held the post of 'Keeper of King's Libraries'. Like Cyriac of Ancona a century earlier, Leland travelled extensively, perusing the libraries of monasteries and colleges; unlike Cyriac, his fieldwork did not involve the rediscovery of sites belonging to a well-known and documented culture, but ill-understood remains of unknown age, or at best fleetingly documented monuments like Hadrian's Wall or Offa's Dyke. His interests were primarily directed towards historical documents and genealogy, and the records which he made of items of interest (whether ancient or contemporary) in the landscape through which he travelled were not published; they may have been intended to accompany a map or an annotated gazetteer. The significance of Leland is his general idea of recording non-literary evidence as part of wider researches; although it was never brought to any completed form, it anticipated the many county histories of the eighteenth century, and illustrated a breadth of interest in the landscape which was characteristic of the new, wider horizons of Renaissance scholarship.

William Camden (1551–1623)

Like Leland, Camden (fig. 7) progressed through a sound education, and eventually held a state appointment which gave him ample opportunity to further his antiquarian researches. After teaching and holding the headship at Westminster School, he became Clarenceux King of Arms in the College of Heralds; although he was less devoted to the study of heraldry and genealogy than Leland had been, it nevertheless formed an essential part of his historical writing. Antiquarianism was his passion from childhood, and he consciously acquired the necessary skills for his purposes – any educated man would possess Latin, but Camden learnt Anglo-Saxon and Welsh in order to study place-names. He travelled extensively and was already an authority of European standing in his twenties; when only 35 his major work was published – *Britannia*, the 'first general guide to the antiquities of Britain'. The first edition of 1585 was in Latin with only one illustration, but further illustrations were added to subsequent editions within his lifetime. The careful organization of the book allowed additions during his life, and indeed for nearly two hundred years after his death. The first English edition appeared in 1610.

Camden's purpose has been interpreted as to set Britain into a respectable position in European culture, largely by emphasizing the importance of the Roman occupation, which linked Britain to the Continental centres of the Renaissance. The book proceeds through the Saxon and medieval periods to stress the re-lationship of the Roman province to the recent historical past; no trace of the wild foundation myths of many Tudor writers can be found in the reasoned prose of Camden. His descriptions of antiquities are thorough and detailed, and sections on coins and language are also included. As with Leland, descriptions of the present configuration of the places he visited form an inseparable part of his account of Britain; indeed, Camden made extensive use of Leland's manuscript, occasionally quoting passages *verbatim*. One observation for which Camden is noted is a concise account of crop marks; the visible effects of buried structures on growing plants which are so important to air photography in the detection of sites today; another is the identification of pre-Roman coins minted by the late Iron Age tribes of south-eastern England – a notion rejected by Leland.

Camden's achievement was to organise his enormous collection of information into a published form, which Leland never managed. His success is indicated by the popularity and updating of the *Britannia* for so many years – and the high price which it commands amongst antiquarian book collectors today.

John Aubrey (1626–97)

The name of Aubrey (fig. 8) is well known amongst West End theatre-goers since his books of biographies of various contemporaries formed the basis for a successful one-man show, *Brief Lives*: his caustic wit and picturesque anecdotes would have made him the life and soul of any twentieth-century archaeological conference.

Aubrey did not have the learned career of Leland or Camden, and has even been described as a 'Wiltshire squire fallen on evil days', but he was part of a new kind of scholarship which came to prominence in the seventeenth century, mainly centred upon the Royal Society, and characterised by a wish to approach any subject from a sound basis of classification and comparison, whether astronomy, medicine, botany, or antiquity. A contemporary of Aubrey, Dr Robert Plot, stated this new attitude, which contrasts with that of Leland and Camden: 'I intend not to meddle

7 The great work of William Camden was *Britannia*, a comprehensive account of the antiquities of Britain published in 1585. It was so successful that editions followed long after Camden's death, brought up to date by various editors. This engraving was used as a frontispiece to an edition of 1789 revised by Gough.

8 A portrait of John Aubrey by William Fairthorne, dated 1666. *Bodleian Library, Oxford*

with the *pedigrees* or *descents* either of families or lands, it being indeed my Designe . . . to omit, as much as may be, both *persons* and *actions*, and chiefly apply myself to *things*; and amongst those too, only of such as are very remoted from the present *Age*.' This is the attitude of a true archaeologist rather than a historian who happened also to be interested in monuments.

An attitude which remained firmly established from Leland and Camden was that antiquities formed only one part of a complete study of the landscape, and Aubrey included all kinds of natural and artificial phenomena in his accounts of his beloved Wiltshire. Sadly, Aubrey's great work of a purely archaeological nature, the *Monumenta Britannica*, was never published except for a summary of some parts which were included in a new edition of Camden's *Britannia* in 1695. Its contents reveal Aubrey's interests and approach. The first part was centred around the great prehistoric monuments of Wessex such as Stonehenge, Silbury, and Avebury, which he was the first to firmly assign to the pre-Roman Celts, and their priesthood, the Druids, who were described by Tacitus and other Classical authors. Part two concerned pre-Roman and Roman camps and forts, and Roman civil settlements, again predominately those of Wessex which he knew best. Part three was more diverse, including barrows, pottery, burials in general, linear earthworks, roads and trackways, mosaic floors, and coins. The fourth part was never finished, and contained an assortment of material of medieval date including a series of features of medieval buildings, from which he deduced correctly that windows were particularly diagnostic for dating purposes – 'the windows ye most remarqueable, hence one may give a guess about what Time ye Building was'. Aubrey was right, but these unpublished deductions remained largely unknown, and they had to be worked out again independently when interest in church architecture was renewed in the nineteenth century. Unfortunately the failure to publish, so characteristic of Leland and Aubrey, is a problem which still bedevils the work of twentieth-century scholars.

The most significant feature of Aubrey's work is the attitude that information was worth collecting and classifying for its own sake, and not simply to illustrate a particular theory, and it finds parallels in the work of his contemporaries in other fields of learning such as botany and the study of fossils. Aubrey's observations and interpretations show the effects of another important feature of his age – the dissemination in Europe of accounts of American Indians. That he did not share the 'Noble Savage' view of North Americans held by some of his contemporaries (which could easily have resulted from reading Tacitus) is clear from the analogies he makes between ancient Britons and Indians. '. . . the inhabitants (of northern Wiltshire) almost as savage as the Beasts whose skins were their only rayment. . . . They were two or three degrees I suppose less savage than the Americans. . . . The Romans subdued and civilized them.' Clearly, Aubrey shared Camden's view that it was the Roman period which made Britain acceptable in the eyes of European post-Renaissance scholarship: remnants of this view survive today in the way in which the archaeology of Roman Britain is often studied with little reference to what preceded or followed it, but in the wider context of the Roman Empire.

William Stukeley (1687–1765)
If ever an individual reflected the spirit of his age, it was Stukeley (fig. 9), to the extent that his early researches belong to one tradition, and his later interpretations of them to another. The early eighteenth century saw a decline in the objective scientific enquiry which had been the mark of the Royal Society, and a shift in popular taste away from severe Classical art and architecture towards fanciful 'Gothic' buildings incorporating medieval features, and 'Romantic' art and literature.

Stukeley was trained in medicine at Cambridge and became a Fellow of the College of Physicians in 1720, having practised as a doctor. He had also studied botany, and this experience probably led him to an appreciation of ancient monuments in the countryside, which captured his imagination, especially after reading the manuscript of Aubrey's *Monumenta Britannica* in

Within the image: *a ſtone*, *Druids tumulus*, *Windmill hill*

1718. Extensive fieldwork in Wessex followed in the 1720s, including accurate and thorough surveys of Avebury, Stonehenge, and Silbury. He went on to travel extensively throughout Britain, from the south coast to Hadrian's Wall, making surveys and excellent sketches. So far, Stukeley would appear to be a typical scholar of the 'Age of Reason'; but signs of 'unreason' are evident in his taste for dramatic landscapes such as the Lake District, Gothic architecture (to the extent of designing mock-ruins or 'follies'), and a change of direction from medicine to religion in the 1720s, leading to his ordination in 1729.

From this point, Stukeley began to use his collected fieldwork from Wessex in an extraordinary attempt to establish a theological connection between the Druids and Christianity. Aubrey had made observations, sorted them into a sensible order, and made limited deductions from common sense and historical information – Stonehenge and its related monuments did not fit into the Roman period, so he attributed them to the pre-Roman Britons; they were obviously ritual, not functional, and he had therefore assigned them to the only known

9 William Stukeley (1687–1765) and friends engaged in fieldwork; even in this light-hearted sketch a number of antiquities and features of the landscape are drawn and labelled. He was an observant and accurate recorder whose plans remain an important source of information to this day. The drawing (by Stukeley himself) comes from a manuscript in the Bodleian Library, Oxford (*Ms. Eng. Misc. b. 65 fol. 43r.*).

cult and priesthood attested by the Classical authors, the Druids. Stukeley accepted this attribution, but went on to invent a vast theological system for the Druids, supported by quite unwarranted connections with features of the monuments: 'The form of that stupendous work (Avebury) is the picture of the Deity, more particularly of the Trinity'. He published two major books – *Stonehenge* (1740) and *Avebury* (1743) – which he claimed were part of a larger enterprise entitled *Patriarchal Christianity, or a Chronological History of the Origin and Progress of true Religion and of Idolatry*. One historian of

27

archaeology has elegantly summarised the curious dualism of Stukeley: 'Just as Dr Stukeley can be said to be the patron saint of fieldwork in archaeology, so can the Rev. William be held to be the evil genius who presides over all crackbrained amateurs whose excess of enthusiasm is only balanced by their ignorance of method' (Casson, 1939, 150). Nevertheless, the basic evidence from which Stukeley worked still forms an invaluable record of monuments which have suffered severely since his day – in fact, an avenue of stones leading from Stonehenge to the river Avon which he recorded but was subsequently destroyed has only been re-located by aerial photography in the twentieth century. His observations were careful and logical, and included the ability to relate whole groups of separate earthworks in an area into a coherent pattern, and on a more individual basis to make observations such as that a Roman road postdated some burial mounds because of its relative position – skills fundamental to both fieldwork and excavation to this day.

These advances in research were not restricted to Britain, of course; historians of ideas, science or archaeology can point to similar phenomena in most of Europe and North America at this time. Developments in Scandinavia and America have been particularly well described in recent years by Ole Klindt-Jensen (1975) and Brian Fagan (1972). After Leland, Camden, Aubrey and Stukeley, field archaeology could not develop from a methodological point of view until some new element was introduced. Accurate recording was continued and extended, and many county histories continuing the style of their work appeared into the nineteenth century, but interpretation of recorded monuments remained static, because of the limited historical evidence available, which scarcely extended back beyond the Roman period. This evidence could be shuffled into a different order, or fanciful theories could be constructed to extend it, but no new source of evidence was forthcoming until the idea of excavation became widely accepted in the nineteenth century, and improved in the twentieth. This development will be followed in the appropriate chapter below, but a further stage in

10 Thomas Howard, second Earl of Arundel, portrayed with part of his collection of antiquities around 1618 by Mytens. The sculptures and inscriptions adorned Arundel House in London, where scientist and philosopher Sir Francis Bacon '. . . coming into the Earl of Arundel's garden, where were a great number of ancient statues of naked men and women, made a stand, and as astonished, cried out "The Resurrection!"'. *Photograph by the National Portrait Gallery, London, of the painting in Arundel Castle, Sussex*

the unravelling of the past remains to be outlined here – the collection and study of objects, rather than sites, which ran parallel to the development of field archaeology, but triumphed in the nineteenth century as excavations began to provide more and more pottery, metal, stone and other objects for study.

TOURING AND COLLECTING

The Renaissance saw a revival of the Roman habit of visiting notable monuments and collecting works of art for purely aesthetic reasons which had been interrupted by the medieval church's concentration upon shrines, and relics amassed for religious motives. The concept spread to north Europe, and educated gentlemen of sufficient financial means began to visit the Mediterranean centres of classical civilization in Italy, Greece, Turkey and the Near East. It was natural that such travellers should purchase 'souvenirs' to adorn their northern residences (constructed and decorated, of course, in a classical manner), and the process was accelerated by sending agents to seek out further items and to arrange for their shipment back to their stately homes. A good – and very early – example of an English 'Grand Tour' aristocrat was Thomas Howard Earl of Arundel (1585–1646), who first travelled to Italy in 1612 with a large entourage, where he purchased and even dug for antiquities. His agent, William Petty, extended the search to Greece with the help of the Ambassador to the Porte, who described him as 'all things to all men that he may obtain his ends'. Petty built up a collection (at a bargain price compared with buying in Italy) which became a centre of great learned interest, known throughout Europe after its rapid publication in 1628 (fig. 10). Arundel's collection suffered neglect and dispersal after the Civil War (although a proportion eventually ended up in Oxford as part of the Ashmolean Museum), but it had generated similar desires amongst other noblemen and even royalty, notably King Charles I, who stated that 'The study of antiquities is by good experience said to be very serviceable and useful to the general good of the State and Commonwealth'.

There were other effects too; learned societies such as the Society of Dilettanti sponsored expeditions to make records of Classical sites rather than simply to loot them, and men of lower social status and wealth also began to form collections which included a wider variety of items. That of John 'Gardener' Tradescant was formed in the first half of the seventeenth century, and a catalogue of its contents appeared in 1656. Although largely made up of botanical specimens, it also comprised 'Mechanick artificial works in carvings, turnings, sowings, and paintings', and 'warlike instruments', mainly from Polynesia, Africa, and America. After his death, the material passed to the University of Oxford through Tradescant's friend, Elias Ashmole. The new museum was opened in 1683 by the future James II, and moved in the nineteenth century to the present building which is known throughout the world as the Ashmolean Museum. Tradescant's name is still widely (if unconsciously) remembered by all growers of that indefatigable house-plant, *tradescantia*.

The Renaissance fashion for collecting thus led indirectly to the establishment of public museums attached to centres of learning or to city corporations, which became the first point of contact with archaeology experienced by many members of the public. Today, the spirit of the early Ashmolean – collecting, scholarship, and public display – is happily to be found throughout the world, and is accepted as an integral part of the cultural (and tourist) life of almost every country. Travel abroad and the collecting of works of art thus inspired a wider kind of museum in northern Europe, and the interest in prehistoric objects and sites displayed by field archaeologists like Aubrey and Stukeley cannot be separated from this phenomenon; indeed, many antiquarians travelled in Britain because they could not afford to go abroad. However, the early field archaeologists concentrated on sites, for until a concept of the great depth of time involved in prehistory became accepted, the idea of using objects to distinguish between various stages of development within it remained extremely limited. We have already seen how late this acceptance came, in the second half of the nineteenth century; the study of objects was therefore similarly late in gathering momentum. Its history, like that of fieldwork, provides a useful illustration of the basic principles which still underly the subject today.

11 Stone artefacts from the Old and New Worlds; the full recognition of prehistoric implements in Europe was greatly assisted by observations of similar objects still in use in other parts of the world. In 1699 Edward Lhwyd, keeper of the Ashmolean Museum and authority on fossils and antiquities wrote in a letter from Scotland: 'I doubt not but you have often seen of these Arrow-heads they ascribe to elfs or fairies: they are just the same chip'd flints the natives of New England head their arrows with at this day; and there are also several stone hatchets found in this kingdom, not unlike those of the Americans.' The artefacts on the left of the photograph come from various parts of North and South America, whilst those on the right are all British, of Neolithic and Bronze Age date.
Photograph by the Audio-Visual Centre, University of Newcastle upon Tyne, of objects from the University's Hancock Museum and Museum of Antiquities

THE RECOGNITION OF HUMAN ARTEFACTS

Roman and later artefacts did not pose problems of identification as the work of man, of course, but they attracted little or no interest unless they possessed aesthetic qualities, and they were only discovered accidentally until excavation became an essential part of archaeology during the nineteenth century. In fact, many of the more sophisticated prehistoric metal objects were commonly assigned to the Romans or Danes, because of the lack of any clear idea of prehistoric material culture. The history of the systematic study of objects thus began with those of the earliest periods.

Casual finds of finely worked flint arrowheads and polished axes would immediately suggest human manufacture to anyone who actually troubled to apply common sense to them, and the idea that they might have been used before metals were known would not have been difficult to reach; Classical and ancient Chinese literature contained concepts of successive ages of stone, bronze and iron which may not have been suggested by actual finds, although they illustrate the kind of thinking involved. The seventeenth-century theologian Isaac de la Peyrere had proposed that stone implements were not 'thunderbolts', but the tools and weapons of the races of men who had preceded Adam; ethnological collections from the South Seas and the Americas soon provided good analogies still in use amongst primitive peoples. The second Keeper of the Ashmolean Museum in Oxford, Edward Lhwyd, an authority on fossils and antiquities, encountered such objects on his travels in the Celtic areas of Britain, and in a letter written from Scotland in 1699 remarked: 'I doubt not but you have often seen of these Arrow-heads they ascribe to elfs or fairies: they are just the same chip'd flints the natives of New England head their arrows with at this day; and there are also several stone hatchets found in this kingdom, not unlike those of the Americans' (fig. 11). A century later, John Frere's celebrated letter published in *Archaeologia* in 1800 (above, p. 15) included drawings of hand-axes of the Old Stone Age. 'They are, I think, evidently weapons of war, fabricated and used by a people who had not the use of metals. . . . The situation in which these weapons were found may tempt us to refer them to a very remote period indeed.' However, Boucher de Perthes was still fighting for their acceptance as artefacts, as well as their early date, fifty years later.

SCANDINAVIA AND THE THREE-AGE SYSTEM

Denmark is particularly rich in finely made artefacts from the prehistoric to Viking periods, and this probably helped to make it fertile ground for the growth of ideas on the classification of ancient objects. However, the contribution of Sweden to the theory of classification should not be overlooked, for Linnaeus published an arrangement of animals and plants in 1735 which is still basically followed, and parallels the careful approach which English field archaeologists like Aubrey had already employed in the previous century and which began to be applied to artefacts in the next, as increased building, agriculture, and

12 C.J. Thomsen in the Oldnordisk Museum in Copenhagen thirty years after its foundation in 1816. His enthusiasm for increasing public awareness of antiquities is well illustrated by this drawing by Magnus Pedersen. *National Museum, Copenhagen*

excavation provided a growing supply of objects of all kinds for study. From the late eighteenth century Scandinavians regularly employed the concept of three successive ages of stone, bronze and iron (whether derived from reading Lucretius, common sense, or observations), and it was particularly well expressed by Simonsen in 1816: 'At first the tools and weapons . . . were made of stone or wood. Then the Scandinavians learnt to work copper and then to smelt it and harden it . . . and then latterly to work iron. From this point of view the development of their culture can be divided into a Stone Age, a Copper Age and an Iron Age.' In 1807, the Danish Government set up a Royal Committee for the Preservation and Collection of National Antiquities, which was intended to protect sites, to establish a museum and to promote *public* awareness of antiquities – the last two ideas obviously being closely connected. The first curator of the resulting National Museum in Copenhagen was Christian Thomsen (fig. 12), who held the post from 1816 to his death in 1865; his achievement was to apply the theoretical ages to the practical classification of the objects in the collection as the basis for its display, which he enthusiastically explained to visitors of all classes, especially peasants, who were likely to find objects themselves with which to increase the collections. The spirit of the Earl of Arundel had been transformed in an exceedingly democratic fashion, and the approach of Thomsen is still characteristic of successful museum workers today. The displays were described in a guide printed in 1836, which received wider attention after its translation into English in 1848. Classification was the necessary prelude to the study of prehistory, so that when the true depth of time was accepted from the 1860s, the Three-Age System provided a framework which survives (with modifications) to our own day.

Thomsen's successor as Director of the National Museum was another remarkable man, J. Worsaae, whose writings on archaeology (including excavation) were decades ahead of other European scholars. The historian of archaeology, Glyn Daniel, has emphasized the quality of his thinking, and singled out a key phrase in Worsaae's writings published in 1843: 'As soon as it was pointed out that the whole of these antiquities could by no means be referred to one and the same period, people began to see more clearly the difference between them.' In other words, if the objects (and sites, for that matter) belonged to a succession of different ages, it was only natural to look for similarities and differences amongst them, and to attempt to establish the order in which they were invented and used.

TYPOLOGY

The 1860s saw the wide acceptance not only of the Antiquity of Man and the Three-Age System, but also Darwin's theory of evolution

incorporated into *The Origin of Species* (1859); Man had suddenly ceased to be a 'degeneration from Adam' and had become a 'perfected monkey' (as one contemporary put it). This concept of progress towards perfection permeated not only the philosophy of the times, but the whole attitude towards the colonization of primitive countries, improvements in industry and engineering, and the way of life of people in general. Theories of progressive stages in social development from savagery to civilization also began to be developed, which powerfully influenced the interpretation of prehistoric archaeology; these will be examined further in connection with the general question of interpreting the past (Chapter 6). The concepts of evolution and improvement were naturally applied to artefacts by both anthropologists and archaeologists. The former are exemplified by Augustus Lane Fox (later known as Pitt Rivers, having taken the name under the terms of an inheritance in 1880), and the latter by Oscar Montelius and John Evans. Pitt-Rivers had collected artefacts from all over the world from the early 1850s whilst serving in the Grenadier Guards. His early professional career was largely taken up with the introduction of the rifle into the British army, and in particular with the testing of various models and modifications for reliability and efficiency. This approach also characterized his collecting policy: he sought to demonstrate the progressive improvements and developments of classes of artefacts, documented by examples of the principal stages involved. Oddities and rarities were not for him, in contrast to most collectors in the tradition of Tradescant; his artefacts were assembled 'not for the purpose of surprising anyone, either by the value or beauty of the objects exhibited, but solely with a view to instruction. For this purpose ordinary and typical specimens rather than rare objects have been selected and arranged in sequence.' This philosophy is also found in the excavations which Pitt Rivers carried out later in his life, which will be examined in their place (p. 58–9).

The theory of typology is clearly seen in Pitt-Rivers' scheme for the derivation of Australian weapons, where a variety of clubs, boomerangs,

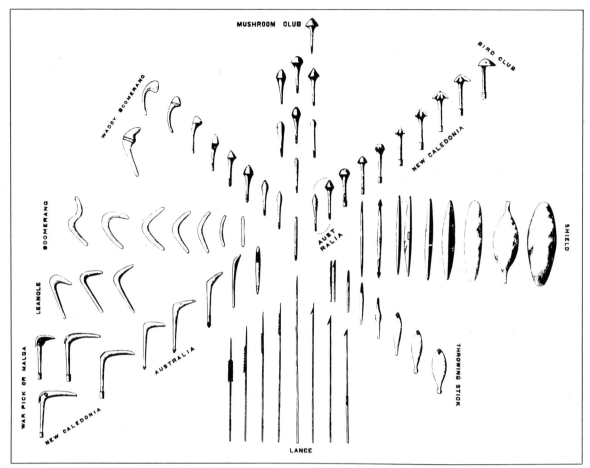

13 Pitt Rivers justified his idea of typology by illustrating the derivation of a wide range of Australian aboriginal weapons from a single common ancestor, a plain cylindrical stick. '. . . but I only ask you to glance at the sequence shown in this diagram . . . in order to convince you of the truth of the statement . . . that although, owing to the complexity of modern contrivances and the larger steps by which we mount the ladder of progress in the material arts, their continuity may be lost sight of, when we come to classify the arts of savages and prehistoric men, the term growth is fully as applicable to them as to the development of the forms of speech . . .' (*Lane Fox 1873–5, pl. III and p. 514*)

throwing sticks, shields, and spears are placed in sequences from simplicity to complexity, all beginning with the common ancestor of a plain cylindrical stick (fig. 13). The same general principle was applied to the stone and bronze implements of the British Isles by John Evans in books published in 1872 and 1881 respectively, whilst the whole of Europe was encompassed in the works of Oscar Montelius from the 1880s, eventually with the added refinement of numbered subdivisions of the Bronze Age, and attempts to fix dates for these stages with reference to dated events and objects from the ancient civilizations of the Near East. Fellow-Swedes Salin and Åberg continued this Scandinavian tradition of research in the twentieth century with typological studies of the objects and ornament of the historical Germanic tribes of the Roman and 'Dark Age' periods; the technique can be applied to artefacts of virtually any kind or date found anywhere in the world.

ACHIEVEMENTS OF EARLY ANTIQUARIANS

The purpose of this chapter has been to demonstrate that the basic principles of contemporary archaeology are most clearly understood by studying how they came about in the first place. The discovery of the 'lost' civilizations of the Ancient World (other than Greece and Rome), the appearance of scientific excavation techniques, and the increasingly sophisticated interpretation of the societies of the past all belong to a phase of archaeology which only really began in the nineteenth century and still continues today, but they embody several of the key factors slowly established during the Renaissance and 'Age of Reason' which have been outlined in this chapter. A thought-provoking historian of archaeological theory, Stuart Piggott, has observed 'that the accurate and precise science which some of us would consider modern archaeology to be, began merely as an episode in the history of taste'. It is certainly true that the pursuits which were considered respectable in intellectual circles happened to include the study, recording, and collecting of ancient sites and artefacts, as part of a wider scientific interest in natural history. Through the efforts of a series of remarkable individuals, usually amateurs and often eccentrics, the methods of fieldwork were laid down: museums were established, staffed, displayed and catalogued; the existence of man on earth was extended from a mere six thousand years back into an immeasurable period; and man's artefacts were collected, organized, and arranged to form a new source for the documentation of his technical progress. Co-operation with specialists in other disciplines was easy in the restricted circles of learning of earlier centuries, and a truly multi-disciplinary approach brought immediate benefits to the study of man, which have continued and increased ever since. Two less welcome traditions were also established early – the almost pathological inability of some scholars actually to publish work of the highest quality and significance, and the distortion of basically sound evidence to support unlikely and fanciful theories. Although characterized by such early antiquaries as Aubrey and Stukeley respectively, both phenomena are still very much a part of archaeology today, and will be examined further in later chapters.

FURTHER READING

The most prolific writer on the history of archaeology is Glyn Daniel, whose most recent popular survey is *A Short History of Archaeology*, 1981. More detailed is his *150 Years of Archaeology*, 1975, whilst an entertaining and instructive anthology of archaeological writings with a commentary can be found in the same author's *The Origins and Growth of Archaeology*, 1967. The place of archaeology in a wider cultural setting of European thought is the theme of Stuart Piggott's collection of papers published together as *Ruins in a Landscape: Essays in Antiquarianism*, Edinburgh, 1976. Piggott's *Antiquity Depicted: Aspects of Archaeological Illustration*, 1979, pursues the changing styles of illustrating monuments and artefacts from the medieval period onwards.

An older but excellent history of archaeology and anthropology was published by Stanley Casson in 1939 entitled *The Discovery of Man*, whilst studies of developments in Scandinavia and America are to be found respectively in Ole Klindt-Jensen's *A History of Scandinavian Archaeology*, 1975, and Brian Fagan's *Elusive Treasure: the Story of Early Archaeologists in the Americas*, 1972. Fagan's *In the Beginning* (3rd ed., 1978) has a concise historical introduction which integrates European and New World archaeology, and brings their history right up to date with the current state of the 'new' archaeology of the 1960s and 1970s.

Many more detailed studies exist about particular phases in the history of archaeology or individual antiquarians – the bibliographies of the books mentioned above will provide plenty of additional references to these.

A facsimile publication of John Aubrey's *Monumenta Britannica* is now under way, edited and annotated by John Fowles and R. Legg.

2 Discovery and Fieldwork

In Britain, we have seen that archaeological exploration usually began for one or other of two principal reasons. Structures were investigated either because they were thought to relate to some historically attested people, period or event, or conversely, mysterious monuments were dug into in the hope of revealing their nature and date. A third factor existed almost universally: treasure hunting, whether for purely financial gain, or on the more intellectual plane of collecting curiosities or *objets d'art*. This physical interest in material remains, especially the concept of excavating them for information rather than treasures, developed fairly late – well after the great period of descriptive study by antiquarians like Camden or Aubrey.

The classical Mediterranean civilizations of Greece and Rome formed such a strong part of European culture throughout its history, with higher points of interest in the Renaissance and Enlightenment periods, that their truly archaeological study was not as significant in introducing new techniques and concepts as either the question of the Antiquity of Man or the exploration of the civilizations of Egypt or Mesopotamia. It so happened that when European gentlemen first began to turn (in the years around 1800) to more systematic forms of excavation, the declining strength of the Turkish Empire was allowing access to these regions. This led to the presence of diplomats and soldiers from France and Britain (and later Germany too) around the vital Red Sea and Arabian Gulf routes from the Mediterranean to India. Many of these individuals came from very much the same aristocratic and landed background as those antiquarians who received a sound classical education, did the Grand Tour, and increasingly turned to the investigation of sites on their estates. It is therefore not surprising to find that Claudius James Rich (agent of the East India Company at Baghdad from 1807) or Paul Emile Botta (French consul at Mosul from 1842) investigated the remains of Babylon and Nineveh, and other sites near the towns in which they were based. National prestige naturally became involved, and vast sculptures and even larger portions of buildings were transported to the museums of London, Paris, and Berlin. Even more striking was Napoleon's invasion of Egypt in 1798; Nelson ensured that it was not a military success, but it was certainly an academic triumph, as the 200 savants who accompanied Napoleon's army established the foundations of decades of detailed research into that country's civilization and prehistory.

The failing grip of the Ottoman Empire in the nineteenth century also stimulated the exploration of Greek civilization; after its independence in 1831 Greek and foreign excavators rapidly cleared the Acropolis of Athens, releasing the remains of such buildings as the Erechtheum and Parthenon from the encumbrances of a harem and mosque respectively (fig. 14). The interest in Egypt and Mesopotamia should not be seen as an entirely separate phenomenon. Egypt had been absorbed by Greece and later Rome, and some indications of its earlier history and antiquities were known from Classical writers. Mesopotamia was even better known through the many references in the Old Testament to Babylon and Assyrian kings; perhaps more important, a wide public could safely indulge in the news of discoveries, for they promised only to enrich and confirm two major roots of European culture – the

14 The Parthenon, Athens, in an engraving published by Stuart and Revett in 1787, showing Turkish houses and a mosque which were rapidly removed after Greece became independent in 1831. Five volumes of Stuart and Revett's architectural studies and drawings were published between 1762 and 1830, and their interest in recording rather than plundering made a welcome change from the attentions of other European visitors to such sites. Their principal motive was to improve the sources of design and decoration for architects building in the Neo-Classical style. *Stuart and Revett 1787, pl. I*

Classics and the Bible. A greater contrast to the suspicious claims being made about unspectacular and dubiously man-made stone tools found in France is difficult to imagine, particularly when such finds were being linked by heretical geologists to the ideas of Charles Darwin, who had the effrontery to deny both the date and nature of the Creation recorded in the Book of Genesis: 'Darwin and the pre-Darwinian theorists had distracted attention from the study of man in his character of *sapiens* and had concentrated on his position in the world as a mere *homo*. . . . To the side of scholarship and literary interest there gravitated, imperceptibly, the bulk of those religious-minded traditionalists who were alarmed at the tendency of the times' (Casson 1939, 207).

'Literary' interest in Egypt and the Near East was soon given a tremendous boost, for the written languages of both civilizations were deciphered by the middle of the nineteenth century. The story of the Rosetta Stone has been told many times: in essence, a single text inscribed on a stone discovered by a French officer in Napoleon's army in 1799 turned out to be written in two Egyptian scripts and also Greek. Despite the loss of the stone to the British after Napoleon's defeat, various attempts to use the Greek text to decipher the Egyptian scripts culminated in success by Jean François Champollion, who was able to publish a grammar and dictionary of Egyptian hieroglyphics by the 1830s. The implications for Egyptology were tremendous, as countless hieroglyphic inscriptions were already known (their use had continued under Greek and Roman rule until at least the end of the fourth century AD), and structures could now be dated according to the Pharoah's names adorning them, by reference to detailed lists compiled from a number of inscriptions and papyrus documents extending back to around 3,000 BC. Egypt thus joined Greece and Rome in having a detailed historical framework for the study of its culture and physical remains; Mesopotamia followed soon afterwards. Henry Rawlinson was appointed British consul in Baghdad in 1844, and was able to complete his study of a gigantic inscription at Behistun in Persia, where an identical text in Persian, Babylonian and Elamite had been carved on a high cliff to expound the authority of the Persian king Darius over his conquests. The decipherment of Babylonian 'cuneiform' writing (named after its wedge-shaped components) allowed the translation of the thousands of clay tablets found on excavations throughout the area, often recording meticulous details of palace stores and accounting, as well as other inscriptions giving historical information. The situation was not entirely beneficial for these civilizations; increased interest led to greater demands by museums and collectors, and greater plunder of sites for impressive carvings and inscriptions. In Mesopotamia, where unlike Egypt even palaces and temples were largely built out of sun-dried mud-brick, the neglect of subtle structures and perishable or unimpressive artefacts was to be widespread for most of the rest of the nineteenth century, and the absence of investigation of any earlier, prehistoric levels underlying the historical sites almost complete. Casson has succinctly summarized this aspect: 'Scientific method existed. But for the archaeologists of the various phases of civilized man there were no

scientific collaborators. . . . This divorce of science from archaeology, in so far as the later phases of civilization were concerned, was largely due to the fact that historical sites fell automatically under the control of literary men' (1939, 215). The division, over forty years later, has still not been healed; only in the most developed countries is the same rigorous, total investigation of all aspects of the available evidence long associated with prehistoric excavations regularly applied to historical sites. Frere, Worsaae and Boucher de Perthes observed stratigraphy because it was their only source of chronological evidence; with hieroglyphs or cuneiform, who needed strata?

So far, then, fieldwork or planned discovery was almost absent from the process of discovery, and inhibited by the course taken by the study of literate civilizations. After Schliemann's major discoveries at Troy in the 1870s, an English request was made for financial support from the Treasury for work on barrows in the same area on the grounds that they were of as much potential interest as the Temple of Diana at Ephesus, also in Turkey, which was receiving financial support. The official reply was mortifying: the work at Ephesus was undertaken '. . . not for the purpose of ascertaining the site or the form of the Temple, objects quite beyond the scope of the Trustees (of the British Museum), but for the sake of such relics of ancient art as might be found buried among the ruins. The ascertainment of the site was a mere incident. . . . The question then is: are excavations undertaken for the purpose of illustrating the *Iliad* a proper subject for the expenditure of public money? I am sorry to say that in my judgement they are not' (Rt. Hon. Robert Lowe, 1873). However, mention of Schliemann does hint that clearer objectives were coming into the study of the early civilizations. The later nineteenth century also witnessed a more systematic approach to the recording of the surface remains of monuments, using improved surveying techniques, and of course the rapidly developing science of photography.

Heinrich Schliemann was born in Germany in 1822, and his commercial skill and gift for languages allowed him to retire at the age of 46

15 Schliemann's excavations at Troy (Hissarlik, Turkey) were far from being a model of archaeological technique. Only solid structures were noticed and recorded – and frequently promptly demolished to reveal earlier features. He recognized that the site had been occupied by a long succession of cities, and the fact that he was mainly interested in finding the Homeric level did at least lead him to take note of the occurrence of artefacts in different levels. It is Schliemann's motivation for digging rather than his practices which is of interest; it was the logical conclusion of a long preparatory process of literary research, fieldwork, and related excavations on several sites in order to discover the physical setting and remains of a culture known only from literature. *Schliemann 1880, facing p. 265*

to devote himself to Greece. Part of the glamour of Schliemann is the romance of an outsider taking on the academic establishment and the Greek and Turkish authorities to pursue his theories – and of course in seeming to be right, and making spectacular discoveries. How far this view is correct may be debated, but the persistence, discipline and intelligence which brought him commercial success and a rapid rise from grocer's assistant to Californian banker can only have been helpful in approaching excavation. Casson has epitomised the popular view of his abilities: 'The grocer who unpacks crates is better equipped to unpack the middens of antiquity than the polite scholar who has never seen the inside of his own dustbin' (1939, 224). Schliemann is certainly important for showing that literary documents need not rule archaeology absolutely. The nature of the epic poems of Homer was hotly disputed in the middle of the last century; German scholars favoured a view which made it unlikely that the *Iliad*'s stories of the Trojan Wars were based on reality, but rather involved miscellaneous separate mythological accounts of heroes. Schliemann held the opposite view and, combining the Homeric text and fieldwork in Greece and Turkey, published observations about Mycenae and the location of Troy in 1869 – two years before he began to excavate the latter site (fig. 15). A rapid series of publications of his work there and on related sites, as well as regular reports to newspapers such as *The Times*, brought wide attention to his finds.

'His results have subsequently undergone considerable revision, first by his co-worker Dörpfeld, who redefined the occupation level of Troy which was to be assigned to the Homeric period only three years after Schliemann's death in 1890, and subsequently as a result of further excavation and research around the Aegean'. The Greek Bronze Age and its antecedents were first exposed to view by Schliemann, and the implications of the pre-Homeric remains are still being researched. His excavations began as a conscious problem-oriented exercise, to answer

questions about a disputed literary tradition, and the hypothesis-testing aspect of his work has a modern ring. The implications of Troy for the development of excavation techniques were also important, and will be discussed in the next chapter. His approach is in stark contrast to the discovery of the Serapeum at Memphis in Egypt by Mariette in 1851; he knew about the site through an ancient Greek account and from references to it in Egyptian papyri, but only discovered it thanks to a good memory and the chance observation of the head of a recurrent kind of sphinx sticking out of the sand; four years of excavation followed (Daniel, 1967, 229). Such happy accidents were the rule rather than the exception in the discovery of the early civilizations; the identification of historically or biblically attested sites usually resulted from the recognition of their names on building inscriptions or clay tablets found in the course of

16 A clay cylinder from Sippar (now Abu Habbah) found by Rassam in excavations in 1881, which describes the building of the temple of Shamash by the Babylonian King Nabonidus (Langdon 1912, 257). *British Museum, London*

plunder for museum exhibits. This is true of the site of Sippar in southern Mesopotamia, the Sepharvaim of the Bible, where Rassam excavated for the British Museum in 1881. Ironically, one of the inscriptions he found recorded an excavation carried out by the Babylonian king Nabonidus, who in the sixth century BC had excavated beneath the foundations of the temple of the Sun-God Shanash to find out who had built it, and had discovered an inscription which answered his question (fig. 16). Nabonidus was evidently a rather more problem-oriented excavator than Rassam.

The final stage in the revelation of the early civilizations of Europe and the Near East took place at the close of the nineteenth century, when Sir Arthur Evans investigated the origins of the Mycenean civilization (revealed by Schliemann in Greece) soon after the independence of Crete in 1898. He excavated the Minoan palace at Knossos, where a literate civilization developed around 2,000 BC. Evans, like Schliemann, was testing an informed hypothesis; he was aware that engraved seal-stones bearing a pictographic script independent of those of Egypt or Turkey had been found in Crete, which indicated that a system of writing long preceded the adoption of the Phoenician alphabet by the Greeks. Arthur Evans did not suffer the opposition and ridicule that Schliemann had met, coming as he did from an impeccable academic background and the Ashmolean Museum, Oxford – not to mention the influences of his father John, whom he had accompanied to Abbeville to see Boucher de Perthes in 1859; Arthur had actually found a flint implement there at the age of eight.

Unlike Egypt, Mesopotamia, or even Homeric Greece, the Minoan world was almost entirely unknown apart from a few legends; the notion of a literate civilization *preceding* Classical Greece was a real revelation. As at Troy, earlier levels extending back into the prehistoric period were also found below the palace at Knossos, emphasizing the great lengths of time which lay behind the literate stages of the early civilizations. Thus, archaeology alone was able to provide almost all of the information about a major literate period, to match the achieve-

ments made by prehistorians in the understanding of the Antiquity of Man. The excavations at Knossos were directly addressed to the solution of a cultural problem, using a variety of evidence, including some small previous excavations on the site, and the results were spectacularly successful. Evans was helped by the fact that he was dealing with a site without subsequent occupation, which had been destroyed along with most of its artefacts and furnishings, allowing detailed interpretation. Unlike most Near-Eastern excavators, Evans consciously preserved the crumbling gypsum masonry as he went along. The comparatively simple plan of the palace (with modifications rather than wholesale rebuildings) also helped him, but, even allowing for these circumstances, the very first excavation photographs show a meticulously cleaned site, and the text demonstrates an attention to the position of finds both as dating evidence and as a way of interpreting the destruction of the palace (Evans, 1899–1900). In Britain, similar attention to detail in the closing years of the last century was also a feature of Pitt Rivers, of course, whose work must have been familiar to Evans, but the same standards were certainly never achieved in any of the 1906–1914 excavations at Corstopitum (Corbridge, Northumberland) (pp. 66–9).

After the Minoan civilization, only that of the Hittites remained unknown until the early twentieth century – like the Mesopotamian civilizations, it was known from the Bible, and like the other Near Eastern areas, it was illuminated by the discovery of large numbers of inscribed tablets found at the large fortified city of Hattusha (now Bogazköy) in Turkey in 1906–08. Further East, both India and China produced evidence of urban civilizations in the twentieth century, dating back to before 2000 and 1000 BC respectively, and in the New World, urban civilization in Mesoamerica was taken back to before the beginning of the Christian Era.

In general, the discovery of the great civilizations did little to advance archaeological techniques, and conscious problem-solving exercises only appeared at a late stage with Schliemann and Evans. Luck, accident and careless plunder were commonplace; historians and art-historians were interested in documents and works of art, and these could be gained without much attention to stratification or planned research. These awaited the growth of a sense of responsibility about antiquities, the systematic approach of men like Pitt Rivers, and the formulation of problems – such as the pre-historic background of Egypt, the early Sumerian development of Mesopotamia, and the origins of the settled Neolithic communities accidentally revealed in the lower levels of Knossos and many Near Eastern tells. Without historical texts and before the advent of radio-carbon dating, these problems required the kind of study which had been current in northern Europe for decades – careful excavation with regard to stratification; the association and physical development of pottery and other artefacts upon which at least relative dates could be based; and fieldwork aimed at eluci-dating known problems by finding new sites to extend knowledge chronologically and geo-graphically or to fill gaps in sequences. The importance of agriculture in the 'urban revol-ution' of settled communities also posed social and economic questions, long after the theories of Tylor or Marx about the development of human societies had been devised. The greater the range of questions demanded, the better archaeologists developed ways to answer them by fieldwork or excavation. The Near East amply made up for its poor nineteenth-century beginnings in the 1920s and 1930s, and a very readable account of the steady pushing-back of the frontiers of knowledge of the prehistory of the area has recently been provided by David and Joan Oates (1976, 50–61). Since the Second World War, Kathleen Kenyon at Jericho, Robert Braidwood at Jarmo, James Mellaart at Catal Hüyük, and many other European and American (and more recently native) excav-ators have continued this progress, with ever more finely-focussed research, right up to the present day.

THE DISCOVERY OF NEW ARCHAEOLOGICAL SITES

In Chapter 1, we saw how antiquaries like Cyriac of Ancona or William Stukeley and the tell-diggers of the Near East relied on straight-forward visual inspection to find ancient sites, travelling unsystematically either to see what lay in unknown areas, or to increase knowledge about regions which had already proved pro-ductive. The limitations of travel obviously imposed severe restrictions on early field-workers, but even today the first approach to fieldwork in any area is very similar, although usually on a more systematic basis. The human eye is an extremely sensitive instrument, par-ticularly when it is tuned in to minor fluctu-ations in the character of the ground surface, or to noticing objects lying upon it. In addition, frequent chance discoveries of artefacts or structures in the course of agriculture or build-ing work continue to add to the basic *corpus* of archaeological knowledge, and are often follow-ed up by more informed examination. Thus, many professional and amateur archaeologists spend a significant amount of their time in simply looking around them.

Discovery is rather pointless without record-ing, and the early antiquaries are often in-valuable and at the same time frustratingly inadequate in their accounts of sites which in many cases may have now disappeared. A slow progression led from terse description to illust-ration, and then from picturesque illustration to accurate surveying. The scientific attitudes which accompanied the eighteenth-century Enlightenment led to an increasing interest in classification, which naturally required more careful observation, whether of the details of monuments or artefacts. In the 1850s recording was revolutionized by the rapid adoption of photography. Both British and French expe-ditions carried out extensive photography in Syria and Egypt in 1851–2, and when the Crimean War began in 1854 the Society of Antiquaries of London requested the English Army to instruct its photographer 'to take and transmit photographic views of any antiquities which he may observe'; only a century earlier, William Stukeley, 'arch-druid of his age', was lecturing to that society on the Druidic associ-ations of Stonehenge, and relating how he and friends had dined on one of its trilithons.

Systematic recording by detailed field note-books, surveying and photography is now standard procedure. An area for examination (such as the route of a planned road, or an open area of highland ground) is marked out with some kind of regular grid which an individual or team can follow to provide even cover; any finds, whether artefacts or surface features, can be recorded quite accurately in relation to this basic grid. The results can be plotted on to a masterplan to give an overall distribution of the results. Careful organization should allow even sampling of parts of a very large area which cannot be totally explored, so that the results can be assessed statistically and extrapolated to the whole area with some confidence. There may be obvious clusters of potsherds, flint flakes, or building debris lying on the surface suggesting *foci* of occupation; the converse does not mean that no occupation existed – the agricultural exploitation or geological weathering of the land can vary widely in even a small area, and affect the results in different ways. Any traces of structures or earthworks such as ditches or field-boundaries can be roughly surveyed with simple equipment, but a more detailed follow-up will usually be desirable for greater accuracy. A grid of spot-heights measured by levelling can be used to provide contour plans which may reveal more subtle surface variations not immediately apparent to the eye, and sophisticated computer analysis of the results can even be used to enhance any variations which occur. A large site will usually be much more comprehensible when the features recorded in a survey are drawn out at a smaller scale – the relationships between its various components are more likely to be evident, and any blanks or inconsistencies will be made obvious, and can be investigated further. The analysis of recorded plans is an important aspect of such surveying, and a combination of field observations and the examination of scaled-down plans can often elucidate the sequence in which overlapping earthworks have been created, altered or superseded, although it must not be forgotten that Stukeley was perfectly capable of making these kinds of deductions.

It is often remarkable how much can be revealed about a site without actual excavation using entirely surface observations; however, these depend on a reasonably good state of preservation of visible structural remains or earthworks. In densely populated, intensively cultivated countries these are very much the exception, and many prehistoric sites must have already been ploughed flat by the end of the Roman period in much of Europe. The greatest single contribution to fieldwork and recording has undoubtedly been made by aerial photography, which can provide either general views of entire sites or areas, or details of individual sites of which little or no surface trace remains, through discolourations in their overlying soil or vegetation. The visual effectiveness of aerial photographs had been appreciated since the 1850s; occasional archaeological shots were taken from balloons, but the First World War stimulated the practice of taking reconnaissance

17 Hypothetical diagram of circumstances leading to the formation of surface characteristics detectable by aerial photography. A: Slight variations in the surface of pasture which might not be apparent to the eye are enhanced by highlights and shadow in morning or evening light. B: The same features will be levelled by ploughing, but the disturbance of the soil may cause noticeable variations in colour or texture on the surface. C: During the initial growth or the later ripening of a crop, variations in the depth and moisture content of the soil may lead to marked variations in its height and colour. Drought will exaggerate these effects and reveal much slighter features, not only in crops such as cereals, but in permanent pasture like A. The post-hole and hearth at the left and centre of the diagrams would not be likely to be revealed except in the most extreme conditions.

The phenomena indicated in this diagram should be compared with the results of geophysical prospecting over the same features (fig. 21).

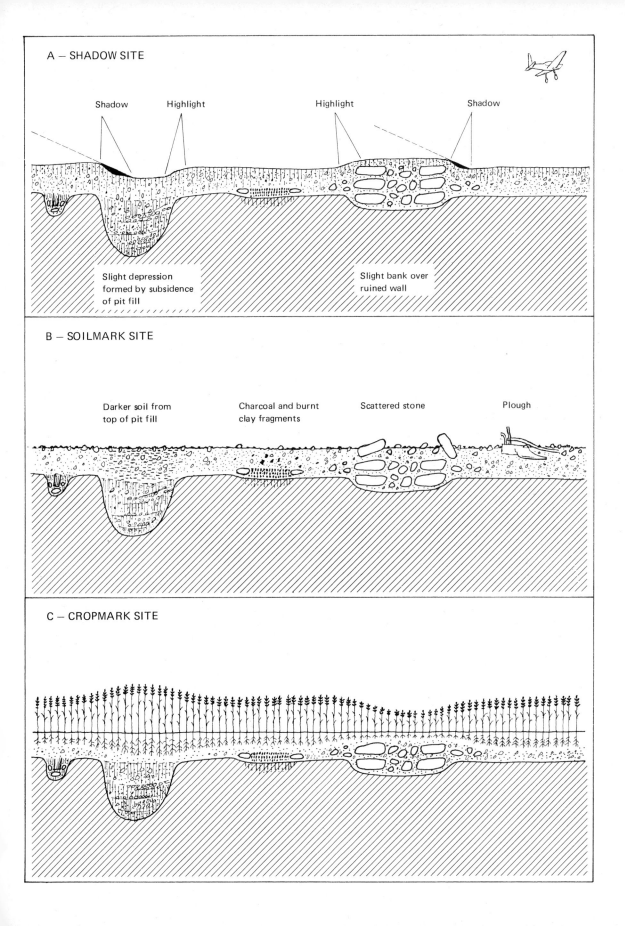

A — SHADOW SITE

Shadow   Highlight   Highlight   Shadow

Slight depression
formed by subsidence
of pit fill

Slight bank over
ruined wall

B — SOILMARK SITE

Darker soil from   Charcoal and burnt   Scattered stone   Plough
top of pit fill   clay fragments

C — CROPMARK SITE

photographs from aeroplanes both for mapping and strategic purposes. Many pioneers of archaeological aerial photography gained their experience in this way, including O.G.S. Crawford, who published a manual on the subject in 1929. The use of the technique has expanded exponentially since then, and the understanding of the conditions for its optimum application have greatly increased, as well as the versatility of cameras and film-types; even remote-sensing from satellites is becoming a credible extension of its scope. Lest twentieth-century technology claim all of the credit for the achievements of aerial photography, it must be noted that Camden and Stukeley in the sixteenth and eighteenth centuries made sensible observations and interpretations of buried features or structures revealed by variations in growing crops (Daniel 1967, 37; 45). The traces of archaeological sites which are observable from the air can be conveniently divided into shadow-sites, crop-marks and soil-marks (fig. 17).

AERIAL PHOTOGRAPHY (Wilson 1982)

Visible sites

Aerial photography can supplement ground observations made during fieldwork on visible earthworks by giving an overall view. Isolated features may be given coherence, and new features invisible or not readily noticeable on the ground revealed. The best conditions are provided by low light, which emphasizes irregularities in the ground surface by highlighting bumps and filling hollows with deep shadow (fig. 18). Temperate countries cannot guarantee that clear sunlight will be available at exactly the right time of morning or evening, of course, and even when it is, the best shadow effects do not last long. It is therefore most suitable for adding details to known sites, rather than as a method of pure prospecting.

Invisible sites

Although many of the most impressive photographs taken by pioneers like Keiller were of visible shadow-sites, more information and discoveries have been provided about sites which have been almost completely levelled, and are therefore unlikely to be spotted during normal fieldwork — even if concentrations of surface finds suggest their existence, their form will not be perceptible. Such sites are commonest in areas of heavy agricultural exploitation, where different settlement patterns and field systems may have come and gone several times during the evolution of the present landscape. Their detection relies on a number of phenomena, affecting vegetation or the soil. **Crop-marks** are created by buried features either enhancing or reducing the growth of plants, usually by affecting the availability of moisture to their roots (fig. 19). Extreme conditions such as drought emphasize such crop-marks, particularly in cereals, either in their growth or ripening, but the effects are not consistent or easily predictable. Many years of observation of the same site under different conditions may be required to provide a cumulative record of its features; as with shadow sites, the optimum conditions do not last very long. Some root crops or pasture are very insensitive, and only reveal marks during extreme drought conditions (fig. 20). Much research continues on the nature and causes of these variations, in order to improve the results obtained — it is an expensive and time-consuming process, which needs critical preparation if the results are going to be worthwhile. **Soil-marks** may be observed on land under plough; human disturbance of the ground may create variations in the character and colour of the topsoil, and like cropmarks, subtle variations need to be seen from above to reveal any coherent plan. The most dramatic example of sites discovered in this way comes from the prospecting by Roger Agache in north-eastern France, where detailed plans of Roman villas show up in white against dark brown soil,

18 A deserted medieval village at Downton, Northamptonshire; the long shadows cast by the trees show that the low angle of the sun's rays have enhanced the low relief of the earthworks delineating the central street and building plots either side of it. The site was cleared and taken into cultivation soon after this photograph was taken in 1963 (St Joseph 1971). *Cambridge University Collection: copyright reserved*

as ploughing turns up fragments of their chalk foundations (Agache 1970). This makes another point: if a site shows up clearly after ploughing, it is probably being severely eroded, and may soon disappear altogether if regularly ploughed; photographs taken from the air may well be the first and last record unless protection is secured.

There are also good examples of the use of frost or light snow to enhance shadow sites, through their reflectiveness, or buried sites through differential thawing. Such conditions are of course rare, and only likely to be found by luck rather than planning.

It should be apparent that aerial photography is not to be undertaken lightly. Like fieldwork on the ground, it needs to be well thought-out and systematic, with a full knowledge of the conditions, crops, and geology of an area to be photographed, so that it can be timed to coincide with the best conditions. As well as this, photographic knowledge is required in selecting the best kinds of cameras and films for the recording of sites. There are colour film emulsions which are specially sensitive to particular colour ranges, and infra-red photography, or the artificial enhancement of colour variations by special developing or printing processes, can all help to clarify the results. Of course, any observations need to be mapped in order to be of use to archaeologists on the ground. Oblique views of sites require complicated adjustments to plot them on to a horizontal plan, and even the best cameras suffer some distortion away from the centre of their lenses. Once again, computer-based techniques have been designed to overcome these problems, but they are obviously restricted to specialized mapping centres, and a lot of patient geometry is the only alternative for most archaeologists, using any fixed reference points available from large scale maps. On sites which are about to be excavated, some geophysical prospection may be advisable to locate prominent features like buried ditches or walls, to ensure that trenches are located in the right places.

Experience is also required not only to photograph the right things from the air, but to recognize and interpret the results – distinguish-

19 A Neolithic settlement at La Panetteria, Foggia, Italy. The enclosure ditches and foundation trenches for timber round-houses show as particularly clear crop-marks, although it should be noted that only the ditches are visible in the less sensitive vegetation at the bottom of the photograph. Many dark spots, lines or patches appear within and outside the enclosures; only excavation could determine whether these are natural geological effects, prehistoric features, or the result of modern farming.

20 It cannot be stressed too highly that the appearance of archaeological sites on aerial photographs is the result of many chance factors – the construction of the site, its location and surface geology, its subsequent agricultural exploitation, and most important, whether a photograph happened to be taken at a good moment when vegetation and climate combined to make recognizable features visible. This photograph shows an Early Christian monastic enclosure at Tarramud, Co. Galway, Ireland, which is visible partly as a surviving earthwork (left), partly as a crop-mark in a standing crop (bottom right) or as a 'parch-mark' in a harvested hay field (top right). In the remaining fields the line of the enclosure is almost invisible in pasture and cut but ungathered hay: if its position had not been indicated by the other parts of the circuit, it would not have been noticed and photographed.

ing between archaeological features and natural geological phenomena, and attempting to classify and date archaeological sites by their form.

Also important is the recognition of areas where sites are absent, and deciding whether they really did not exist, or whether conditions simply do not reveal them. One of the first effects of aerial photography was to reveal cropmark and soilmark sites on agricultural land in valleys which had previously been considered too densely forested for occupation until comparatively recent historical times. This has caused an upward revision of estimates of early populations, but has perhaps led to the neglect of the areas where earthwork sites had already been recorded – obviously, photographers tend to concentrate on the most promising areas. A further problem is that much low-lying land which was once under plough may have remained under pasture for a considerable period, in Britain perhaps showing the tell-tale traces of medieval ridge-and-furrow ploughed strips. These conditions will not only have destroyed any earthworks which preceded them, but mature pasture will prevent the detection of buried sites except under extreme conditions. The use of land for arable or pasture depends on factors such as the surface geology, drainage, climate, and altitude. Thus, a map of sites in an area is incomplete unless it shows how the sites were discovered, and marks the relevant conditions for the presence or absence of phenomena likely to show. It is important that new photography should be as carefully planned as any other form of fieldwork; ideally an area should be subjected to repeated study over many years in a variety of weather and crop conditions, in the hope that a much fuller record of sites may be accumulated than would be achieved in a single season's flying. Such programmes are less exciting and more expensive than unplanned exploration, but their results of course allow much firmer conclusions to be reached about site distributions, settlement patterns, and other features of ancient landscapes.

GEOPHYSICAL SURVEYING

It will be apparent that in the case of buried sites there are many chance factors affecting the visibility of crop- and soil-marks – the kind of vegetation, the level of moisture in the soil, and the agricultural state of the land. Some sites may never show up at all, others may show different parts at different times, and others may be partially revealed but extend into adjacent land where conditions are unsuitable. When the excavation of a site known from photographs of this kind is planned, more detail may be required of parts which do not appear clearly on photographs, and even the precise location of

the site on the ground may be difficult if only oblique photographs with few reference points exist. Here, a useful range of geophysical prospecting devices which can detect buried features is available. Their use is valuable wherever details need to be checked and where trial excavation would be inefficient. For example, at Usk, Gwent, the position of one side of a Roman legionary fortress including one of its gateways was found during the excavation of an area threatened with redevelopment. The fortress could reasonably be assumed to have been of a regular plan, but its overall area might vary by ten acres or more, and the exact form from squarish to rectangular. About half of the site lay under modern buildings, but its south side was likely to be in fields under pasture, insensitive to crop-marks. It was a comparatively simple exercise to take measurements along a line within and parallel to the known rampart, and two major anomalies were found which would be consistent with the existence of two buried ditches lying outside the former rampart (which had been destroyed long ago). With two sides known, the others could be deduced – a possible north ditch had been revealed by building work, and the survey of the southern limits had also suggested a break in the ditches which presumably indicated the position of its gateway. By combining the precisely known east side and gateway, the possible north ditch, the south side suggested by the geophysical survey, and the limits for the east side imposed by a river, a plan could be drawn up which (assuming a symmetrical layout) would give a fortress of 48 acres, fitting neatly within the range of comparable sites in Britain and abroad. On a site of such size, trial trenching would have been far too time consuming, and experience of the difficult subsoil had shown that features could only be reliably detected when large areas were uncovered (Manning 1981, 86–8).

Geophysical surveying is often used within known sites to suggest areas where excavation might be most profitable. At Anstiebury and two other Iron Age hillforts in Surrey, a limited research excavation was successfully guided to promising anomalies suggesting *foci* of occupation debris or pits likely to produce dating

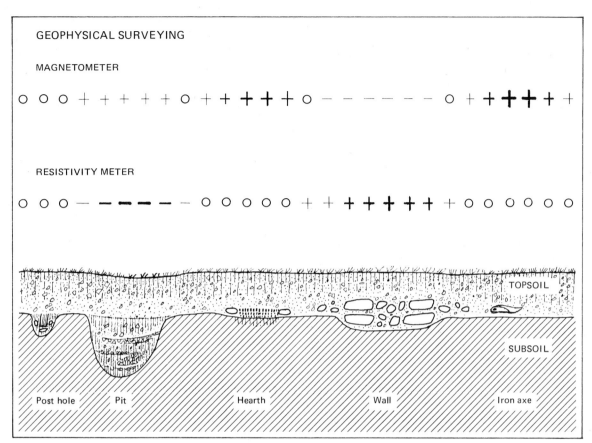

GEOPHYSICAL SURVEYING

MAGNETOMETER

RESISTIVITY METER

TOPSOIL

SUBSOIL

Post hole   Pit   Hearth   Wall   Iron axe

evidence for the site (Thompson 1979, 250). Some of the most important applications of this kind occur in rescue situations, where excavation is needed to locate suspected sites or structures whose position is only vaguely known, but where an enormous area excavation would not be a feasible or sensible way of recovering them. Such guidance can be misleading, however; at South Cadbury Castle (an Iron Age hillfort with additional Dark Age occupation) an area of the interior was excavated because a geophysical survey had suggested a rectangular building, potentially a Dark Age timber hall. On excavation it was found to be a fortuitous combination of entirely unrelated features of different dates, but a timber hall was indeed found in an adjacent area; however, its construction was largely based on post holes which were too small to have shown up in this kind of survey anyway (Alcock 1972, 71, fig. 8; below, fig. 52).

There are two main classes of instruments for

21 A hypothetical example of the ability of the two main methods of geophysical prospecting to detect buried features, using the same soil profile as fig. 17, where their appearance on aerial photographs is assessed. **0** indicates an average background reading, **+** a positive reading (stronger magnetic field or higher resistance to the passage of an electrical current), and **−** a negative response (lower magnetism or resistance) compared with the site average. Lighter or darker symbols give a rough impression of the relative strength of these likely results. It is apparent that the instruments do not react to the same things with equal strength, and that neither can be expected to detect minor features such as the posthole. Experience, and the nature of the particular site to be explored, will determine which method is employed.

geophysical prospecting, which detect either the resistance of a subsoil to the passage of an electrical current (resistivity meters) or variations in its magnetic characteristics (magnetometers). It must be stressed that these instruments are only used on sites whose location is already known or suspected, as their procedure is too elaborate and time-consuming to be applied 'blind' to large areas. As with aerial photography, the main purpose is to detect anomalies, hopefully man-made variations from the general background (fig. 21).

Resistivity surveying

This is a method by which an electric current is passed through the ground between electrodes, and the resistance to its flow measured. The current will pass relatively easily through damp soil, but drier compact material such as a buried wall or cobbled road surface will create a higher resistance. Resistivity surveying was first used for archaeological purposes in 1946. The method is rather cumbersome, because it requires a number of electrode probes (usually four) to be pushed into the ground at precise intervals for each reading. A variety of configurations have been tried in order to speed up the surveying. For instance, instead of forming a line, probes have been fixed in a square table-like arrangement with the instrument mounted on top for single-handed surveying. Needless to say, an even well-drained subsoil is best for resistivity, with features buried at a fairly constant depth. Otherwise, natural disturbances and variations may confuse resistivity readings. Because of the laborious procedure involved, the method is best suited to the detection of linear features, such as roads, walls or ditches, by taking measurements along a straight line across the approximately known or suspected position of the feature. The results are normally presented in the form of a graph with its peaks and troughs indicating high and low resistance, and marking the position of the buried anomalies. This is clearly demonstrated by J.J. Hus, who traced a Roman road at Sauvenière in Belgium in this way. By taking measurements along more closely spaced parallel traverses, Hus has also used a computer to

filter the results and to produce a contour-plan of areas of higher and lower resistance which effectively revealed the plan of a slight circular feature seen on an aerial photograph taken by C. Léva (Léva and Hus 1975).

Magnetic surveying

Like resistivity, this relies on the detection of variations from the general background of the soil, in this case indicated by differences in its magnetic field. Several aspects of human occupation cause anomalies. Heat (from hearths, kilns, furnaces, etc.) causes the magnetic particles which occur naturally in most soils and clays to align themselves along the prevailing magnetic field of the Earth at $c.$ 700°C or above – and to retain their alignment on cooling. The digging and refilling of ditches and pits also affects the normally random alignment of magnetic particles, whilst solid features such as walls or road surfaces contain less magnetic minerals, and therefore provide lower readings compared with their surroundings.

Unlike resistivity surveying, no probes into the ground are required; the instrument can simply be carried by an operator along traverses or a grid. If conditions allow its use, it has generally been preferred to resistivity for this reason since its first successful application in 1958. One form of instrument, the **proton magnetometer**, takes readings of the absolute magnetic field at given points on a grid; less sensitive but in many ways easier to operate is the **proton gradiometer** which measures the differences between two separate detector bottles at either end of a two-metre pole held vertically by the operator. Buried anomalies affect the lower bottle more than the higher, and the difference is recorded, rather than the absolute field. This allows rapid surveys of areas threatened by development to be made, particularly when there is a 'bleeper' mechanism to produce an audible sound when an anomaly occurs. Even more effective is the **differential fluxgate gradiometer**, which behaves in the same way as a proton gradiometer but can take continuous rather than spot readings. Gradiometer results are easier to interpret than magnetometer readings, which are more liable to disturbance by natural variations in the subsoil, surrounding wire fences, and electrical storms or railways. All of these detectors are connected to the basic instrument by a cable. As well as the person carrying the detector, another operator is normally required to record readings in relation to the surveying grid, unless an automatic system is being used (fig. 24). Like resistivity results, computer processing is useful in 'filtering' the results – particularly those from the sensitive proton magnetometer – and plotting them on a plan (figs 22–3). Practically, there are some difficulties with the readings, for they are usually displaced from the centres of the buried features which they represent for reasons which lie firmly in the realm of physics, but which must be taken into account before excavation. In fact it may often be the case that a portion of a site needs to be excavated to see what kinds of features are responsible for different kinds of anomalies before their interpretation can be extrapolated to the rest of the surveyed area.

Electromagnetic surveying

Electromagnetic instruments include the widely-used 'metal detectors' which have received such a bad press from archaeologists, but show every sign of growing popularity amongst the general public. In fact, the readily available types have been shown to be extremely inefficient, and to penetrate the soil only to a very limited extent. A larger more sophisticated device (the **pulse induction meter**) has been used with rather more respectable motives in Greece and Italy to give advance warning of ferrous and non-ferrous metal objects in graves which are about to be excavated. For detecting archaeological features, their depth penetration is poor compared with resistivity or magnetometer instruments, and few successful applications have been made.

Thus, the combination of fieldwalking, aerial photography, and geophysical surveying has increased the powers of observation of archaeologists to a remarkable extent during recent decades. However, the use of geophysical prospecting is not restricted to archaeology on dry land. Magnetometers are effective in surveying wreck sites on the seabed, although echo-sounders and sonar scanners take the place of aerial photography for detecting anomalies in the seabed, except in clear shallow water. Fieldwork underwater is not unlike that on land, and relies on visual scanning of areas of the seabed by divers; photography, recording, and surveying practices on wreck sites and cargo scatters use the same general principles, but are more time-consuming and cumbersome.

Scientific location instruments have by no means replaced some of the traditional pre-excavation observation techniques, which may be as simple as hitting the ground with a mallet to see what kind of resonance it produces (light over a buried wall or thin topsoil, a dull thud over a humus-filled ditch, for instance). Probing or augering are also useful, either simply to test the depth of soil, or to remove samples as well as to gain some idea of the buried stratification. The latter is dangerous on a small complex site – a regular series of bore-holes could easily damage slight traces of structures or fragile artefacts; it is more commonly used to provide soil samples for pollen analysis or to test their phosphate content. An early medieval site at Vallhagar on the island of Gotland in the Baltic was thoroughly sampled for phosphate analysis; the site consisted of a widespread scatter of buildings and enclosures representing a farming community, and concentrations of phosphates derived from animal urine and dung were found adjacent to some buildings as well as in open areas, presumably resulting from milking and byre areas (fig. 25). A less predictable technique (normally employed to locate underground water sources) is dowsing, with a Y-shaped twig or whatever else the exponent finds suitable; its occasional success in finding archaeological features is difficult to explain, and relies on the intuition of the dowser. I have surveyed a buried rock-cut ditch which enclosed a Romano-British farmstead in South Devon which a local farmer had noticed as a crop-mark and accurately located by dowsing with a forked hazel twig cut unceremoniously from the nearest hedge; probing and a small trial excavation confirmed its position and recovered dating evidence (Greene and Greene 1970).

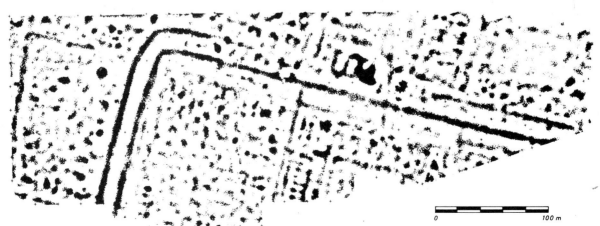

0   100 m

22–23 Magnetic prospecting at Colonia Ulpia Traiana, Xanten, near Düsseldorf, Germany. The aerial photograph shows some crop marks in the triangular field in the centre – pale lines indicating walls near the tree-lined road, and an indistinct darker band across the middle. The results of the magnetic survey are striking; the dark band emerges as two distinct ditches which make a right-angled turn in the adjacent field in which crop marks are not visible. The walls shown on the photograph form part of a much larger structure, in fact the forum of the Roman town. The whole area shows intensive occupation which is not apparent on the aerial photograph. *Rheinisches Amt für Bodendenkmalpflege, Bonn*

24 The Xanten survey was carried out by a mobile recording unit: the operator takes measurements at metre intervals along a grid, which are recorded on equipment in the van in the background of the photograph. The results are processed by computer in Bonn, and plotted out as in fig. 23. *Rheinisces Amt für Bodendenkmalpflege, Bonn*

25 A soil survey at Vallhagar, an early medieval settlement in Sweden. Buildings and enclosures extend over a considerable area, and more information has been provided by the analysis of soil samples for their phosphate content, which will have been increased by intensive agricultural use, such as manuring or the herding of animals. *After Stenberger 1955*

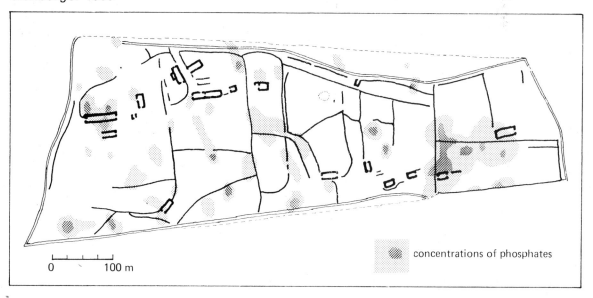

0   100 m

concentrations of phosphates

CONCLUSIONS

The archaeological fieldworker of the later twentieth century needs to be a master of many skills, some of them subjective and with a long history of development, others scientific and relying on new techniques. In addition, in developed and densely-populated areas of the world, the fieldworker may also need to be a local historian capable of using documentary evidence as well as geology and geography in the study of mature rural or urban landscapes. These approaches will be examined in Chapters 3 and 6, in connection with research carried out in advance of excavation and the interpretation of fieldwork by methods loosely described as 'spatial archaeology'. The more technical methods of archaeological prospecting outlined in this chapter are sometimes applied to individual sites with the limited objective of maximising the understanding of its nature and extent in advance of excavation. They might also be employed in a specific research project into a particular phase in the history or prehistory of a selected region. Today however there is an increasing tendency for information to be gathered more objectively, with the aim of collecting it as thoroughly as possible for all periods, to provide what in computing circles would be called a 'database', which can be used for a number of different purposes, and by many individuals who may not have been involved in its collection. One of the most positive results of 'rescue' archaeology is the stimulus to this kind of recording, in order to actually estimate the nature and extent of the threats to particular areas, and to assist in the best selection of sites for excavation. There is also a pre-emptive factor: if planning authorities and contractors can easily consult records of sites at an early stage, they may well be able to adjust developments to avoid sites, or at least take note of them so that excavation can be arranged well in advance without the costly unforeseen disturbance of building schedules. Thus another layer of responsibility is added to fieldworkers – not only to discover, record and interpret sites, but to present the results in a convenient and comprehensible form for consultation by non-specialists.

Further reading

This discovery of the ancient civilizations and the growth of fieldwork techniques are described in the historical accounts of archaeology by Glyn Daniel and Stanley Casson referred to at the end of chapter 1 (p. 34 above). Individual accounts can be found together with current views in books in the Elsevier/Phaidon series *The Making of the Past*, which include historical introductions to the particular civilizations or periods which they cover: particularly good is the account of research in the Near East by David and Joan Oates, *The Rise of Civilization*, 1976, 25–68.

Something of the excitement of the discovery of the ancient civilizations can be recaptured in Edward Bacon's *The Great Archaeologists*, 1976, which contains extracts from *The Illustrated London News* from 1842 onwards about major finds in many parts of the world.

Fieldwork techniques and scientific location devices are to be found in most archaeological manuals. Basic fieldwork in the historical period employing technical as well as documentary work is described in *Fieldwork in Medieval Archaeology* by Christopher Taylor (1974). Aerial photography is introduced by Leo Deuel's *Flights into Yesterday: the Story of Aerial Archaeology*, 1971; case studies are included in D.R. Wilson, (ed.), *Aerial Reconnaissance for Archaeology*, (Council for British Archaeology Research Report 12), 1975. Geophysical surveying devices and the principles upon which they are based are to be found in several books on the sciences in archaeology, for instance M.S. Tite, *Methods of Physical Examination in Archaeology*, 1972. The French archaeological magazine *Les dossiers de l'archéologie* has devoted several lavishly-illustrated numbers to aerial photography and geophysical prospection in many countries, notably issues 1 (1975), 22 (1977), 39 (1979), and 43 (1980). New techniques of location and detection appear in journals such as *Journal of Archaeological Science* and *Archaeometry*.

3 Excavation

Excavation is one of the most important sources of new information in archaeology: if the data recovered is to be reliable, the excavation techniques must be sound. Although large modern excavations may appear technically complex with 'virtuoso' directors, the basic principles are simple and have changed little since their importance was first realised. Their application has been slow, and is far from complete in many parts of the world. Excavation consists of two components which are at times in conflict – the *vertical* sequence of layers, structures and the finds they contain, and the *horizontal* plan of an occupation area or individual structure. The most important development of the twentieth century has been an improved understanding of the vertical aspect, and the design of excavation techniques to reveal it most carefully. The most recent large excavations have gone further, and have attempted to maximise the horizontal aspect while still recording the vertical sequence in all necessary detail.

Many early excavations were simply treasure-hunts which sought to recover objects of commercial or aesthetic value by random digging on known sites, or the systematic plundering of individual monuments such as burial mounds, in a manner requiring the minimum physical effort. Others were a form of more academic exploration, where sites were uncovered on a large scale to reveal structures and finds. Frequently, the two objectives could be combined – many ancient sites in Egypt and the Near East were extensively cleared; the best sculpture and objects were usually transported to museums, leaving behind impressive foundations or ruins, from which much of the most important evidence had been shovelled away

for ever. Finely-engraved architectural plans and elevations are no substitute for the information which might have been gleaned from the unspectacular layers of accumulated soil and debris and the modest artefacts they once contained. Many of the most familiar views of ancient Greek or Egyptian sites frequented by tourists in their thousands today are the product not of abandonment and natural decay, but eager clearance by archaeologists in the nineteenth century (fig. 14). These at least remain visible; it is instructive to consider one of England's richest discoveries in order to perceive most clearly the loss of information which must have occurred on other sites.

The royal Anglo-Saxon burial mound at Sutton Hoo in Suffolk (Bruce-Mitford 1979) was one of several barrows excavated in an exploratory manner in 1938 and 1939 on behalf of their landowner. When an undisturbed burial was found, more expert help was sought, and in 1939 a rich deposit was excavated. It included personal ornaments, weapons, drinking and table vessels of extraordinary richness in both precious metal and decoration. The sandy conditions had seriously weakened iron and bronze, however, and years of laboratory work have been devoted to the reconstruction of such items as a decorated iron helmet. By combining historical documents relating to East Anglia and the gold coins found in a purse in the burial, it has been widely accepted as the grave of King Redwald, who died in *c.* AD 625. The whole deposit was enclosed in a burial chamber in an eighty-foot ship, buried in a deep trench below the burial mound (fig. 26); only this saved the find. A hole had been dug into the barrow in the sixteenth or early seventeenth century, but fortunately its centre did not lie directly over the

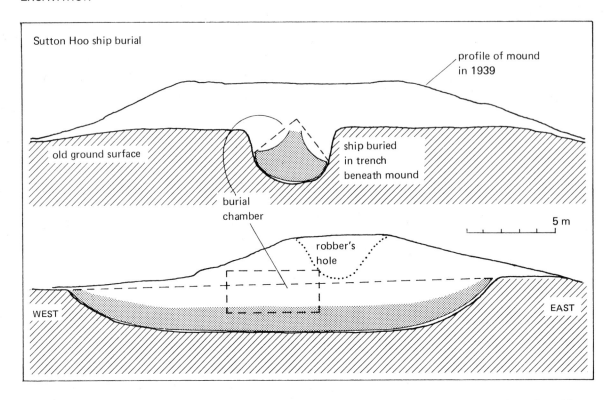

Sutton Hoo ship burial

profile of mound in 1939

old ground surface

ship buried in trench beneath mound

burial chamber

5 m

robber's hole

WEST

EAST

26 The Sutton Hoo ship burial, Suffolk: the ship was hauled from a nearby river into a deep trench and subsequently covered by a large mound. The burial chamber amidships contained an extraordinarily rich group of armour, weapons, silver tableware and other items from an Anglo-Saxon royal household of the early seventh century AD. Only the partial erosion of the mound and the depth at which the ship was buried saved the treasure for proper excavation in 1939; the seventeenth-century robbers' hole was off-centre and made no allowance for the extra depth. *After Bruce-Mitford 1979, 72 fig. 65*

burial chamber, and the hole was not taken below the surrounding ground level. If that attempt *had* been successful, very little would be known about the find. Some objects would undoubtedly have been melted down or sold off; others would only be known from unconnected fragments, and many more would have been discarded immediately as worthless. The ship

(only represented by discoloured sand and iron nails) would be unknown, as would the existence of the burial chamber and the layout of the grave goods. The date, identity and cultural connections of the dead king, and the relevance of the boat burial described in the Anglo-Saxon poem *Beowulf* would remain unknown; we might not know whether the surviving finds came from a single burial or several, or even the exact location of the original find.

Sutton Hoo is of course an extreme case, but its lesson applies to most of the 'great' excavations of the nineteenth and early twentieth centuries. The problem continues in many areas of the world where state archaeological services are small and the policing of sites difficult, but where sites regularly produce items desired by museums and collectors (Meyer 1973). Even in well-protected countries like Britain, the proliferation of metal detectors has revived the plundering of sites on a large scale. What always suffers is the *quality* of information – the context of a coin, precious object, or carving in relation to adjacent levels and structures. However, this seems to be a concept which archaeologists find particularly difficult to communicate to the public, and is often interpreted as professional jealousy or fun-spoiling.

Even after the above paragraphs were written, news came of further plundering at Sutton Hoo, remarkably reminiscent of the sixteenth- or early seventeenth-century attempt on the famous ship-burial: we can only hope that it was similarly unsuccessful. The *Newsletter* of the Council for British Archaeology for April 1982 carried the following comment:

In early February a hole measuring 10ft × 6ft × 4ft deep was discovered dug into the top of one of the unexcavated mounds at Sutton Hoo, one of the most famous and important archaeological sites in the British Isles. Although this was widely publicized in the local press, it passed almost unnoticed in the nationals. The Sutton Hoo mounds are on private property but they are, of course, Scheduled Ancient Monuments and protected under the Ancient Monuments and Archaeological Areas Act 1979. Damage to a protected monument is a criminal offence, carrying a maximum penalty of two years' imprisonment.

A Parliamentary Question by Baroness Birk asked what steps were being taken to improve the protection afforded to the 13,000 Scheduled Monuments in England against vandalism and clandestine excavation in the light of what had happened at Sutton Hoo. In his reply, Lord Avon stated that no steps were being taken; it was the responsibility of owners of monuments to do what they reasonably could to protect them from damage and vandalism.

It looks as though England's treasure hunters are becoming more ambitious, and that their activities will soon rival those of the TOMBAROLI of Italy or the HUAQUEROS of central America. The national heritage seems to be up for grabs.

STRATIFICATION

The most fundamental principle upon which excavation is based is the succession of levels, and the examination of the finds which they contain. We have already traced the origins of this understanding among geologists, palaeontologists, and students of human origins such as Frere, Boucher de Perthes, and McEnery. The study of later periods lagged sadly behind, and racy accounts of barrow excavations in Kent by Thomas Wright in the 1840s continue to provide a curious mixture of amusement and horror (Daniel 1967, 222). Stratification – if

27 General Pitt Rivers (1827–1900), portrayed by Frank Holl R.A. in 1882, shortly after he had inherited a large estate in Hampshire and Dorset containing many archaeological sites. Three elements in his approach to the study of the past are symbolized in the painting: the prehistoric shield and the pickaxe relate to his collection and intense study of ancient weapons which led him to excavate in order to recover more information, whilst his observant stance and notebook are a reminder of his surveying, recording and protection of ancient monuments. Although his perception of stratigraphy and recognition of archaeological features in excavations were not particularly advanced, his standards of recording and publication set a standard which is difficult to better even today. *Pitt Rivers Museum, University of Oxford*

noticed at all – was usually passively observed, rather than actively sought; good examples of such observations can be found at least as early as the seventeenth century in Scandinavia. In the 1840s J.J. Woorsae wrote lucidly and rationally on the requirements of controlled excavation (Daniel 1967, 103), which was a logical consequence of the Three-Age System put into effect by Thomsen some years earlier. Modern excavation practice does not have a single 'founding father' but the kind of progress made in the late nineteenth century is exemplified by **Pitt Rivers** (1827–1900; fig. 27). We have already seen that Pitt Rivers played an important part in the development of the study of artefacts in the mid-nineteenth century; he would undoubtedly be remembered for his contributions to typology, as well as fieldwork and surveys carried out in Ireland. Later in his life, through an unlikely course of inheritance, he came into possession of a large tract of one of the most archaeologically productive areas in Britain – Cranborne Chase in Wessex.

He devoted the rest of his life (1880–1900) to the study of this area – together with a host of other interests of an educational and 'improving' nature which give fascinating insights into the cultural atmosphere of Victorian England. The wealth derived from his estates allowed him to employ full-time assistants and to use his own estate labour to carry out a number of excavation projects on monuments of a variety of dates, from a Neolithic barrow (fig. 28) to a standing medieval building. It must be remembered that his first excavations predated this phase of his life, and had been undertaken in order to recover artefacts to place into his typological studies, and only secondly to elucidate sites or structures. It was the importance which he attached to *all* finds, however trivial, that gives him his modern aspect, and led him to record contexts as well as the artefacts themselves. In fact, it was not really his *excavation* technique which was revolutionary – it was neat and methodical, and accurately surveyed, in accordance with his military training – but the publication of these details in a series of massive volumes with copious illustrations and 'relic tables' which are still usable today. It was the

later combination of this approach with a clear perception of stratification, and an ability to excavate a site layer by layer, with detailed regard to the stratification which first properly fulfils the requirements of 'scientific' excavation. Contemporaries of Pitt Rivers such as Schliemann and Petrie working in Turkey, Egypt and Palestine were more advanced in their understanding of stratigraphy and the use of artefacts for dating the observed layers.

Three elements had emerged by the beginning of the twentieth century. Horizontal observations had improved considerably, with accurate recording and more careful examination; the vertical sequence was increasingly important, particularly on the deeply stratified 'tell' sites of the Near East. Orderliness, carefulness, and close attention to all classes of finds was the newest and most important element, which gave rise to authoritative publications and catalogues through which others could critically examine the work of the excavators. Glyn Daniel has commented:

It is difficult to overestimate the contribution made to archaeological method in the last quarter of the nineteenth century by Schliemann, Pitt Rivers and Petrie. It would be no exaggeration to say that, with the experience of the Danes and the Swiss behind them, they forged the essential technique of archaeology (1975, 177).

In the 1920s and 1930s the three elements outlined above were most notably combined in **Mortimer Wheeler**, a man with a military background and bearing like Pitt Rivers, but who, unlike him, trained many others (fig. 29). He also organized museums and wrote for the public, and in his later life communicated through radio and television in a remarkably successful way. Wheeler is chiefly remembered as the excavator who perfected the 'box system' and 'grid system' by which a site was divided up into square areas, with baulks between them left standing as a permanent record of the stratification on all four sides of each excavated square (fig. 30). But Wheeler did not always excavate in this fashion: some of his work at Maiden Castle (Dorset) was very similar to modern open-area practice. His techniques emphasize

28 The excavation of Wor Barrow, Dorset, by Pitt Rivers in 1893. Despite the quality of the recording, the actual excavation technique is crude, moving forward against a vertical face; sloping layers of barrow material can be seen on the sections, but there is no attempt to remove these individually. Worse, the excavation has been taken down below the old ground surface, whose buried soil shows as a dark layer at wheelbarrow height in the left section. Pitt Rivers was lucky to find the outline of a timber mortuary structure which had stood in a foundation trench beneath the barrow; many slighter features must have been dug away with the old ground surface. A model of the barrow before excavation can be seen propped up at the front of the excavation. *Photograph by courtesy of Salisbury and South Wiltshire Museum*

29 Sir Mortimer Wheeler (1890–1976) casting his experienced eye over the excavation of a hill-fort at South Cadbury in Somerset in 1968, in the company of the site director Leslie Alcock, who had assisted him on his excavations in India in the late 1940s. Wheeler had first entered professional archaeology in 1913, and his perceptive appreciation of sites and the landscape was soon increased by artillery experience during the First World War. He remained a vigorous and colourful figure active in archaeology until his death in 1976. *Photograph by courtesy of Prof. L. Alcock*

32 An early example of open-area excavation in Denmark – the Iron Age settlement at Nørre Fjand, explored by Hatt from 1938–40. The faint traces of timber buildings, fragmentary stonework, and superimposed floor levels could only have been revealed by the systematic uncovering of large areas, and piecemeal examination of individual features and layers. *Hatt 1954, 75 fig. 50; photograph National Museum, Copenhagen*

30–31 The different roles of box trenches and open-area excavation in the Iron Age fortification at Stanwick, Yorkshire, excavated by Wheeler in 1951–2. **30** shows a typical grid of baulks providing four permanent sections in each individual square trench; wooden pegs at their intersections are reference points for surveying and the plotting of important finds. In **31**, the baulks have been removed to reveal a circular timber building; there is no depth of deposits requiring the number of control sections visible in **30**. The grid of baulks would in fact conceal many important features and mask the continuity of the gulleys – much effort would have been saved by an open-area excavation from the outset.
Photographs from Wheeler 1954a, pl. VIII, facing p. 8

the conflicting requirements of lateral and vertical excavation: to understand the sequence of the site, the stratification is essential; but when an arbitrary grid of vertical baulks is imposed on a site, it may mask important horizontal features (fig. 31).

The concept of revealing stratification in a key section which is then drawn to provide the basic record of a sequence obviously demands straight-sided trenches, which need not be very large if the sequence alone is being studied. Wheeler discussed this basic conflict (1954. 126–9), and admirably summarized the optimum compromise:

With the proviso, then, that all horizontal digging must proceed from clear and comprehensible vertical sections, the question of priority is fundamentally not in doubt. Careful horizontal digging can alone, in the long run, give us the full information that we ideally want (*ibid.*, 129).

This compromise cannot always be reached even today, and when Wheeler was first excavating, he was undoubtedly well aware of the problems of huge 'tells' in the Near East, where it had become standard practice to sink deep shafts ('*sondages*') to sample the successive occupations and their artefacts.

At the other extreme was the digging of many very small trenches on large shallow sites; it has sometimes been described as 'keyhole excavation', and was much used in Roman military archaeology to check critical details of fairly predictable plans of forts and their internal structures – Ian Richmond produced overall plans of vast Roman forts and fortresses in northern Britain by the judicious use of small narrow trenches. In Northern Europe, the same inter-war decades saw the development of open-area excavation of both stone and timber sites, where there was little build-up of occupation layers (fig. 32). The lowlands of Scandinavia and the Netherlands, and the river terraces of Germany contain many rural sites of this kind, from 'Danubian' Neolithic villages right through to the early medieval period, lying on flat alluvial land with subsoils favourable to the recognition of pits and structural remains of buildings. Such sites could not be predicted in the manner of Roman forts, and complete uncovering was essential to their understanding. A German archaeologist, Gerhard Bersu, carried out an influential excavation in England in 1939 on an Iron Age farmstead at Little Woodbury, Wiltshire, and demonstrated clearly that pre-Roman Celts lived not in minute pit-dwellings but substantial round timber houses, plans of whose post holes could only be recovered by stripping large continuous areas (Bersu 1940). The history of excavation techniques is brought up to date by examining the extension of this idea to sites which *do* have an accumulation of layers.

It may be repeated that good excavation

33 The excavation and dating of a post-hole

Left: the post stands in its hole, with some packing stones for extra stability. The topsoil and subsoil mixed up during the digging of the hole give its filling a different texture from its surroundings.
Right: a new layer has accumulated after the demolition or decay of the structure, filling the cavity left by the post ('post pipe'); a new topsoil has also developed.
Dating evidence
The rim of a pot datable to c. AD 1300 is 'residual', left over from an earlier occupation and accidentally incorporated into the filling because it was already in the topsoil through which the hole was dug. The position of the coin of AD 1520 amongst the packing stones shows that it could not have entered the hole *after* the erection of the post; it was presumably dropped by one of the builders during construction. A second coin is present in the soil which overlies the hole and fills the post-pipe; this soil provides a *terminus ante quem* for the end of the life of the structure, and the coin can only have reached this position after the decay of the post or its extraction during demolition. Thus, the date of the potsherd is irrelevant, but the coin of AD 1520 provides a *terminus post quem* for construction; likewise, AD 1600 is the *t.p.q.* for whatever activity is represented by the layer in which it was found. A life of c.1520–1600 could thus be suggested for the timber structure, but of course neither coin need have been new when lost; other dating evidence from the rest of the site must also be considered, as well as numismatic information on the likely circulation periods of the coins, before any precision can be reached.
NB If the coin of AD 1520 had not been found, a misleading *t.p.q.* two centuries too early would have been given by the residual potsherd. Furthermore, only precise stratigraphical excavation could have revealed the exact positions of the

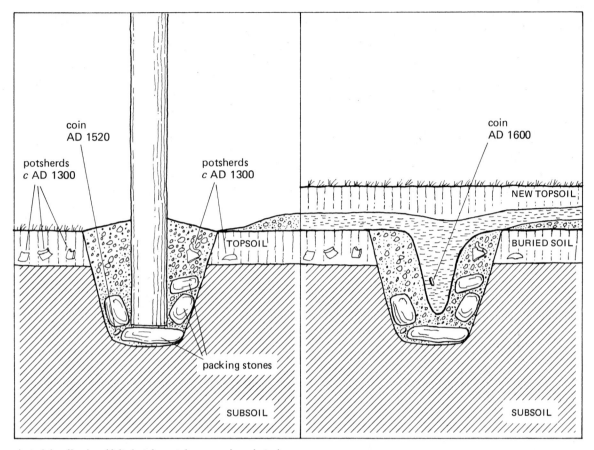

coin
AD 1520

potsherds
c AD 1300

potsherds
c AD 1300

coin
AD 1600

NEW TOPSOIL

TOPSOIL

BURIED SOIL

packing stones

SUBSOIL

SUBSOIL

datable finds; if it had not been absolutely clear that the latest coin came from the *post-pipe* rather than from the *packing*, a false *t.p.q.* of AD 1600 might easily have been assumed.

satisfies the requirements of both the vertical and horizontal aspects of a site. On sites excavated by a grid system, and particularly in the case of mounds excavated by quadrants, the final stages of excavation usually consisted of removing the baulks; the most recent open-area excavations never have baulks at any stage. On sites of limited depth, this causes no problems; the disturbed ploughsoil can be stripped off and the various features revealed for individual study. This can also be done on sites with deep stratigraphy, by careful contoured planning of the extent, depth and consistency of each layer that is removed, so that in theory a section could be drawn on any given line from the site records alone. Alternatively, fixed section lines can be

selected, and the cross-section of each layer drawn during its removal, so that a cumulative drawing is built up. These techniques suffer one considerable drawback, however; unlike the sides of a trench or a baulk, they are never actually seen by the excavator all at once, and they can therefore never be checked. However, on sites where the full exposure of each horizontal level and phase is very important, this is a justifiable sacrifice.

THE INTERPRETATION OF STRATIFICATION

John Frere's observations published in 1800 clearly embodied the commonsense notion that in a series of layers, those at the bottom will be earlier than those at the top, and geologists used the same principle to arrange fossils from different strata into developmental sequences. Today, even the simplest archaeological situations are approached from the same point of

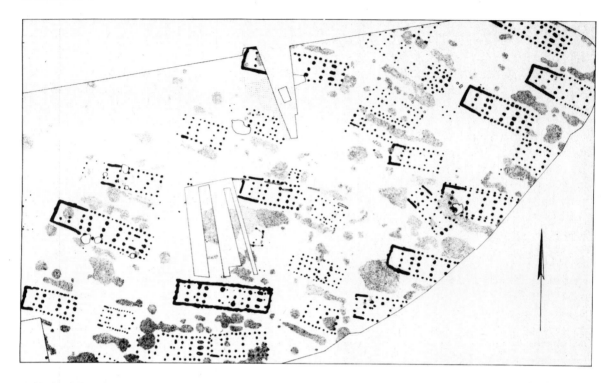

34 The Neolithic settlement at Elsloo in the Netherlands illustrates the problems of open-area sites where no occupation levels survive to provide stratigraphical relationships – only the chance intersection of individual features can give a clue to the sequence of overlapping structures. How many of the large timber buildings were contemporary? *After Modderman 1975, fig. 86*

view, whether long sequences in sections are being studied, or the direct relationship between intercutting or intersecting features in an area excavation. An additional element is the introduction of dating; this gives rise to the clumsy but apposite terms *terminus post quem* and *terminus ante quem* (fig. 33). These concepts can occasionally be extended to draw conclusions about features which do not directly interrelate at all, often by assumptions which are not objective and are a reminder that excavation is by no means a 'science'; it is up to the reader of an excavation report to decide whether or not they are reasonable assumptions.

Thus it can be seen that the use of sections to

reveal and elucidate relationships is very important – especially on open-area excavations with little stratification to link buildings together by their floor levels, construction and destruction debris, etc. In fact, on many sites, it is impossible to ascertain any relationship between structures. At Elsloo in the Netherlands a large number of plans of timber buildings of Neolithic date has been revealed; a few can be shown to be of different dates because their plans overlap, but most of them do not (fig. 34). Did the site last for a comparatively short time, crowded with buildings, or were there just a few at any one time over a longer period, gradually being replaced in slightly different positions? At best, informed guesses can be made that particular buildings were contemporary (similar alignment, constructional details, etc.) but frequently the final interpretation is purely a personal judgement by the excavator – a fact which again underlines the necessity to check the original report, and not to accept its conclusions at face value, especially when they are quoted in a secondary source.

An increasing awareness of the complexity of stratification and the large size of many modern excavations have combined to make the interpretation of stratification (= **stratigraphy**) very difficult. The first stage in writing an excavation report usually involves integrating the stratification and structures with the dating evidence recovered from them, whether it is pottery, coins, radio-carbon samples, or whatever else may be of chronological significance; of course it is essential that such excavated material has been carefully recorded in relation to the deposits in which it was found. One development has greatly assisted the study of stratigraphy – the Harris Matrix (fig. 35). Harris has emphasized the fundamental validity of Wheeler's approach to stratigraphy, but demands a more systematic approach. His term 'unit of stratification' rather than 'stratum' or 'layer' conveys the importance of **interfaces** between layers – for example the sides of a silted-up ditch have no actual existence other than as the boundary or interface between its filling and the material through which it was dug, but they

35 The recording of a stratigraphic sequence using the *Harris Matrix*. The simple section (top left) and the exploded three-dimensional diagram show the same stratigraphic units and the order in which they were formed (note that (2) and (6) are *interfaces* rather than actual layers). Bottom left is a Harris Matrix showing all of the stratigraphical relationships by lines; in the centre, this has been reduced to a clear summary of the original section by the removal of superfluous or duplicated lines.

This process can be carried out during the course of an excavation, and when simplified, such diagrams make a convenient method of summarizing the stratigraphy in a published excavation report. *After Harris 1979, 87, fig. 28*

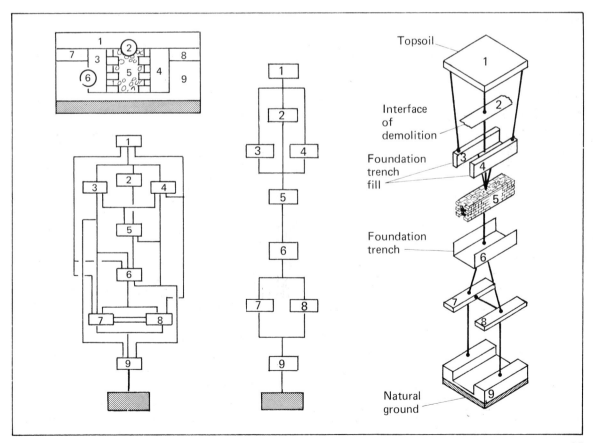

nevertheless represent an actual human operation which can be allotted its correct place in the sequence of layers.

The recognition of interfaces is a great aid to the analysis of the stratification of complex excavations. It is not always fully appreciated that the interfaces represent a period of human activity just as much as the visible layers and other features, and that the only way to make sense of them is to study the whole extent of each interface in order to understand that activity:

No amount of sectional drawing is of the slightest help in such a composition of these period plans, as it becomes clear that the horizontal record of stratification is far more important than the vertical. . . . What is needed is not a grain-by-grain plan, but a record of scaled drawings with each stratigraphic unit on a separate sheet, and which shows, at the very least, the area of the stratum and spot heights of its surface – as recorded prior to excavation. With such an archive any desired configuration of stratigraphic units can be made at any time . . . (Harris, 1977, 94).

Harris matrices have by no means replaced the traditional section-drawing in archaeological reports; there are many crucial relationships which the director will want to illustrate, as well as details of individual features – the composition of silted-up ditches, or rubbish-pits, for instance. Even colour photography will rarely bring out the amount of detail required (and it would be prohibitively expensive to publish anyway), so that a section drawing is by definition an interpretation, and can be expressed in a variety of different ways, from baldly diagrammatic to naturalistic. Some excavators go further, and attempt reconstruction drawings of the structures whose decay has resulted in a particular section – this is a valuable discipline which can generate many useful ideas which will improve the quality of an interpretation. A subjective aspect of section drawings is also important – an impression of the actual *appearance* of a stratigraphic sequence can be given, and supply a level of information which cannot be included in a matrix.

CASE STUDY: THE DEVELOPMENT OF EXCAVATION TECHNIQUES AT CORBRIDGE, NORTHUMBERLAND

The Roman site, *Corstopitum*, lies just west of this medieval town in the Tyne Valley, 24 miles from the mouth of the river. It lay at the junction of two important Roman Roads, Dere Street and Stanegate – the former led from York into Scotland, while the latter continued west to Solway and actually formed the northern frontier of the Roman Empire for some years. The history of the exploration of this site clearly illustrates the changing aims and techniques of archaeological excavation, from treasure-hunting to area excavation.

Stone robbing and treasure-hunting
As early as the seventh century AD, Corbridge was being used as a source of building stone for Anglo-Saxon churches, which were the first major stone constructions in the area since the end of the Roman period. Degradation of the site by this kind of quarrying went on for over

1000 years before any real archaeological excavation was carried out, but it was probably still impressive in the thirteenth century, when it attracted the attention of King John during a visit to the region in 1201. The contemporary record is terse, and sounds better when embroidered by the comments of the Tudor antiquary Camden:

No inconsiderable remains of antiquity, however, are to be found here, among which King John dug for treasure supposed to be buried by the antients; but fortune mocked his vain pursuit, as he had formerly done Nero when searching for Dido's treasure at Carthage. He found nothing but stone with marks of brass, iron, and lead. Whoever views the adjoining heap of ruins called *Colecester* will pronounce it a station of Roman soldiers (Camden, trans. Gough, 1789, III, 235).

Antiquarian observations
Following Leland and Camden in the sixteenth

century many other travellers commented on the visible ruins well into the eighteenth century. In addition to the long tradition of stone robbing, the expansion of agriculture must have had severe and cumulative effects; indeed, a wholesale clearance of an area of the site took place in the first decade of the nineteenth century for the specific purpose of agricultural improvement. A notable local antiquarian, John Horsley (1684–1732), gathered information in the first quarter of the eighteenth century, and in his *Britannia Romana* observed: 'It is now almost intirely levelled. . . . Pieces of *Roman* bricks and pots were lying everywhere on the surface of the ground in tillage, when I was on the spot.' He also commented on the numbers of antiquities discovered at the site (1732, 397). Stukeley's *Iter Boreale*, an account of a tour made in 1729, confirms this with an alarming observation. 'They tell us with some sort of wonder, that it is the richest and best thereabouts for ploughing: they discern not that it is owing to the animal salts left in a place that had been long inhabited. Corbridge is built out of its ruins, which are scattered about there in every house' (1776, 63).

Excavation (fig. 36)

Archaeological excavations were mounted in 1861; '. . . a labourer had been placed by Mr. Cuthbert of Beaufront at the service of Mr. Coulson, . . . for the purpose of making investigations at Corbridge.' The Roman road (Dere Street) and bridge across the Tyne and some internal structures were examined (Bruce, 1865, 18–19). In retrospect from 1906, the aftermath was predictable: '. . . . the results obtained were apparently of great interest. Unfortunately the plans, reports, and drawings made by Mr. Coulson have entirely disappeared, and the only record of his work is an inadequate *resumé* given at second hand . . .' (Woolley 1907, 162).

The early twentieth century witnessed a new investigation. The reasons for the excavations of 1906–14 relied partly upon past accounts of buildings and rich finds, and present ignorance. The best insight is provided not in the excavation reports, but in the autobiography published in 1953 by the first director, Leonard Woolley (1880–1960):

My first experience of digging was at Corbridge in Northumberland, and I know only too well that the work there would have scandalized, and rightly scandalized, any British archaeologist of today. It was however typical of what was done forty-five years ago, when field archaeology was, comparatively speaking, in its infancy and few diggers in this country thought it necessary to follow the example of the great pioneer, Pitt Rivers. *The Northumberland County History* was being written and the writers wanted to know more about the Roman station at Corbridge, so proposed a small-scale dig to settle the character of the site. The committee naturally appealed to Professor Haverfield as the leading authority on Roman Britain, and he, as he had intended to take a holiday on the Roman Wall, agreed to supervise the excavations. Somebody, of course, had to be put in charge of the work and because I was an Assistant Keeper in the Ashmolean Museum my qualifications were, in the eyes of an Oxford professor, *ipso facto* satisfactory. Haverfield arranged with Sir Arthur Evans, the Keeper, that I should go to Corbridge. In point of fact I had never so much as seen an excavation, I had never studied archaeological methods even from books (there were none at the time dealing with the subject), and I had not any idea of how to make a survey or a ground-plan; apart from being used to handling antiquities in a museum, and that only for a few months, I had no qualifications at all. I was very anxious to learn, and it was a disappointment to me that Haverfield only looked in at the excavation one day in the week and then was concerned only to know what had been found – I don't think that he ever criticized or corrected anything' (Woolley 1953, 14–15).

The excavations of 1906–14 explored enormous areas of the site, and resulted in a series of annual excavations reports which totalled 676 pages. In addition, Volume X of the *Northumberland County History* appeared in 1914, and contained a 48-page synthesis of the results, written by Haverfield (this was of course the *raison d'être* of the excavations described above by Woolley):

It seems plain that we have here something that was neither an ordinary fortress nor an ordinary town. The castramentation of the one and the street-planning of the other are alike wanting. We may rather guess that Corstopitum was now a store-base for armies operating further north and possibly even

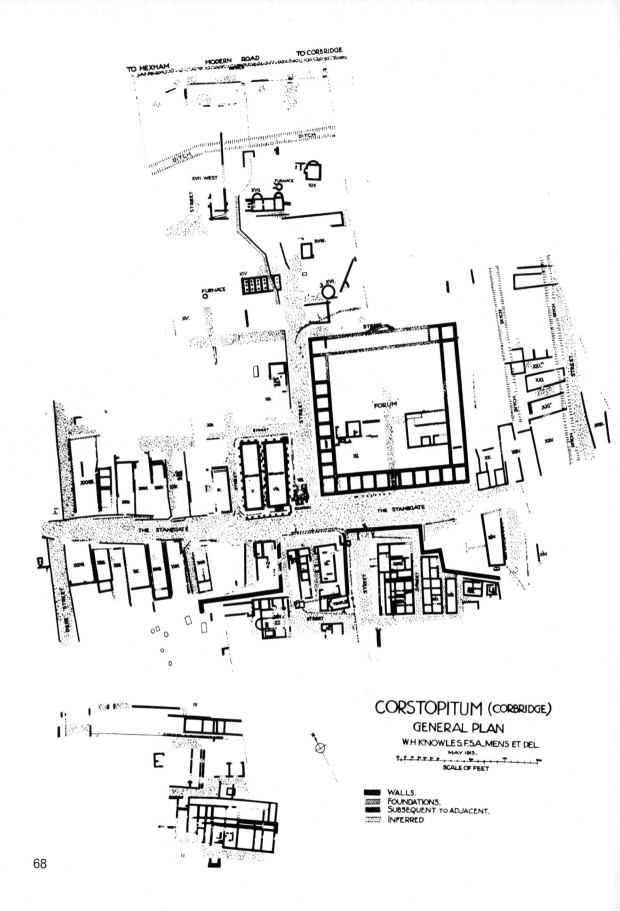

TO HEXHAM   MODERN   ROAD   TO CORBRIDGE

DITCH

DITCH

XVII. WEST

FURNACE

STREET

XVII

XIX

XVIII.

FURNACE

XIV

XVI.

STREET

XV.

FORUM

DITCH

DITCH

STREET

XXI.

XXI

STREET

XXI.

XX

XX

XXIV.

XXV.

XL

STREET

STREET

DERE STREET

THE STANEGATE

THE STANEGATE

STREET

XII.

STREET

STREET

E

CORSTOPITUM (CORBRIDGE)

GENERAL PLAN

W.H.KNOWLES.F.S.A.,MENS ET DEL.

MAY 1913.

SCALE OF FEET

WALLS.
FOUNDATIONS.
SUBSEQUENT TO ADJACENT.
INFERRED

68

36 Plan of the area excavated at Corbridge before the First World War. Good plans were obtained of major stone structures in the centre of the site (the granaries and 'forum', labelled X, VII, and XI, and walled compounds to the south of Stanegate). To the north and west, however, buildings had been at least partially constructed in timber or had been disturbed by agriculture. Along the Stanegate, the positions of shops opening onto the road were only indicated by stone gutters and gravel or paved floors. The existence of four major timber forts built successively on the site before the large stone structures were erected was entirely unsuspected until excavations were renewed in the 1930s. *Plan from Craster 1914, pl. VIII, facing p. 481*

37 Excavation techniques at Corbridge; this photograph was included in a short interim report published in 1910 by Knowles and Forster. It shows the clearance of the porticos of the two stone granaries (X and VII on the plan, fig. 36); the bases of the columns have become deeply embedded in a build-up of surfaces of the main road (Stanegate), and a gutter can be seen against them. All of the deposits which would have contained the layers linking the road surfaces to the granaries and their loading platforms have been removed without record – everything except solid masonry. Not only was the evidence removed, but it was totally destroyed without leaving anything for later excavators to re-examine.

for the eastern garrisons of Hadrian's Wall, with a half-military, half-civil population which would gather round such a base (*op. cit.* 479).

As the [fourth] century advanced, Corstopitum declined. It survived . . . only as an ill-built town of hucksters and mechanics, whose mean shops intruded on the nobler ruins of the Antonine Age; a town of vanishing wealth, on the extreme border of a sinking empire (*op. cit.* 11).

It was known, then, that coins, pottery and dated inscriptions indicated occupation throughout the Roman period, from the late first century AD (when the area was first invaded) until the late fourth or early fifth. But most of the information centred upon the structures assigned to the second century – what preceded or succeeded them was largely unknown. A glance at the seven photographs which Haverfield selected as illustrations shows why. The whole exercise had consisted of stripping soil until stone structures were found, and then uncovering them completely or simply following the walls (fig. 37). Some digging around beneath the foundation levels was carried out, but actual structures were rarely revealed, although 'disturbed ground' containing recognizably earlier Roman finds was frequently encountered. This was no longer treasure hunting; the horizontal aspect of the site – plans of buildings in particular – was being actively explored with the clear (if undefined) purpose of finding out more about the site, simply by carrying on digging until finds and structures ceased to be found. In fact, only the Great War intervened:

At the time of writing the question of continuing the excavations in 1915 remains in suspense. . . . If it should be necessary to suspend operations till the end of the war, it is hoped that the Committee will then be able to resume their work and carry it to completion. A considerable part of the east field still remains untouched, and a fair amount of work will be necessary in the field immediately to the south of it. The unexcavated part of the south field is indicated above, and in the west field a large area awaits examination (Forster and Knowles 1915, 231).

Excavations between the wars

Durham University Excavation Committee began work at Corbridge in 1934 under the joint direction of Ian Richmond and Eric Birley; the reason for the work was the preparation of the central portion of the remains found in 1906–14 for public display by His Majesty's Office of Works. The remaining topsoil from the central areas of the site (which are displayed to this day) was removed *before* the new excavations. Birley had been asked to write the official guide in 1933, and had recently hypothesized four firmly-dated periods of construction, occupation and destruction for Hadrian's Wall as a result of his excavations in one of the Wall forts, Birdoswald. By this date, stratigraphic excavation was familiar, and artefact studies – notably the dating of pottery – had advanced considerably. The excavations of the later 1930s were therefore carried out with strict reference to stratigraphic deposits and relationships, which could then be dated by their associated artefacts. Furthermore, the directors had a distinct working hypothesis in mind: 'It seemed axiomatic that the four main Wall periods should be reflected in the structural history of Corstopitum too', said Birley in retrospect (1959, 3). The work was a mixture of replanning and analysis of the stone structures which were to be conserved and displayed to the public, and new trenches dug to examine specific relationships between the structures and to assign them to their appropriate historical period.

One important aspect which was studied was the nature of the layers below the stone buildings; they had been recognized, but neither understood nor explored since 1909. The new excavators not only knew how to recognize remains of timber structures, but were fully aware of the nature and planning of Roman forts; thus, using a series of small trial trenches, a late first-century fort gateway, its ditch system, and parts of internal buildings were identified. More layers belonging to later forts were recognized between this first phase and the overlying stone structures (fig. 38); the 1936–38 excavation report speaks with an air of confidence entirely lacking from the 1906–14 series:

. . . it is impossible . . . to correlate with history all the periods of occupation so far discovered. . . . The

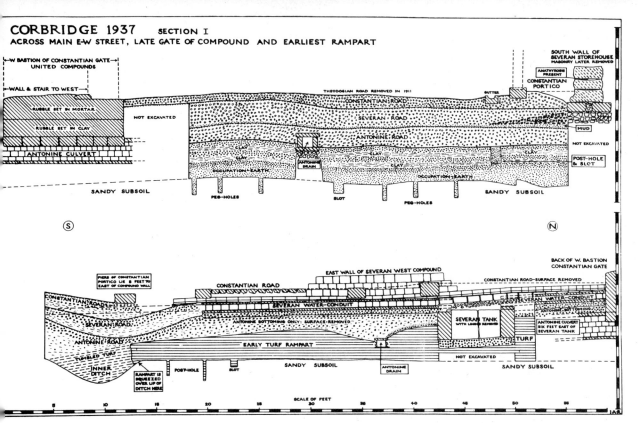

deep sections, however, by relating to the subsoil and to one another buildings of which the planning has long been known, mark a new departure in our understanding of the site. It is not possible both to describe and to date the work of later periods; while the fact that the problems concerned with early periods can be defined, may be regarded as the first step towards their solution (Birley and Richmond 1938, 260).

Excavations proceeded (broken only by the 1939–45 war) every year until 1973; new details were added, old ones were confirmed, modified, or rejected. Excavation was on a comparatively small scale, and used for training purposes as well as research; it was heavily constrained by the consolidated remains of major late second-century stone structures of the central area of the site. Four successive superimposed forts – two of them with additional phases of internal modification – were gradually disentangled by a cumulative series of detailed stratigraphic observations of intercutting features made in small trenches over the years; in addition, a native farmstead which had existed before the first fort was built was discovered. Correlations between historical events, dated buildings inscriptions found on the site,

38 Sections drawn by Ian Richmond from trenches which explored the relationships between the structures discovered at Corbridge before the First World War. The buildings are related to road levels assigned to specific historical periods (Antonine, Severan, etc); underlying the lowest road are several layers belonging to timber forts of the late first and second centuries AD, and settings for timber structures can be seen extending into the subsoil. With hindsight, the interpretation seems rather over-simplified and the dating arbitrary, but it is a considerable advance over the treatment of the same road a few metres away shown in fig. 37. *Birley and Richmond 1938, facing p. 254*

and stratified coins and pottery were all used to provide dating for these phases, whilst comparative studies have suggested the size and nature of the army units occupying each phase.

The stone structures on the site were more difficult to assess, particularly their later history after the second century AD, because of the removal of the crucial overlying strata either by the early excavators or during clearance for display. Debate has raged, often relying only on observations recorded in the early reports from the 1906–14 excavations, but the data simply cannot be checked: it has gone forever. Much of the surrounding area has not been touched since 1914 and lies under farmland outside the limits of the remains open to public display. To the west it is known that open-fronted shop buildings flanked a main street – but when were they constructed, and what was their history? Many must have been built of timber, but the only traces recorded were occasional stone gutters, hearths, or gravel levelling and floors; their existence was often suspected, but it was outside the technical competence of the excavators to find them. To the north, the plan is even less satisfactory. Fragments of building plans, minor roads, ditches, and furnaces indicate intense activity; it was probably a civilian industrial area, overlying the northern parts of the early timber forts. In some places, stratigraphic sequences were actually recorded on the plans, where major features overlapped each other (fig. 36), and occasionally structures were dated by associate finds, but little else can be said in the absence of further excavation.

Thus, excavations at Corbridge from the 1860s to the 1960s illustrate the general development of modern excavation techniques. The story does not end there, however, and in the 1970s and 1980s it has been brought up to date with large open-area rescue excavations instigated by the construction of a new museum on the main site and by road building nearby. The latter is a classic example of the combination of planned research, chance discovery, and systematic fieldwork, which revealed a whole new phase in Corbridge's early military history.

Area excavations

In the very last season of the annual training excavations at Corbridge in 1973, several fragments of a decorated pottery bowl were found sealed in the foundations of the headquarters of the very first fort on the site, providing a textbook example of a *terminus post quem*. The bowl was of a well-known form of samian ware, imported from southern France, and closely datable by historical evidence from other sites, including Pompeii, and expert opinion concurred that it was unlikely to be earlier than *c.* AD 90, and certainly later than *c.* 85. This created an immense problem, for the first fort was assumed since the 1930s to have been built during the campaigns of the governor of Britain, Agricola, who first garrisoned the area in the *early* eighties AD.

However, a Roman bath-house had been discovered by accident in 1955 one kilometre west of the main site (fig. 39), and its excavation had produced pottery of a date appropriate for the time of Agricola. Informed fieldwork suggested a level river terrace immediately east of the bath-house as the likely site for the fort which must have accompanied such a structure, for a civilian context would be unthinkable in this area at such an early date. As it happened, a dual-carriageway by-pass was about to be constructed, which had been routed north of the *known* site, but cut right across the suspected site of the newly-envisaged Agricolan fort. Rescue excavations were mounted, and the patience of the road contractors allowed a reasonable amount of information to be obtained. A continuous open strip over 150 metres long was uncovered, including remains of fifteen timber buildings (fig. 40). Associated pottery and coins

39 Location map showing the relative positions of *Corstopitum* (Corbridge main site) and the Red House site excavated in 1974 in advance of the construction of the Corbridge by-pass. The structures shown in black on the main site are those found in 1906–14 (fig. 36), and the rectangular outline of one of the underlying timber forts revealed between the 1930s and 1970s is also indicated. *Hanson* et al. *1979, 3, fig. 1*

40 Rescue excavations at the Red House site, Corbridge. A narrow strip was cleared along the line to be taken by a new road, although space had to be left for contractors' vehicles working further along the route. The outlines of foundation trenches for timber buildings can be seen in the foreground. *Photograph courtesy of Charles Daniels*

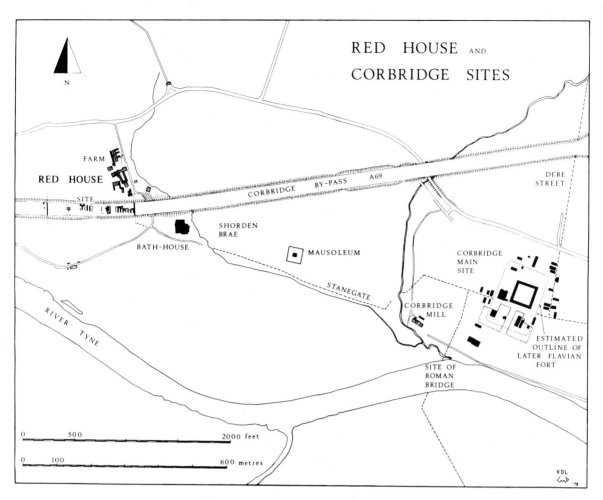

RED HOUSE AND
CORBRIDGE SITES

N

FARM
RED HOUSE
SITE

CORBRIDGE BY-PASS A69

DERE
STREET

SHORDEN
BRAE

BATH-HOUSE

MAUSOLEUM

CORBRIDGE
MAIN
SITE

STANEGATE

CORBRIDGE
MILL

RIVER
TYNE

ESTIMATED
OUTLINE OF
LATER FLAVIAN
FORT

SITE OF
ROMAN
BRIDGE

0   500   2000 feet

0   100   600 metres

KDL
'79

could be dated to precisely the appropriate period for the governorship of Agricola (and the nearby bath house), and provided conclusive evidence that the first period of Corbridge's military occupation lay here on the Red House site, and that it shifted to the well-known main site soon after the date provided by those critical pottery sherds found there in 1973. A tremendous rise in expectations of publication standards is reflected by the fact that this excavation of a small percentage of a single-period site, without occupation levels or rubbish deposits, generated a report of 98 pages in the 1979 issue of the same periodical (*Archaeologia Aeliana*) that had carried the 1906–14 report series. The earlier seasons involved incomparably more extensive and complex areas with abundant structures and other finds but were presented in an average of 85 pages per season.

Since 1974, only one very small excavation had been carried out on the main site (to check an outstanding detail of interpretation) until 1980, when a curious threat to the site gave rise to further rescue excavation. Temporary site-huts built before 1914 had served as a site-museum and store right up until their demolition in 1979; a new purpose-built replacement will soon be built, but its planned basement intrudes into archaeological levels. As a result, an area was excavated to record any details which might thus be destroyed; it is not often that a site has to be rescued from one of the instruments of its preservation. The area was badly disturbed by earlier excavation trenches, and confirmed the inability of the 1906–14 excavators to detect anything not built out of solid stone. In 1908, a deep trench had been cut below the stone buildings, which revealed only that there were four to five feet of 'disturbed soil', which were in fact the remains of the successive west ramparts of the early forts. This trench was emptied again in 1980, and allowed a useful section drawing of their structure to be made by the excavators, John Dore and John Gillam.

EXCAVATION PROCEDURE

Selection of a site

The proliferation of discoveries of new sites, and the limited resources available for excavation make it important that a site should be chosen with care. Two considerations often recur – a site may be a well-preserved example of its class, and attract attention from its owner or people in its vicinity, or a site may be threatened with imminent destruction by building or agriculture. Are these good reasons for an excavation? A basic question of approach is raised here: should archaeology be built up from a gradual accumulation of independent observations (the 'detective story' image), or should there be an overall strategy? The problem is perhaps best illustrated by an analogy.

Suppose that an area has been extensively examined by fieldwork of various kinds, and that twenty sites of a similar nature and Roman date are known. Ten are on marginal land, and well preserved from past or present destruction; of the other ten, nine are on active farmland, gradually suffering from the effects of ploughing, and one is about to be totally destroyed by building work. Sufficient funds are available to excavate *one* site completely. What should be done? Some choices may be suggested:

a   The site threatened with complete destruction should be totally excavated to save its information for posterity.
b   One of the well-preserved sites should be totally excavated, because it is likely to be in better condition and can be approached at a more leisurely pace, as it is not threatened; the quality of information should therefore be high.
c   Several sites, including that threatened with imminent destruction, should be partially examined in order to provide some basis for comparisons between them.
d   None of this class of site should be excavated at all; instead, resources should be devoted to investigating a different period for which fewer sites are known. The destruction of one out of twenty similar sites can be tolerated.

A number of problems are apparent – there are good points about all of the choices, and the decision will probably rest with a committee or individual who will need a lot of confidence to take choice (b); no two sites are ever identical, and surface indications may be deceptive – information of more precision may just as well be found on a damaged site as a well-preserved one. If either (a) or (b) are selected, how far can the results be safely generalised to the other 19? Few scientists would accept results gained from only five per cent of a sample. Choice (c) may therefore seem to be a good compromise, but partial excavations always leave unanswered questions, and complete knowledge of one site may be more informative than one-quarter of each of four. However, the problems of sampling in archaeology are a fertile area for debate, and opinions would vary over this solution (Mueller 1975). Whether (d) is better than any of the others may depend on the particular interests of the decision-maker; a Bronze Age specialist might well prefer to increase aerial survey and fieldwork on prehistoric sites rather than to explore a Roman site.

A further question may be added at this point: what should be done about 'unique' sites? Stonehenge, Avebury or Silbury Hill are all 'unique' prehistoric sites in Wessex – mainly in terms of their size in relation to similar stone circles, henge monuments, or mounds. Should they be ignored, and effort concentrated on a large number of more 'typical' sites, or can they be expected to give a clearer insight into their times because of their remarkable character? In a historical period, the same question may be framed; for example, which will tell us more about medieval Kent – Canterbury cathedral, or a selection of churches from surrounding urban and rural parishes? Again, there is no obvious answer – a compromise would seem reasonable, but may well be beyond available resources.

The only common theme to emerge from this discussion is the need for conscious decisions and policy, based on a well-informed overall knowledge of the significance of any given site in its region or country, and its relevance to current academic questions.

Planning an excavation (fig. 41)

Most excavations are planned by a single director who will take responsibility for preliminary research, setting up the actual excavation, and writing up the results. Of course, there is a broad range, from an individual engaged in a small research project digging a minor site with a few volunteers, up to the

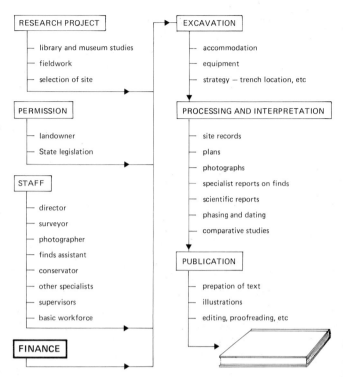

41 Theoretical flow-diagram of the organisation and excavation of a small excavation.

director of a permanent excavation unit involved in a major research or rescue project with a full-time team of special assistants and a paid labour force. Assuming that a site has been selected in the light of a sensibly-conceived programme of fieldwork, there is an enormous amount of research and organization still to be done. It will vary little, whatever the period of the site, or the country in which it lies.

Background research

The more information that can be amassed before excavation starts, the better the director can plan a detailed excavation, and respond to the information revealed as it goes along. Library work is essential; any accounts of the appearance of the site in past centuries by antiquaries, reports of previous excavations, or records of stray finds recovered from it must all be carefully examined. The last two may have left material in museum collections, which can be re-examined both before and after a new excavation. In countries where documentation extends far enough into the past, archive offices may hold maps and plans, such as those drawn up for land ownership or tax purposes, showing features of the site itself or its physical surroundings which have subsequently disappeared, such as earthworks, field systems, or trackways. Informative place names may also be recorded in such sources. In England, an area may be featured in Anglo-Saxon charters, the earliest surviving land-documents, although these are more likely to have been useful during the general background research leading up to the site's selection for excavation.

Among the more up-to-date sources of information which must be thoroughly explored, any aerial photographs which may have been taken are very important – the more varied the conditions, the better they may reveal slight surface earthworks or the effects of buried features on growing crops (above, fig. 17). Maps of soils, drift and solid geology should provide insight into the kind of natural subsoil conditions likely to be encountered. Frequent visits should be made to the site with the knowledge gleaned from the above sources, and detailed surveys made to locate the site in relation to modern reference points, and to record its contours – particularly on a research excavation, where the original form of the monument is to be restored. If resources are sufficient new aerial photographs can be taken specially, additional exploration carried out with resistivity equipment or magnetometers, and professional surveyors employed. On the basis of all the information gathered, the director can plan his priorities, and decide how best to lay out trenches in order to answer them.

Staff and equipment

It is impossible to generalize for all situations as the number and nature of staff on an excavation is directly related to its size, resources and complexity. Certain basic requirements exist, however; on small sites, many tasks will be performed by the director himself. Because excavation actually destroys a site and its information, **recording** is perhaps the most important part of the process. The records come in three forms – written, drawn and photographic – and staff with sufficient experience,

both archaeological and technical, are required to maintain them. A large excavation producing many finds will also require a full-time finds assistant with a team of pot-washers, and also cataloguers to compile the vital finds lists for each excavated context, and to label, bag, box, and store everything. Conservation may be needed on some sites where delicate finds are abundant; an on-site laboratory to carry out immediate cleaning and stabilization is now common on large excavations. Environmental evidence may require carefully-taken soil samples, and sieving or flotation equipment in order to recover small bones, seeds, etc. On sites where radio-carbon dates are likely to be required, it is fundamentally important that samples of the optimum quantity and material can be selected, and stored in conditions to protect them from contamination. As long as it is realised that the quality of the interpretation and publication of a site is directly related to the comprehensiveness and skill of its recording and finds preservation, a sensible selection of capable staff should be a basic priority.

Excavation strategy

The experience of the director combined with all of the background research which has been carried out in advance will be necessary in deciding how best to approach an individual site. Aerial photographs and geophysical prospecting may help to suggest the most informative parts of the site on which to begin – this is obviously particularly important if it is only being sampled, not totally excavated. Exploratory 'sondages', larger trenches, or extensive open areas can be employed in various configurations, according to available resources and the nature of the site; their applications are discussed on pp. 58–62.

Even the best-prepared director will rarely find that a site conforms exactly to expectation, and the strategy should allow for modifications to be made in the light of discoveries. Such flexibility is important, and depends to a great extent on the quality of the specialist staff of the excavation; detailed site planning and interpretation, combined with provisional dating and other observations about the finds recovered, should continuously feed information back to reinforce, modify or reject the working hypotheses. In a few cases, it has been possible to compile computer-files of site information for this purpose actually during the course of an excavation, and to carry out analyses as the work progresses.

The use of trenches or open areas, standing or cumulative sections, or the recording of each layer in such a way that no actual sections are required at any given point (see above, pp. 63) will depend on the preferences of the director, the size and nature of the site, and the available resources of money and manpower. It should be readily apparent from what has been said that a good excavator is not only an archaeologist, but also a manager and decision maker.

Excavations: some technical aspects

Underlying all theoretical and practical discussions of excavation is the fact that the process relies on largely subjective perceptions of the buried deposits which are revealed. There is no substitute for experience, based on an understanding of how buildings decay, occupation layers accumulate, ditches silt up, or any other of the many processes which go together to form an archaeological site. The recognition of the importance of stratigraphy led to the idea of removing layers or other features in strict order, and keeping detailed records of each, together with any finds. The procedure is often likened to dissection – an appropriate analogy where care and order are involved, but misleading in two major ways. If a dissection goes wrong, there is always another hamster; furthermore, layers of muscle, bones, and organs are far more predictable and recognizable than archaeological features. The first observation reminds one that no two sites are ever identical, and the second emphasises the fact that layers of soil may merge into each other without clear interfaces, leaving it to the experience of the excavator to decide what divisions will be made for the purposes of recording.

The size of many modern excavations has led to the role of a director resembling that of a general manager, whose site supervisors actually control the detailed excavation; only on small sites can the director hope to keep an overall check on the entire process, with the help of diary-like site notebooks in which occasional insights can be jotted down to add to the basic records. The increasing demands on excavators for precision, combined with the complexity of, say, a major multi-period urban excavation have led to the widespread use of pre-printed standard recording forms which considerably reduce chances of error or omissions (e.g. Barker 1982, 148–9). If carefully designed with future analysis in mind, such forms can be computer-coded so that the information can be transferred easily into data files – perhaps even during the excavation itself. Indeed, such records are now having serious implications for the manner in which excavations are published; should such detailed information be published in a fairly undigestible and expensive printed report, or left in a computer archive to which specialists are allowed free access? Such site record forms are used to describe the position, extent, characteristics and significant finds from each context; to support these basic records, various categories of material such as pottery, bone, scientific samples, and photographs all require separate files, fully cross-referenced to the contexts to which they relate. A point which can be made with confidence is that an excavation can only be as good as its recording system; a director's personal observations can no longer be accepted without adequate documentation.

However scientific the appearance of a site's information recording processes may seem, the subjective element remains – an individual working with a trowel is having to make continuous observations and judgements about the texture, colour, and significance of a deposit or feature, as well as recognizing all kinds of finds from solid stone or pottery to fragile corroded metal, or even discolourations left by organic materials which have decayed away completely. The history of archaeology shows with frightening clarity how much information can be lost; clearance of stone-built sites could take place oblivious to the presence of traces of timber structures, or, in the Near East, sun-dried mud-brick. Excavators need not only experience, but *informed* experience, including an understanding of a variety of constructional techniques which may have been employed on a

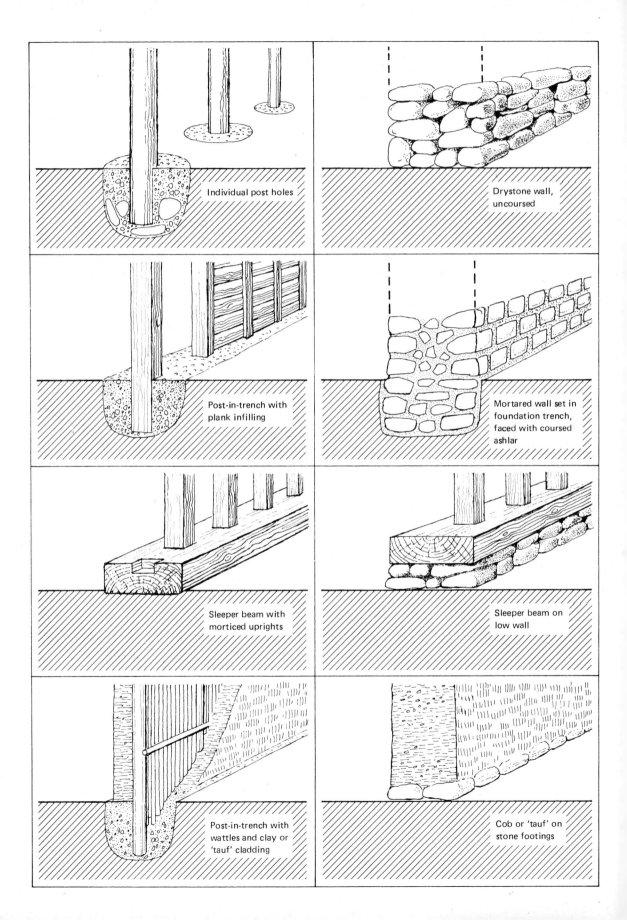

Individual post holes

Drystone wall, uncoursed

Post-in-trench with plank infilling

Mortared wall set in foundation trench, faced with coursed ashlar

Sleeper beam with morticed uprights

Sleeper beam on low wall

Post-in-trench with wattles and clay or 'tauf' cladding

Cob or 'tauf' on stone footings

site. For this reason, two sections will be devoted to the problems of stone and timber in excavations.

Stone structures

Second only to burial mounds and other major earthworks, stone structures were easiest for early archaeologists to recognize and excavate; in many cases quite reasonable conclusions were drawn from them, for an architectural background was much more prevalent amongst excavators of the last century than those of today, particularly where Greek and Roman archaeology was concerned. J.T. Wood, excavating at Ephesus in Turkey in the 1860s, could explore Roman theatres and the Temple of Diana, knowing what to expect, and how remains of columns and architectural sculpture probably fitted into the original structure (Wood 1877). On sites about which less was known, a common procedure was to dig narrow trenches until buried walls were struck, and then to follow them by digging along each side to reveal off-shoots or junctions until a complete plan was recovered. The islands of soil in the rooms could then be cleared in the hope of recovering objects to indicate their date and function. The effect of this was that all the vital stratigraphic relationships between walls, floors, occupation, and destruction levels were entirely removed, making critical reappraisal

42 The interpretation of excavated remains of structures is greatly aided by an understanding of construction techniques. This diagram presents eight imaginary examples of wood, stone and clay used in a variety of combinations or alone; many other possibilities exist. It is instructive to see how many would actually be found on a site which had suffered from agriculture or surface erosion – only four have holes or trenches dug into the ground. The remainder could be built directly onto an existing ground surface, and could only be detected in ideal conditions by scrupulously careful area excavations such as those at Wroxeter which have been described by Barker (1982).

by re-excavation impossible, even if the rooms were not completely cleared. Unfortunately this technique provides visibly impressive results quickly, and is still practised in many parts of the world today.

The excavation of stone structures

It is important to state at the outset that, except in the case of monumental architecture, stone construction need not have any significance in terms of either technical ability or wealth and social status. Stone buildings are commonest in areas where stone is conveniently available: if it is not, timber, mud-brick, or any other useful local material may be used for most buildings. For instance, there are upwards of 40,000 ring forts of Iron Age and Early Christian date in Ireland. Some are built with earthen ramparts (raths), others with stone (cashels), others with varying quantities of each, for instance in stone-faced earthen banks. Their internal structures may be of stone or timber, and like the defences, reflect not status but geographical position. The most picturesque and frequently illustrated examples lie in western Ireland, where limestone often outcrops naturally in convenient blocks and slabs, whilst in the east, raths predominate on the low-lying fertile farmland (Norman and St Joseph 1969).

Early Irish laws define the social status of ring forts according to the number of ramparts, not their building material – the danger of falsely assuming differences in status or function simply because archaeologists have classified them according to one particular criterion is obvious. A further factor compounds this problem; stone ring-forts in thinly-populated western Ireland are more likely to have survived in better condition than those in the east, where demands for agricultural land are stronger, and where the natural decay of the timber and earth structures will in any case have been faster, facilitating their levelling by agriculture. This is a recurrent problem in most countries, which introduces severe distortions into the evidence of many periods which will be discussed further in Chapter 6.

Assuming the availability of building stone, a great variety of construction techniques exists. The simplest is drystone walling, which uses uncut natural boulders or roughly quarried blocks, relying on gravity and friction for their stability. This kind of construction is not un-skilled, but no tools or other materials are required. In many areas, stone outcrops or boulders cleared from farmland would have provided very convenient sources of stone. Some kinds of stone break naturally into regular rectangular blocks, but otherwise a certain amount of basic shaping can produce a much more regular wall face, made up either of stones of varying size, or in regular courses. Strength can be increased by bonding the stones together with tough clay or mortar, which also improves the comfort of buildings by reducing draughts and water penetration. In Roman architecture, many buildings relied more on the strength of the thick concrete cores of their walls than on the visible stone surface, of which the most important function was to form a mould for the concrete while it set. Mixtures of stone or tile courses and details, and thin ornamental wall-claddings of sheets of marble or mosaics are characteristic of many buildings of the second century AD and later. Many now appear un-sightly, with their concrete cores exposed, strip-ped of facing by later stone-robbers, particul-arly where building stone is not easily available locally.

Much of the final work on Greek, Roman, and medieval buildings of finer stone was carried out on site by masons; blocks were cut roughly to shape at quarries, to minimise their weight during transport, and then trimmed to exact requirements during building, and any decorative carving completed. Small chippings of stone and discarded tools from this process can often be detected, and provide a useful device for relating the stratigraphic record to the building. At the Roman palace at Fish-bourne, Sussex, spreads of builders' mortar, and splashes of wall paint were also found by the excavators, in addition to debris left over from cutting blocks of fine imported stone into geometrical shapes for decorative wall cladding (Cunliffe 1971, pl. 11).

Structure

When remains of stone walls are uncovered on an excavation, it is easy at first to assume that they result from a stone building. However, in many cases, low stone walls are simply a method of providing sound dry footings for structures such as clay-walled or timber-framed buildings (see fig. 42). Their effectiveness can be judged by the large numbers of picturesque cob or half-timbered thatched cottages which have sur-vived for many centuries in the south of England; the combination of dry footings, and a thick overhanging thatch throwing rainwater well clear of the wall face, is most effective. Mud or clay walls are of course better suited to dry climates, and quite complex structures are already to be found on classic early agricultural sites of the seventh millenium BC in the Near East, such as Çayönü, in Turkey or Jarmo, in Iraq (fig. 43); stone footings were used as a base for packed mud walls, and curious 'grill plan' foundations in stone supported floors made from bundles of reeds covered in clay (Oates 1976, 83–4).

Another variable is the presence or absence of foundations set in a trench dug into the subsoil. Two factors are most relevant: if the above-ground structure was only low, or perhaps not stone at all, substantial foundations would be superfluous; the same would be true if sound bedrock lay immediately below the surface, rather than soft earth or sand. In Northumber-land during the Roman period, timber round-houses on native farmsteads were often replaced by dry-stone walled round-houses, which unlike their predecessors rested directly on the surface of the ground without creating any subsoil features – a real problem for excavators, when agricultural clearance has removed most of the stone from a site. At the other end of the spectrum Hadrian's Wall was originally plan-ned without foundations, but, when a change of plan reduced its thickness from ten to eight feet during construction, foundations were con-sidered necessary.

A general problem applies to all buildings which normally have timber roofs resting on the top of stone walls. When the roof ages and needs replacing, it will probably be possible to remove and replace it with little or no disturbance of the wall itself. However, timber houses will need

fairly frequent repairs to, or even complete replacement of, their walls, and such changes will usually leave detectable traces in the sub-soil. It is therefore impossible to trace the detailed history of a stone house of this kind even when the walls remain substantially complete. A long chronological span for artefacts from the site may be the only indication of the duration of such a structure. This problem is not restricted to simple buildings; a glance at any standing medieval structure usually reveals inserted and blocked windows, changes in roof line, extensions and rebuildings stretching over several centuries. If only the foundations and a few of the lower courses survive, most of this inform-ation will have disappeared; only features such as a blocked doorway or an extended found-ation may betray such alterations. Further details might again be gleaned from datable artefacts, or fragments of masonry showing distinctive architectural styles; if the excavator is fortunate, documents containing building

43 Stone paving and wall-footings for buildings of sun-dried mud on the early Neolithic village site at Jarmo in north-eastern Iraq. In the background, a number of small square excavation trenches can be seen, by means of which the extent of occupation and structures over the whole site could be defined; larger areas were opened in order to examine interesting structures more fully. *Photograph by courtesy of the excavator, Prof. Robert J. Braidwood*

accounts or illustrations made before complete ruin may be found in archives – but such records should of course have been revealed in the preparatory stages before excavation even began.

Internal features of stone buildings may also have been constructed from perishable mat-erial, such as wooden partitions, screens and flooring; once again, even their existence may be hard to detect unless traces extended below ground level. Floors of stone or beaten clay can be more helpful as the ground was frequently levelled up with rubble and other material before they were laid, and this may contain architectural fragments from earlier phases, masons chippings, or even domestic rubbish; if datable sherds or even coins were included, these may provide a useful *terminus post quem*.

Survival of stone structures

Most of the preceding discussion has assumed that stone structures survive reasonably intact. In reality, one of the consistent problems in their excavation is that buildings which had gone out of use were normally treated as quarries, particularly for ready squared-off ashlar facing blocks, except in areas now deserted or where abundant building stone is readily available. In areas where stone is particularly scarce, not only the walls but the very foundations may have been carefully dug out and removed, leaving nothing more than discarded fragments and scattered mortar in the resulting 'robber trenches'. Needless to say, the stratigraphic relationships between walls and their floors and other surrounding levels will have been destroyed in exactly the same way as in 'wall-chasing' archaeological excavations. However, the stone robbers tended to shift the very minimum of soil in their quest for stone, and their trenches normally follow the foundation very closely, leaving a negative plan of the building. Wheeler recognized 'ghost walls' in this way at Verulamium (St Albans, Herts: Wheeler and Wheeler 1936, pl. 88a) and was able to recover the plan of a monumental Roman gateway into the city of which in places not a single stone survived; at Winchester, the impressions of individual blocks removed from the lowest levels of the foundations of part of the Saxon Old Minster were still visible on excavation in 1969 (Biddle 1970, pl. 47a–b).

Reconstruction

One of the most informative disciplines in understanding the excavated remains of any kind of building is attempting to draw, or even build a scale model of, the possible structure to which they originally belonged. Various finds may assist the procedure – the size, depth and strength of foundations, pillars, or walls; architectural details such as window or door frames; voussoirs from arches or vaulting; roofing slates or tiles, etc; many of these may also have chronological significance. Comparisons with contemporary structures can be made, and any documentary evidence brought to bear; specialist help may be needed from an architect or engineer to estimate load factors on proposed walls, roof structures or vaulting. The results will largely consist of informed guesswork, but nothing enhances the display of an ancient site for the public more than a high-quality scale model reconstruction, with figures and activities relevant to its function. The excavator will also benefit from the process; examination of various hypotheses will require very close scrutiny of the excavated remains, and indeed may suggest new interpretations or direct further research to points which still need clarification.

Standing structures

As far back as the seventeenth century, John Aubrey worked out a dated sequence of window styles by looking at medieval buildings, although this unfortunately remained unpublished; classical archaeologists could follow architectural styles of column capitals, etc, from ancient authors and notable surviving buildings in Greece and Italy. The Neo-Classical architects of the Renaissance and more particularly the eighteenth century often examined and drew surviving fragments of classical architecture in their search for details or designs to incorporate into their own work, and of course the rediscovery of Herculaneum and Pompeii added impetus to such studies. Medieval buildings returned to favour in the nineteenth century, and many of the great Gothic Revival architects designed new or reshaped existing buildings in a meticulously academic fashion – particularly churches, even if it meant destroying genuine medieval features which got in their way. Indeed, it is only in the present century that the notion that an interest in the remains of the past should be dedicated to their preservation has really gained hold. Twentieth-century urban renewal, involving the permanent destruction of large percentages of the historic centres of cities on an unparalleled scale in many countries, the redundancy of many rural churches, and massive repairs to major European cathedrals such as York and Trier, have all caused the archaeological and architectural study of buildings of many dates to converge. The analysis of standing structures by traditional methods of architectural analysis are now frequently supplemented by such activities as the stripping of wall plaster to reveal earlier decoration and the original wall faces (fig. 45), the excavation of levels both within and outside the buildings (fig. 44), the sampling of mortar from different phases, and even the dating of tiles used for building by thermoluminescence (p. 119).

The procedure of analysing a standing structure relies on principles akin to those of stratigraphy, through the placing of their various features into sequence, and tying down any fixed points with whatever dating evidence is available. The establishment of the original form of a building is a prime objective, by the gradual elimination of later features. Tell-tale indications include **blocking** and **insertions**; redundant doorways or windows may be walled up, and new openings pierced through an existing wall to insert new windows, doors, or other functional features – or perhaps just to bring it up to date with new fashions. It is surprising how frequently existing walls were adapted and modified in this manner rather than being demolished and replaced.

Extensions to an existing building are usually detectable through differences in the size, style or geological source of the stonework, and new walls may simply butt up against existing surfaces rather than being properly bonded in; conversely, demolished walls usually leave vertical scars on a wall face marking their original junction. A problem may arise here; if an adjunct which was never bonded in is removed, the original wallface will simply be revealed again and give no hint of the adjunct's existence, although occasionally, sockets for roofing timbers or angled grooves may mark the position of vanished roof extensions. However, there are alarming examples of buildings which had

external adjuncts as part of their original layout which were never bonded in the first place, for reasons of convenience in their construction.

Medieval parish churches are among the best examples of this process of analysis, and should be studied carefully, particularly by excavators of entirely buried structures who need to be reminded of complexities which never affected the foundations. A fruitful combination of excavation and the study of standing remains may teach the reverse lesson to architectural historians – significant phases may have come and gone without leaving any visible traces in the above-ground structure (Rodwell 1982).

Excavation of timber structures

Timber is only preserved in exceptional circumstances, notably extremely wet or dry conditions which have remained constant over a long period. Otherwise, wood will decay completely, leaving only differences in the colour and texture of soil, which can, however, be detected by careful excavation. Three examples of boat archaeology display these conditions well. In Sweden, archaeologists have raised the hull of the seventeenth-century warship *Wasa* in excellent condition, thanks to the fact that the brand-new ship sank into deep silt and in water which does not support the sea worms which normally eat hulls. In Egypt, the oldest surviving ship in the world was excavated in 1954; it had been dismantled and placed in a pit beside the Great Pyramid of Cheops (*c.* 2590 BC) and has recently been re-assembled – the arid conditions had protected it from decay. As a complete contrast, the Anglo-Saxon royal grave at Sutton Hoo in Suffolk included a complete ship buried in a long trench cut into a sandy subsoil and covered by a mound. It had completely disappeared apart from one fragmentary plank from the bottom of the hull, leaving traces which were nevertheless recovered by meticulous excavation; only layers of stained soil remained, whose shape was confirmed by the positions of the corroded iron nails which had originally held the ship's planks together. The alternating wet and dry conditions of the sand were the reason for the complete decay (Bruce-Mitford 1979, frontispiece).

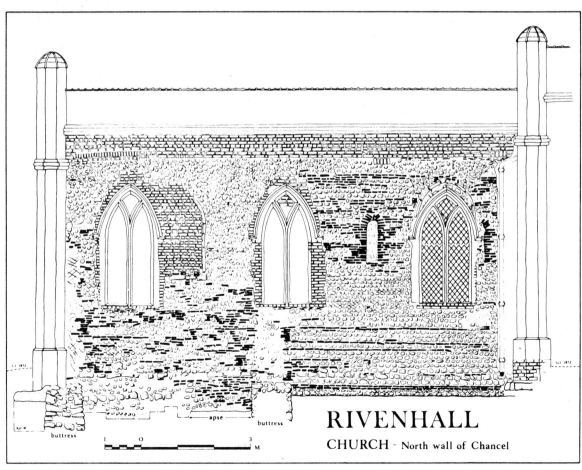

RIVENHALL

CHURCH - North wall of Chancel

buttress

apse   buttress

1   0   3
M

In the case of buildings, a knowledge of methods of construction is important if their remains are to be excavated and interpreted correctly.

Construction of timber buildings (fig. 42) Most forms of timber buildings require foundations of some sort – but not always, and some quite substantial structures can be built without leaving any traces in the subsoil. Rigidly jointed timber-framed buildings, or log-cabins of interlocking timbers rely on their joinery, not earthfast upright posts, and they can rest directly on the ground. Fortunately, the problems of uneven terrain and damp usually required a spread of gravel or rubble make-up, or low stone walls to lift the bottom timbers off the ground. Only indirect evidence may remain for the actual timber building, and one of the greatest achievements of recent open-area excavation has been the revealing of traces of extensive late Roman structures of this kind overlying the

44–45 Churches present some of the most complex problems of archaeological and architectural analysis. **44** shows the excavation of structures and burials stretching back over 1000 years in the church of St Peter at Barton-on-Humber, Lincolnshire; the earlier the remains, the more they are likely to have suffered later disturbance or to be masked by later masonry which cannot be removed. **45** is a detailed drawing of an external wall of a church at Rivenhall, Essex, drawn to emphasise differences in the masonry. A wall with distinctive Saxon windows, marked in black, was retained throughout the life of the church, and that successive larger windows were simply inserted into holes created in the existing Saxon structure. Significant details such as these are frequently masked by wall-plaster; at Rivenhall, even the exterior had been plastered, and the structure was thought to be of much later date according to the only visible windows. *Photograph and drawing by courtesy of Dr W. Rodwell*

Roman baths at Wroxeter, Shropshire (Barker 1977). Many earlier excavators of the site had simply dug through a layer of rubble lying near the surface, using narrow trenches to trace the plans of the underlying Roman masonry buildings, dismissing the rubble as debris left by the demolition and decay of the Roman town, disturbed by later agriculture. Only the kind of open area (and open-minded) excavation employed by Philip Barker could possibly have recovered the existence of a hitherto unsuspected final phase in the occupation of the town. Unfortunately, such excavation would be virtually impossible on most other Roman towns more heavily disturbed by medieval and modern building, wells, pits, etc. – particularly as much smaller areas are normally available for excavation. The implications of Barker's work are universal: wherever timber buildings were erected on simple rubble levelling and have left no surviving floor levels, no claims can be made with complete certainty for the *absence* of buildings during a phase of a site. Also, where deep ploughing has occurred on open sites, traces of this kind will have been utterly destroyed; there may in practice be few places where the lessons learned at Wroxeter can actually be applied.

The importance of recording is also emphasized by excavations such as Barker's. Building platforms may be indicated by nothing more than a slight difference in the size and character of one area of rubble compared to its surroundings. Artefacts, too, require the same kind of scrutiny – fragments of flint, pottery or small coins may appear outside the limits of such structures, where they have been broken or dropped in use and trampled into the surrounding ground surface. Only accurate surveying and planning will allow their exact distribution to be studied, and any guidance to the site's interpretation obtained. Such information may only emerge after the excavation has finished, and echo the words of Pitt Rivers, that everything should be recorded, even if its significance is not apparent at the time of discovery.

Having discussed the rather esoteric question of timber buildings which leave no direct traces, attention will now turn to structures which possess below-ground foundations. One of the most recurrent archaeological features where timber was employed is the **post-hole**. The simplest method of erecting a firm upright is to dig a hole, stand a post in the bottom, and pack the upcast from the hole firmly back around the post, perhaps with the addition of some packing stones; the process can be used for a single post, or for each separate post in a large complex structure. Only rarely is a subsoil suitable for large posts to be rammed directly into the ground without some kind of pile-driving equipment.

Large buildings with regular rows of posts may employ a **foundation trench** rather than individual post-holes; the principle is the same, but a continuous trench is emptied, and refilled around a line of posts. It is a useful technique where large posts need to be set deeply and close together; individual holes would tend to inter-cut, and could be most inconvenient during the manoeuvring of heavy posts. Roman military timber granaries are amongst the best examples, but the technique occurs widely. In the case of houses or fences, the gaps between individual posts in a foundation trench were frequently filled in with horizontal or vertical planks, usually extending below ground level, but perhaps only just penetrating the foundations; particularly careful excavation is required to detect these traces during the emptying of the fill. **Palisade** walls or ramparts combine both features – a continuous screen of posts or planks is set into a trench to provide both walling and support for any roof structure.

Post-holes and foundation trenches, with individual posts, plank walls or palisades are not mutually exclusive methods of construction; they may coexist on different parts of a single site, and may indeed be employed in a single building. Neolithic long houses of the Linear Pottery or Danubian culture in Europe, Bronze and Iron Age roundhouses in Britain, and Iron Age to early medieval aisled halls of the Netherlands and north Germany often combine two or more of these features. This clearly demonstrates that there is a limited number of basic possibilities in timber construction, which were discovered early, and ensured the repetition of closely comparable building forms over wide chronological spans and geographical areas.

An alternative to setting vertical timbers into the ground is to use **sleeper beams**, which are large timbers laid horizontally, into which uprights can be morticed to provide the structure of a building; time and effort saved in digging post holes is offset by additional carpentry, of course. The beams were sometimes set into bedding trenches, but more often lay on the surface or, to be more damp-resistant, were raised up on rubble platforms or low stone sleeper walls. Many of the buildings at Wroxeter could have been of this form, and the inherent difficulties of recognizing their remains has probably reduced the apparent importance of this technique compared with the others outlined above. The sleeper beam technique brings the discussion back to a point at which it merges with stone construction, and the possibilities of combining stone footings with a timber or half-timbered superstructure.

Interpretation of timber structures

A knowledge of the building techniques outlined above is very important for both the excavation of timber remains, and their interpretation. As with stone buildings, comparative information is best gained from more recent structures which are still standing, or the well-preserved remains of ancient structures which have survived through waterlogging or dessication. Excavated remains of burnt buildings may also be informative, as timber can be reduced to charcoal, which resists further decay, and often preserves the shape of former woodwork.

The size and depth of post-holes or foundation trenches are a good guide to the size of the timbers which they once contained, and the kind of load which they might have had to bear; the locations and dimensions of the posts themselves can usually be gained by careful excavation of their filling. The understanding of the fact that features which were not load-bearing need not have penetrated the ground is important – if a site is not deeply buried, and has been ploughed, such traces may easily have been lost; this applies to internal partitions, and even the walls of buildings whose roofs are supported on internal pillars. The aisled structures found at Feddersen Wierde, near the German North Sea coast are instructive in this connection (Haarnagel 1979). Substantial traces of these buildings were found well preserved in damp silt levels, dating to the first four centuries AD. The typical plan consisted of a rectangular house, with two rows of stout roof supports (hence their description as aisled long-houses); one end contained a clay-floored living area with a central hearth, and the remainder was divided up into individual animal byres. The house walls and byre partitions were mostly made from hurdles of thin interwoven branches, with little or no penetration into the ground (Dixon 1976, 58). On a less well-preserved site, the floor, hearth, and byre divisions and possibly even the walls might easily have disappeared leaving only the post holes of the principal timbers supporting the roof – and requiring much more imagination and subjective reconstruction from an excavator.

The height and nature of the roofing of timber buildings discovered by excavation is even more difficult to assess. Within the limits of the load-bearing capacity of particular sizes of timbers and the stresses created by particular kinds of roofing (matters which will probably require advice from a specialist), a number of plausible reconstructions are frequently deducable from a single plan. In fact, it may be most reasonable for several interpretations to be offered in an excavation report, rather than for one to be arbitrarily singled out from a number of competitors. One thing is sure, however – the complexity of joinery and the elaboration of purely decorative detail observable on many surviving medieval and later timber buildings certainly must also have existed in earlier times. The lesson of the American Pacific-coast Indians should be learned: their timber buildings, ships, textiles and everyday objects are still normally covered with elaborate painted and carved designs derived from animals, birds and fish (Holm and Reid 1979). It would seem very likely that pre-Roman Celts or Migration period Germanic peoples would have done the same thing, and that the complex animal and geometric ornament which we only now know from

their metalwork also appeared on timber buildings. Norwegian stave churches are a good European example (Christie 1978–9); if none had survived, who would have believed an archaeologist who proposed the ornate superstructure of Urnes church on the basis of its ground plan? And did the decayed Sutton Hoo ship once bear ornament as elaborate as that of the surviving Viking ships? (Graham-Campbell 1980, 136–9). Reconstruction drawings and models should be treated as no more than economical hypotheses.

A further complication in the study of the excavated remains of timber buildings is again caused by the perishable nature of wood, particularly in the conditions of a temperate climate. If timbers of different kinds or sizes were employed in the construction of a building, decay may have affected them at different rates, requiring running repairs to have been carried out during the life of the structure. Such post replacements were rarely in exactly the same holes as their predecessors, and multiple postholes may result. Precise excavation and recording is necessary to sort out the sequence in which intercutting holes were dug, and to separate out any significant dating evidence. When an entire building needed replacement, rather than individual posts, a very similar new structure may have then been constructed on almost exactly the same site – possibly several times in succession; again, careful area excavation is needed to recover the separate plans of the successive structures, and crucial points at which post holes or other features overlap will need particular attention in order to establish their sequence. Warendorf, a seventh-eighth century AD settlement near Münster in Germany (Winkelmann, 1954) provides a good example; at first sight, the plan of the site gives the impression of having been densely packed with timber halls and outbuildings, but closer examination indicates that four or five similar plans of individual structures may overlap to some extent, making it clear that in fact only a small number of buildings existed at any one time, and that they were replaced many times, showing great continuity (Dixon 1976, 61). On sites where ploughing has removed all traces of floor levels, it is possible to find overlapping plans of post-hole structures, whose features do not actually intercut – there is no way of establishing the sequence in a case like this. Even worse, on sites occupied for particularly long periods by structures with no consistent or obvious plans, it may be quite possible to hypothesize numerous rectangular or circular structures in an area studded with unrelated post-holes. In cases like this, exceptionally precise recording systems may allow different shapes, depths, soil fillings, etc, to be correlated, and suggest sets of features which belonged together – a computer database would be particularly useful for marshalling such information, and plotting out the results.

Other building materials

Emphasis on stone and timber overlooks one of the most important ancient building materials, which is dependent not only on the availability of materials, but also climatic conditions. The early stages of incipient food production and village farming led to a more sedentary life style, and the construction of permanent buildings. These developments centred upon western Asia, where hand-made bricks of sun-dried clay began to be used around 8000 BC. They first appear at Jericho in the 'pre-pottery Neolithic A' phase, in circular houses – astonishingly, lying within an enormous stone circuit wall whose precise function has still not been explained. When available, stone could be used to provide footings, and bundles of reeds or timber were sometimes combined with the clay walls, particularly in Greece and the Balkans, where the more temperate climate made the unfired mud building technique less suitable; Nea Nikomedia (Greece) and Karonovo (Bulgaria) provide good examples of mud and timber construction (Piggott 1965 pl. 2a). Mud bricks went on to become the standard building material of the first urban civilizations of Mesopotamia, Egypt and India, and still remain the dominant construction medium of the region today (Oates 1976, 99).

More durable **fired** bricks began to be used in Mesopotamia by 3500 BC, but were mainly restricted to the ornate or exposed parts of

46 One of the commonest forms of archaeological site in the Near East is the 'tell', a man-made hill resulting from centuries of successive building, demolition and rebuilding in mud-brick. Most important tells now have the additional feature of large spoil heaps from excavations; several can be seen around this mound, which is Mound III at Nippur, including the Temple of Bel with an overlying fortress. *Fisher 1905, pl. 21*

47 Unfired mud bricks bonded together with wet clay are notoriously difficult to locate and excavate. This scrupulously cleaned section at Tepe Ali Kosh, Iran, makes it perfectly clear why excavators of tells in the Near East failed to find any structures other than those finished in fired brick or stone until well into the present century. *Hole* et al. *1969, pl. 9b*

ceremonial buildings. Mud bricks have a very important implication for archaeology. They have a limited life, but are easily demolished and replaced, and the building of successive structures over many centuries leads to a tremendous build up of stratified deposits, which form the characteristic tells of the Near East (fig. 46). They are however difficult to excavate, because the demolished remains compacted by overlying levels are similar in consistency to any surviving structural remains (fig. 47). Furthermore, when exposed by excavation, they decay rapidly – as many of the pioneering excavators of the Near East discovered, when monumental structures simply crumbled to dust after their exposure. Eventually, the depth of most tell

deposits led to an increased awareness of stratigraphy, and the sequences of various kinds of artefacts in successive levels. One of the first and most famous of such excavations was by Schliemann at Hissarlik in Turkey, better known from its identification as Troy. In his later seasons, he was assisted by skilled Germans who applied the high standards developed during their excavation of classical sites in Greece; from the same background came Koldewey and Andrae, who investigated Babylon and Asur in Mesopotamia. These excavators were well aware of the horizontal and vertical requirements: they were interested both in exploring large areas of town buildings, and in completing stratigraphical sequences from the top to the bottom of tells. The sinking of such 'sondage' trenches through mounds was an obvious technique, but the horizontal aspect was more innovative, and has been placed into context by Daniel:

In Egypt every monument was built of the stone or cut in the solid rock, and the arid climate permitted the preservation in a remarkable manner of objects . . . which would have been destroyed elsewhere. It was, therefore, in Mesopotamia that the classical techniques were reshaped and that new techniques of stratigraphical excavation, and of the excavation of perished and semi-perished materials, were developed. The architecture of Mesopotamia is executed in sun-dried bricks; the techniques of tracing these were quite unknown to earlier excavators. Koldewey and Andrae first successfully traced the walls of sun-dried brick, and this work reached its highest technical achievements in the work of Delougaz, at Khafajah, where every single brick was articulated, the chips being blown away by compressed air. The excavations at Ur were a noteworthy model of the whole modern technique of archaeology, from extraction and preservation to interpretation and publication (Daniel 1975, 290–1).

Here the wheel turns full circle, for one of the most prominent excavators of Ur in the 1920s was Sir Leonard Woolley – who, whilst Koldewey and Andrae were already at work in Mesopotamia, was making his first fumbling beginnings in archaeology at Corbridge in Northumberland in 1906 (above, p. 67).

Fired clay bricks form part of the archaeology of many parts of the world, of course, and in many periods the use of unfired clay is very strongly associated with half-timbered construction for infilling, or coating of wickerwork hurdles to make wattle and daub. Such structures do not survive well, unless destruction by burning has had the effect of firing the clay. With good drainage and protective roofing, this form of construction is perfectly well suited to temperate climates; indeed, the surviving stone temples and other buildings of the classical world make it easy to forget that their form owes much to their timber and clay predecessors. Greece and Asia Minor abounded in good building stone, but in Roman times brick buildings make more of an impression around the West Mediterranean and in Europe: the Emperor Augustus (27 BC–AD 14) claimed that he found Rome a city of brick, and left it a city of marble. However, surface appearances can be deceptive, and as we have already seen, most marble-clad Roman buildings depended for their grandeur on brick arches and vaulting, backed by the strength of concrete.

Sun-dried clay is not restricted to the Old World – *adobe* is in common use in Mexico, and is often found in combination with other materials. For example, the vast pre-Columbian city of Teotihuacán (which around AD 500 was more extensive than Imperial Rome) is famous for its pyramids, which are made of adobe, with a protective facing of stone or plaster – a combination reminiscent of Mesopotamia. The importance of locally-available resources has been stressed throughout this discussion of stone, timber, and other materials; at Teotihuacán, the same phenomenon is encountered in the private houses:

The basic building materials of Teotihuacán were of local origin. Outcrops of porous volcanic rock in the valley were quarried and the stone was crushed and mixed with lime and earth to provide a kind of moisture-resistant concrete that was used as the foundation for floors and walls. The same material was used for roofing; wooden posts spaced at intervals bore much of the weight of the roof. Walls were made of stone and mortar or of sunbaked adobe brick. Floors and wall surfaces were then usually finished with highly polished plaster (Millon 1967, 43).

The study of buildings, whether fortifications, temples, palaces, houses or workshops, is fundamental to archaeology, which can be defined as the study of the past through its material remains. The development of photography and then television have greatly expanded the potential of the Renaissance and Neo-classical interest in *seeing* the physical trappings of classical civilization, while archaeological techniques have proportionally increased the information which structures of any culture, area, or age can provide. Their study not only provides a visual dimension for the perception of the past; their technology, materials, planning and decoration all contribute elements to a well-rounded knowledge of the social organizations, religious life and economic activity of a culture, when taken into consideration alongside its artefacts and settlement patterns. This is as true of the earliest known man-made structures – some Palaeolithic oval wooden huts at Terra Amata, Nice, in France (de Lumley 1969) which date back to 300,000 BC – as it is of the factories of the Industrial Revolution.

CASE STUDY: DATING EXCAVATED STRUCTURES BY HISTORY, ARTEFACTS, AND STRATIGRAPHY AT SOUTH CADBURY CASTLE, SOMERSET

This site consists of a large hillfort of pre-Roman date, which had been associated with the King Arthur of medieval romance as early as 1532, when local tradition was recorded by John Leland. It is upon the 'Arthurian' period, its structures and their dating that this study will concentrate. The hill had been chosen for investigation because of the interests of the excavator, Leslie Alcock, in early post-Roman Britain – the 'Dark Age' period in which Arthur is supposed to have led a successful resistance to the Anglo-Saxons around AD 500. Leland's record of a local tradition that the hill was the site of Arthur's 'Camelot' was not the main reason for excavation; some sherds of rare kinds of pottery imported into Britain from the Mediterranean and Gaul in the fifth–sixth centuries AD had been ploughed up on the site. Structural features encountered in the excavations carried out in 1966–70 which have been assigned to this period consist of a defensive rampart around the hill, a timber gateway and its road levels, and a timber hall in the interior of the hillfort; these will be examined in turn. The excavator has published an excellent popular account of his

excavations (Alcock 1972).

The defences – rampart E (figs 48–9)
The hillfort possessed three large earthworks, which are still formidable today; the innermost enclosed 18 acres, and in all of the five trenches cut across it, it showed seven main phases of development, labelled A to G, including a roughly-built drystone bank, rampart E. A general *terminus post quem* was provided by the fact that phases A–D belonged to the pre-Roman Iron Age, but more precision could be given. It *rested* on plough soil which had built up during the Roman period; it *contained* re-used Roman masonry, and it sealed a coin of the Emperor

48 A broad section through the sequence of ramparts at South Cadbury. The Saxon wall is well preserved, and has been removed in the left half of the trench to reveal the coarser rubble of the 'Arthurian' stony bank. Note the relatively stone-free soil between the two ramparts, indicating a period of abandonment and soil formation. The section can be seen on fig. 49. *Photograph by courtesy of L. Alcock*

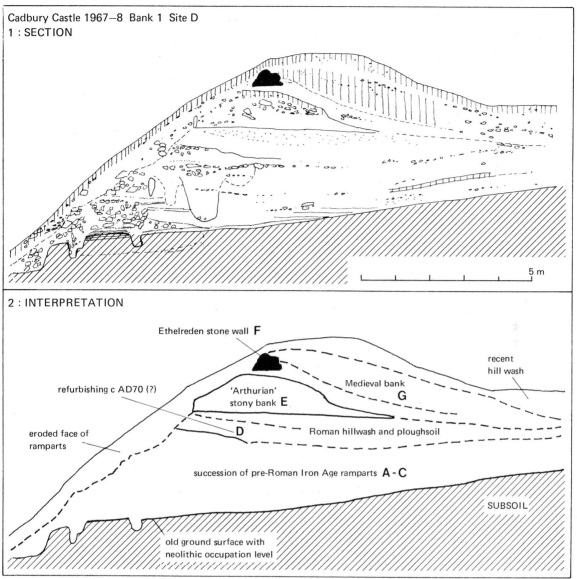

Cadbury Castle 1967–8 Bank 1 Site D
1 : SECTION

5 m

2 : INTERPRETATION

Ethelreden stone wall **F**

recent
hill wash

refurbishing c AD70 (?)

'Arthurian'
stony bank **E**

Medieval bank
G

eroded face of
ramparts

D

Roman hillwash and ploughsoil

succession of pre-Roman Iron Age ramparts **A-C**

SUBSOIL

old ground surface with
neolithic occupation level

49 The rampart sequence at South
Cadbury, simplified from the excavator's
section drawing (Alcock 1972, 66–7); the
various levels can be seen partially
exposed in fig. 48.

Honorius (who brought the Roman rule of Britain to an official end in AD 410), datable to AD 393–402, and a fragment of imported 'B-ware' Mediterranean amphora, of the later fifth century AD. Its construction therefore must belong to the post-Roman period, and the admittedly imprecise dating of B-ware would suggest a specific *terminus post quem* of the later fifth century AD the period to which Arthur is normally allotted. But a *terminus post quem* is only a fixed point *after* which something took place – an upper limit was also required for the rampart in question. Fortunately, it was overlain by

rampart F, a solid mortared wall which provides a particularly precise *terminus ante quem*; it is assignable by analogy to the late Saxon period, when it is recorded historically that Cadbury was occupied by Ethelred the Unready from 1010 to 1017 – silver pennies bearing the name *Cadanbyrig* were actually minted there. This wall

93

rested on a build-up of soil in some places, indicating a period of disuse between phases E and F. Rampart E thus fitted into a definable date range beginning in the fifth century AD,

50 The south-west gateway at South Cadbury. The rough metalling of the 'Arthurian' roadway can be seen running across the foreground of the photograph, interrupted by two narrow trenches in which timber beams were once set (marked by surveying poles). On the far side of the area demarcated by these trenches, remains of the stony bank can be seen, with some large blocks of stone at its faces. The core of the bank ends abruptly at the edge of the road, where some sort of retaining planking must have existed. The Saxon mortared stone wall can also be seen further down the slope in front of the earlier 'Arthurian' structure. The depth of stratified deposits visible in the section shows how soil has been eroded from the hill by agriculture at various dates and built up behind the ramparts, and contrasts with the minimal soil cover overlying the timber hall (fig. 52). *Photograph by courtesy of L. Alcock*

and ending by the eleventh. For further narrowing of the date we must examine the south west gate and its roadways.

The entrance (fig. 50)

A gap in the ramparts at their south-west corner marked one of the Iron Age entrances to the site, and, superimposed on their remains, a timber gate structure was excavated. A pair of large post-holes lay either side of a cobbled road, together with evidence of stout planking holding back the weight of rampart E, to which it obviously belonged. The road surface had been remetalled once, and the repair included a small Anglo-Saxon brooch or buckle with animal decoration roughly datable to the mid-sixth century AD. This provided a *terminus post quem* for the second road surface, and a possible *terminus ante quem* for the first, and therefore by implication the whole gateway and associated rampart; it is only a *possible* t.a.q., because it could conceivably have been lying around for a considerable length of time before being included by chance in material gathered together to provide a new road surface. One observation suggests that it may give a true indication of date; the timbers of the gateway were not replaced at any stage, suggesting that their use

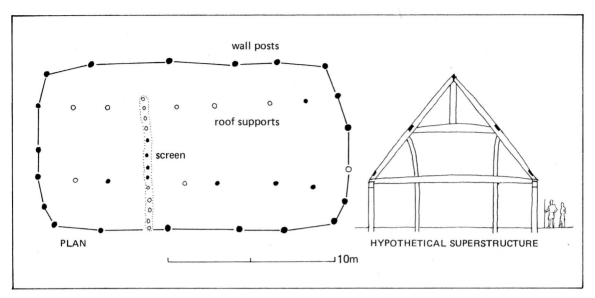

PLAN

wall posts

roof supports

screen

HYPOTHETICAL SUPERSTRUCTURE

10m

51–52 The 'Arthurian' hall at South Cadbury. **51** Plan and possible superstructure of the hall (after Alcock 1972, 179, fig. 30). Definite post-holes are shown in black, and open circles represent inferred posts. Sherds of pottery were found in the trench (dotted line) containing the posts which formed the screen. **52:** Open-area excavation on the hilltop at Cadbury; the positions of the post-holes of the 'Arthurian' hall are indicated by white stakes. It can be clearly seen that a thin ploughsoil rests directly on the bedrock, and that no archaeological features could survive unless they were dug into the rock – the round patches of soil which can be seen are Iron Age grain storage pits, awaiting excavation. *Photograph by courtesy of L. Alcock*

could not have extended far beyond the later sixth century. Thus, the gateway, its first road, and rampart E could plausibly be dated between the late fifth and mid-sixth centuries AD. Their construction would thus conveniently precede the famous British victory over the Saxons at Mount Badon (? c. AD 490 or 518), which was followed by a period of peace, whilst a mid-sixth century resurfacing of the road would fit equally happily with the resumption of the Anglo-Saxon advance which culminated in the capture of Gloucester, Bath and Cirencester from the British in 577.

The timber hall (figs 51-2)

History, legend, and stratigraphy converge in a most impressive manner in the analysis of rampart E, and it may be repeated that imported pottery of the same general date, also suggesting occupation of a high social status, had been ploughed up in the interior of the hillfort. Here, the excavation faced a very difficult problem; instead of trenching a deep stratified sequence of deposits, a large area of the interior was examined on top of the hill where only a few centimetres of disturbed ploughsoil covered a soft limestone bedrock, which had itself suffered from both natural and agricultural erosion. The only stratigraphic relationships which could exist were either between features cut into the bedrock which happened to overlap, or layers within isolated features. Many structures, ditches, and storage pits had been dug in the Iron Age, riddling the surface of the bedrock with disturbances of many shapes and sizes. The problems of assigning individual features to particular phases or structures is discussed elsewhere in relation to timber buildings (p. 87); a further complication at Cadbury was that native Iron Age pottery is extremely durable and plentiful, whereas in the 'Arthurian' period, no native pottery was in use at all – only rare and luxurious imported fine tableware, or jars that contained wine and oil. Thus, if a post-hole was dug in c AD 500, the chances of a contemporary potsherd falling into it before it was refilled would be low, whereas the likelihood of Iron Age sherds from disturbed features or the topsoil being included would

have been extremely high: what follows must be considered in that light.

After excavation had been carried out over a wide area, a small trench, 9.5 metres long, 0.6m wide, and 0.35m deep was found; it had been cut into the rock, and contained traces of a number of posts. Amongst the packing around them were sherds from a 'B-ware' amphora, datable to the later fifth or sixth centuries AD: an extremely well-placed *terminus post quem* for the construction of whatever structure the foundation trench had originally held. By examining other features nearby, several lines of individual post-holes could be incorporated into the plan of a rectangular building approximately 10 × 19 metres, with two internal rows of posts forming aisles, and the foundation trench discussed above lying across it at right angles, dividing off one third of its interior. Without floor levels, or other dating evidence from all of the post holes, the structure can never be *proved* to have existed at all; but Alcock has summarised the situation:

The wall-trench itself formed part of a palimpsest of Iron Age, Arthurian, Aethelredan and medieval pits and gullies, and it was not easy to establish which other features belonged with it. Some parts of the palimpsest could readily be attributed to other periods because of their character or associated finds. From the remainder, it is possible to select those post holes which form lines parallel to the screen-wall or at right angles to it, and which make up a coherent and rational plan' (1973, 226).

As we have seen in the case of the silver brooch or buckle from the gateway, a *terminus post quem* is open-ended; all that the amphora sherds show is that the hall (if the wall-trench is indeed accepted as part of its structure) was not constructed *before* the 'Arthurian' period. Alcock has decided that it is indeed 'Arthurian':

Now it is at first sight conceivable that the trench might be eleventh century rather than fifth/sixth century in date, on the grounds that the amphora sherds could have been lying on the surface when an Aethelredan building was erected, and so came to be incorporated in its wall-trench. But the amphora sherds, despite the softness of their fabric, had sharp, unabraded edges, and there can be no reasonable doubt that they were buried in the trench-filling shortly after the vessel from which they came had been shattered (1973, 226).

The almost legal-sounding choice of words 'no reasonable doubt' is a clear reminder that a judgement has been made, and that anyone else is entitled to accept or reject it, within the bounds of the available evidence. Aisled halls are known from defended sites of both the Celtic West of the Arthurian period, and southern England in the late Saxon period; Cadbury has occupation of both kinds. If, instead of assuming contemporaneity, it were suggested that the 'sharp unabraded edges' of the potsherds resulted from a large 500-year old amphora sherd being crushed into smaller fragments while the packing was being rammed into the wall-trench, there would be no real objection to a late Saxon date for the Cadbury hall.

Thus, the Arthurian phase at South Cadbury Castle illustrates the way in which dating evidence is used on an excavation (fig. 53); it has a historical dimension which would be lacking from a purely prehistoric site, of course, but the technical problems are exactly the same. What is clear is that some conclusions are more precise than others, and that a considerable quantity of subjective judgement is required in order to construct a coherent interpretation of an excavation. As long as the basic evidence is properly excavated and fully published in a manner which allows the director's hypotheses to be re-examined independently, it is above criticism, unless it contains basic logical errors. Other people's interpretations will be no better than the basic evidence, and neither theirs nor that of the original excavator should ever be taken on trust without checking the original observations.

53 A diagrammatic summary of the dating of the 'Arthurian' period structures at South Cadbury; rectangles indicate physical features, and ovals activities or artefacts. The features linked by double horizontal lines are structurally contemporary, but the hall is assigned to the same phase by dated pottery, not a physical stratigraphical relationship like that of the rampart, gateway, and road surface.

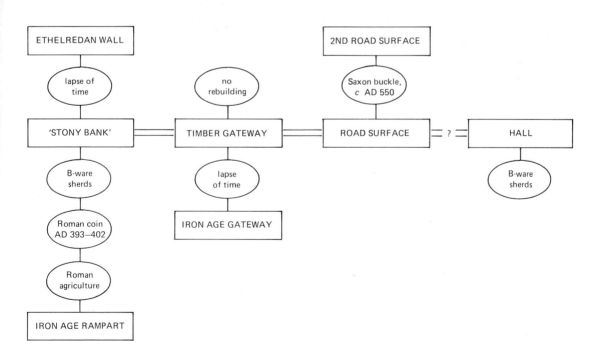

Further reading

As usual, various books by Glyn Daniel provide surveys of the development of the aspects of archaeology covered in this chapter, and the reader is referred to the works cited at the ends of Chapters 1 and 2 (above, pp. 34, 54). Deeper insight into Pitt Rivers can be obtained from M.W. Thompson's recent biography, *General Pitt-Rivers: Evolution and Archaeology in the Nineteenth Century*, 1977; unfortunately the four massive volumes which Pitt Rivers had printed and distributed privately (*Excavations in Cranborne Chase*, 1887–1898) are not easy to find, but repay the effort. For Mortimer Wheeler, a summary of his approach and techniques is contained in *Archaeology from the Earth*, first published in 1954 but reprinted many times, while his racy autobiography *Still Digging*, 1955, traces the major part of his professional career. A biography of Wheeler by Jacquetta Hawkes has recently been published: *Mortimer Wheeler: Adventurer in Archaeology* (1982).

Most general archaeological books discuss excavation, although rarely from the same point of view, but two more specialized works taken together probably clarify the underlying principles better than these – Edward Harris' *Principles of Archaeological Stratigraphy*, 1979, and Philip Barker's *Techniques of Archaeological Excavation*, 1982. They are both written by expert practitioners who have had to test their theory against demanding complex urban sites and large scale open-area excavations. The range of responsibilities of an excavator can be appreciated from *The Directing of Archaeological Excavations* by John Alexander (1970), although the book faces an almost impossible task in attempting to provide a 'manual' for directors;

any book of this kind will tend to reflect the author's own experience rather than being truly representative.

The complexities of stone and timber structures can best be understood by studying vernacular architecture; an instructive selection of English buildings recorded by the Royal Commission on Ancient and Historical Monuments, with excellent explanatory drawings and commentary is *English Vernacular Houses* by Eric Mercer (1975). The study of standing structures is covered by Warwick Rodwell's *The Archaeology of the English Church*, 1982, whilst the excavation, interpretation and reconstruction of Roman military timber buildings may be studied in *Report on the Excavations at Usk: the Fortress Excavations 1968–1971* by W.H. Manning (1981).

Once the general principles of excavation have been grasped, it is likely that readers will gain more from reading individual accounts of specific excavations, such as Leslie Alcock's *By South Cadbury is that Camelot . . .* , 1972, than from textbooks which attempt to provide a general survey. Every site is different, and no two directors would adopt the same strategy or methods for the same site. Many current excavations are reported in magazines such as *Current Archaeology* and *Popular Archaeology*, the American *Archaeology* or the French *Archéologia*.

The best insight into the process of excavation is however gained from actual participation; most university archaeology departments, museums, or larger libraries should be able to provide information, and a monthly calendar of excavations which require volunteers is published in Britain by the Council for British Archaeology, 112 Kennington Rd., London SE11 6RE.

4 Dating the Past

The dating of the past is the key to the organization of archaeological evidence. The gradual erosion of the Biblical account of the Creation and peopling of the world was described in Chapter 1; not until the 1860s was Bishop Usher's date of 4004 BC for the Creation finally undermined by scientists. Before then, in 1816, Thomsen had used the concept of the Three Ages as an innovative criterion for sorting antiquities of stone, bronze, and iron into a sequence. The abandonment of 4004 BC opened a trap-door beneath the feet of chronology, however, and the immense possibilities of slow evolution for Man and his artefacts soon led to subdivisions of prehistoric time, and more refined classifications of artefacts. Geological and archaeological observations of stratification provided physical evidence for the validity of sequences of fossils or artefacts, but only in a *relative* sense; *absolute* dating remained firmly in the hands of historians, and those archaeologists studying the literate civilizations of the Near East, whose scripts began to be deciphered in the early nineteenth century. It was perhaps at this point that history and prehistory first seriously diverged, as what Glyn Daniel has

called the technological model of the past superseded the mythological, theological and historical models; the use of the term 'prehistory' is first recorded in 1833, and became widely established by the end of the century. The growth of awareness of stratification gave more information about sequences of artefacts, and also allowed successive phases of cultures to be defined in terms of ranges of distinctive artefacts, but unfortunately the classification of objects and cultural stages preceded the development of better excavation techniques by several decades. Many of the sequences thus remained largely hypothetical, without any time element other than guesswork.

54 The engraving from Montelius' explanation of his typological methods (1903, 22) shows the transition of the axe head from stone to metal. The first copper axes (nos. 2–3) closely resemble their stone counterparts, but very soon metal was saved by making them thinner and effectiveness was increased by hammering out a wider cutting edge.

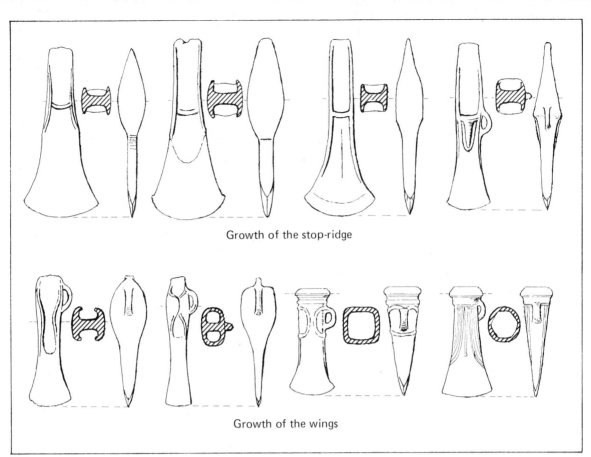

Growth of the stop-ridge

Growth of the wings

55 A series of further modifications gradually appeared during the Bronze Age. Some of the principal stages are illustrated (after Smith 1920); the technical reasons for these changes were well expressed by Pitt Rivers in 1875:

. . . the celt of the neolithic period, chipped only at first and subsequently polished . . . gave rise to the copper celt of the same form having convex sides, which grew into the bronze celt with flat sides. Then the bronze celt was furnished with a stop to prevent its being pressed too far into the handle by the blow. Others were furnished with projecting flanges to prevent them from swerving by the blow when hafted on a bent stick. Others had both stops and flanges. By degrees the flanges were bent over the stops and over the handle, and then the central portion above the stops, being no longer required, became thinner, and ultimately disappeared, the flanges closed on each other, and by this means the weapon grew into the socket celt. On this socket celt you will see that there is sometimes a semicircular ornamentation on each side. This . . . is a vestige of the overlapping flange of the earlier forms out of which it grew, which, like the rings on our brass cannon, are survivals of parts formerly serving for special uses. (Lane-Fox 1875, 507).

Development ceased at this stage, for although a socket formed a very effective hafting method, the use of iron from c. 1000 BC in Europe provided a superior metal with completely different manufacturing techniques which gradually ousted bronze for making edge tools.

Chapter 3 has already examined the dating of sites by stratigraphy, and explored the concepts of the *terminus post quem* and the *terminus ante quem*. This chapter will survey other independent dating techniques which must of course be firmly tied to stratification if the objects or samples to be dated come from excavations.

TYPOLOGY

Pitt Rivers was perhaps the first exponent of

A

B

C

D

RED.

56 Cross-dating by pottery; Sir Arthur Evans was able to use a number of Egyptian artefacts to date contexts in which they were discovered in his excavation of the Palace of Knossos in Crete. In addition, Cretan pottery from his site could be dated by means of similar sherds found in contexts in Egypt. A, B, and D are from Crete, and bear decoration of Evans' Latest Middle Minoan II Phase, whilst C was found at Kahun in Egypt. *Evans 1921, 267, fig. 198*

detailed typology, in the 1850s, but his ideas of its universal validity were too abstract to have any chronological promise. In Sweden, Oscar Montelius advanced typology into the realms of firmer dating through his comprehensive studies of European artefacts published from the 1880s onwards. There were three essential elements in Montelius's framework. The first was to arrange classes of artefacts into **type-series**, normally assuming progress from simplicity towards greater elaboration or efficiency (figs 54–5). Secondly, **associations** between different types were sought, and usually found in individual groups of grave-goods, or hoards of objects buried in times of trouble or stock-piled by craftsmen. These allowed separate type-series to be related to each other, and for **assemblages** to be defined – particular ranges of contemporary artefacts at specific stages of development which often occurred together. These two elements are perfectly acceptable today; the third, **cross-dating**, although logical in theory can be seen in retrospect to have been very misleading. It worked in a number of ways. Sometimes, resemblances between types of artefacts found in different areas were used to link their respective series together; rather better, individual artefacts were sometimes found far from their area of manufacture in association with local types, and thus provided fixed points by which the various type series of the areas concerned could be interlocked (fig. 56). There are obvious criticisms of this method; resemblances between artefacts found in different areas may be coincidental and not contemporary at all, and far-flung objects may have been treasured for long periods before being lost or buried in association with local items. The strongest form of cross-dating took account of artefacts from historically dated areas such as Egypt or Mesopotamia appearing in association with others belonging to undated cultures. These provided actual dates to which the undated cultures could be related. One obvious flaw is that nowhere do historical dates extend before 3000 BC, so that the age of any earlier artefacts could only ever be guessed at. Sir Flinders Petrie was first to achieve this kind of dating, by finding Cretan pottery in Egypt in contexts around 1900 BC, and Egyptian exports datable to c. 1500 BC at Mycenae in mainland Greece. By using the other less reliable forms of cross-dating, Montelius extended these connections right across Europe into Britain and Scandinavia; whereas Petrie's were based on direct associations, each of Montelius's connections added the possibility of a weak link in the chain. Apparent support for these connections was provided by the notion that all cultural developments in Europe were the result of inspiration from the civilizations of the Aegean and Near East, more and more delayed in time as they reached northwards (fig. 88). The effects of this 'diffusionism' lasted up to the 1960s, when a wave of modified radiocarbon dates suddenly snapped the chain into many unrelated links: this issue will be discussed in Chapter 6.

Typology has not been superseded, but the framework of radiocarbon dates now available for prehistory has reduced the burden of chronology that it was made to carry. Type-series remain extremely useful for the description and classification of artefacts, and in understanding their technology and function; associations and cross-dating are still commonly used in building up detailed studies of prehistoric cultures, with the support of as many absolute radiocarbon dates as possible to provide fixed points. In the historical period where the chronological framework already exists, their use is similar; Roman exports of metalwork, pottery, glass and coins reached Scandinavia, Central Europe, and even India, and provide valuable associations for local artefacts. In the Migration period, the typology of brooches and buckles linked to various barbarian peoples is still intimately connected to the study of the bar-

barian settlements which took place within the ruins of the late Roman Empire in the fifth and sixth centuries AD. In many respects the operation of cross-dating and association is comparable to that of the *terminus post quem* and *terminus ante quem* defined in Chapter 3, in the way they can be used to establish fixed points or brackets, whether absolute or relative, in relation to regional typologies or cultures.

SEQUENCE DATING AND SERIATION

These techniques of dating are related to typology but rely on careful excavation and recording, for they both place **assemblages** into relative order, rather than individual artefacts. Sequence dating was used by Petrie in an attempt to work back from the earliest historical phases of Egypt into Pre-Dynastic Neolithic times, using grave-groups, which could be assumed to consist of contemporary artefacts deposited together at a single time (Petrie 1899). Decisions were made about 'early' and 'late' artefacts in graves, by the same kind of typological judgements Montelius had used. The graves were then arranged in a sequence between extreme examples of early and late character, in a kind of 'multiple typology' which simultaneously weighed up the developments of all of the items found in a grave. The graphs which Petrie drew to illustrate the occurrence of pottery types in his numbered sequence of fifty pre-dynastic phases show that types did not suddenly appear and disappear, but gradually gained in popularity and then equally gradually declined again (1920, pl. L). This is of course still an observable feature of twentieth-century fashions, whether in ceramics, clothing or virtually any other innovation which goes beyond purely functional design; the same principle underlies *seriation*, which has been applied to grave groups, strata, or other assemblages found either on single sites or over a wider area.

A range of assemblages is chosen, with a number of definable characteristics occurring in them such as types of pottery or flints, particularly those illustrating change rather than continuity. Each assemblage is reduced to comparable terms, usually by converting the numbers of its selected characteristics into percentages (fig. 57). Assemblages of unknown order can then be arranged to find the optimum sequence, where the percentages of artefacts increase and decline in an orderly manner. For small numbers of assemblages, the process can be carried out by eye using strips of graph paper with the percentages marked on them to represent each assemblage, and shuffling them to find the best fit. A perfect fit will be unlikely, because of random statistical effects and differences in the character of the assemblages compared. Seriation is only relative, and like individual artefact typologies, is mainly used today for examining details within an absolutely dated framework. In fact, the enviable position of modern archaeologists is underlined by Petrie's discussion of an absolute date for the beginning of his prehistoric Egyptian sequence, which is a desperate exercise in grasping at straws and comes to no firm conclusion (*op. cit.* 4–6).

THE ADVENT OF SCIENTIFIC DATING TECHNIQUES (fig. 58)

At the beginning of the twentieth century, it must have seemed impossible that prehistory would ever be dated further back than the tenuous connections established between Egypt and the Aegean in the second millennium BC. Indeed, it is only since 1950 that *absolute* dates have become a reality for archaeology outside limited areas of Scandinavia and the south-west of the United States. However, a number of *relative* dating techniques were developed which gave alternatives or additions to typology and stratification.

Pollen analysis (Dimbleby 1969)

Geologists dealing with very general changes in the surface conditions of the Earth had long been able to equate similar rock structures and their fossils across whole countries and even continents, allowing accurate (relative) cross-dating of local sequences of deposits. Such information was of little help to archaeologists except in relation to the Ice Age and its effects on Palaeolithic man. However, pollen analysis provided a similar comparative framework for

the period since the last Ice Age. The technique used in recovering and identifying the microscopic wind-blown pollen grains, which survive well in damp soil conditions, is described in Chapter 6. It was first used in Scandinavia in the 1920s, and as work progressed a gradual accumulation of pollen records from deep deposits gave detailed confirmation of a consistent series of vegetational changes since the last Ice Age throughout northern Europe, which had already been proposed from visible plant remains. This became a dating technique because the **climatic zones** defined from these changes could be assumed to be fairly uniform over the whole area (fig. 82). Thus, a pollen sample from an archaeological site could be fitted into the sequence at the point indicated by its constituent plant species. As more sites were examined in this way, correlations between sites and zones could be extrapolated to other countries where the technique had been explored as a form of independent cross-dating. Because the zones have now been dated absolutely by radiocarbon, pollen analysis has gone out of use as a chronological indicator, for the sites themselves can of course be dated by the same method; the technique continues to supply important evidence for the interpretation of the environment, however.

Fluorine, nitrogen, and uranium tests (Oakley 1969)

A persistent problem with artefacts excavated from a single level is their contemporaneity – was there some undetected disturbance of the stratum which allowed more recent items to intrude into it? Are some really much older items which have entered the stratum after having been eroded or dug up from an earlier context? These three related techniques can provide effective answers in the case of bone. Bones change over time, and in simple terms, the levels of fluorine and uranium increase through the percolation of water containing minerals which react chemically with the bone, adding fluorine and uranium, whilst nitrogen decreases through the decay of bone protein (collagen). Fluorine and nitrogen levels can be measured by straightforward chemical analysis,

PROJECTILE POINT TYPES

Site	Levanna	Jack's Reef	Fox Creek	Greene	T
Turnbull					187
Black Rock					29
Weinman 4					67
Tufano					44
Barren Island					34
Dennis 6					12
Ford (Dump)					56
Westheimer 2					57
Fredenburg					41

POTTERY: RIM FORMS

Site	Flat	Round	Pointed	T
Turnbull				42
Black Rock				60
Weinman 4				56
Tufano				19
Barren Island				24
Dennis 6				27
Ford (Dump)				67
Westheimer 2				30

SURFACE TREATMENT

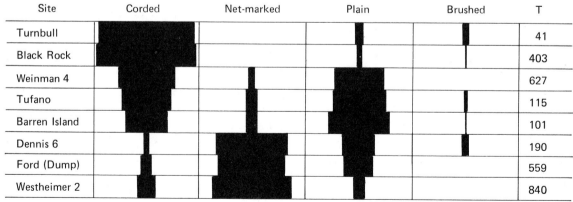

Site	Corded	Net-marked	Plain	Brushed	T
Turnbull					41
Black Rock					403
Weinman 4					627
Tufano					115
Barren Island					101
Dennis 6					190
Ford (Dump)					559
Westheimer 2					840

100%

57 Seriation: artefacts from a number of 'Middle Woodland' Indian sites in New York State, USA, have been arranged into their theoretical order, according to the hypothesis that the popularity of each item will have waxed and waned in an orderly manner (Funk 1976, 282–3). The clearest results can be seen in the case of projectile points (arrowheads, etc.). Two types – Levanna and Fox Creek – show complementary trends; if the sites are ordered from Fredenburg to Turnbull, a gradual decline in the dominance of Fox Creek is apparent, together with the gradual appearance and rise to 100 per cent dominance of the Levanna type. The two remaining minor types do not conflict with this view.

Two aspects of the pottery (rim forms and surface treatment) produce encouragingly similar results, with only two changes in the order of the sites preferred by Funk, indicated here by arrows. Support for the *direction* of the series through time is provided by radiocarbon dates (Fredenburg: AD 360 ± 100; Westheimer 2: 410, 450 ± 80; Dennis 6: 630 ± 65; Tufano: 700 ± 100; Black Rock: 850 ± 95). The columns headed 'total' show differences in the sizes of the samples from each site, from which perfect results would be unlikely: 'Minor irregularities . . . are counterbalanced by the evident continuities and the broad trends of development' (*op. cit.* 282).

58 The range of applicability of a variety of scientific dating methods.

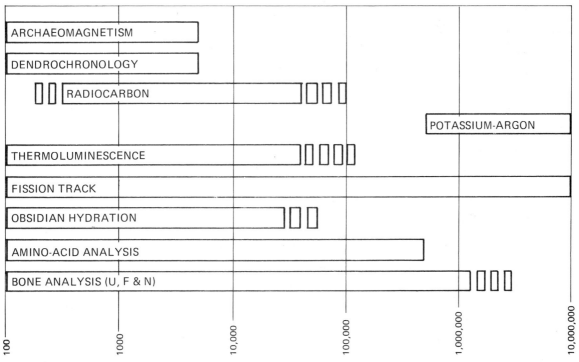

years before present

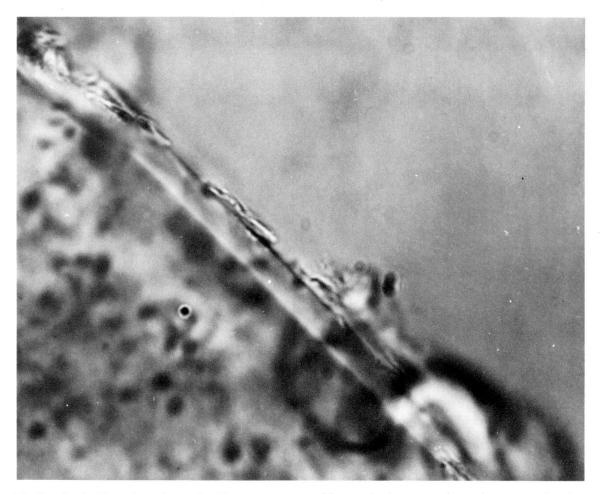

59 The **hydration rim** of an obsidian artefact. The photomicrograph shows a section through the specimen, with its interior to the left; the diagonal band is the layer of weathering beneath the surface, and its extent is demarcated by the **diffusion front** which shows up as a paler line. The photograph shows how clearly the hydration rim can be seen, and therefore accurately measured, although in this case it is only three microns thick. *Photograph by courtesy of Prof. J. Michels*

whilst radioactive uranium can be detected by a Geiger counter. All of the bones found in a single context should have been equally subject to the conditions which cause these changes, and their results should be fairly uniform. Older survivals,

and in particular recent intrusions, may thus be detected by their anomalous levels. Usually, two or all three of these elements are tested where doubt exists over the contemporaneity of fossil bones. Early human remains have been studied in many countries with very clearcut results – none more so than the revelation of the forged 'Piltdown Man' skull and jaw 'excavated' in Sussex in 1912, which had been fraudulently assembled out of fragments of bones of different ages and origins.

The trends of chemical change in bone are reliable and consistent all over the world, but unfortunately depend very much on the environment in which the bone has been buried. There is therefore no possibility of this technique being considered in any way absolute, or for results from different deposits to be compared with each other.

Obsidian hydration dating (Friedman *et al.* 1969)

A further dating technique relying on the decay of substances is concerned with the measurement of a microscopically thin layer which forms on the surface of obsidian (fig. 59), a natural volcanic glass which was a popular alternative to flint for flaked tools in many parts of the world (fig. 72). It is formed by the absorption of water and commences as soon as a fresh surface is exposed, but unfortunately obsidian does not undergo this change at a constant rate and seems to be particularly sensitive to changes in temperature. Like the analysis of bone, it can only be considered a relative dating technique. Furthermore, samples of obsidian from different geological sources may also weather at different rates. However, in regions where supporting dates can be supplied by radiocarbon large numbers of measurements can be compiled to provide a standard against which the rim thicknesses from individual artefacts or assemblages can be compared. This has been carried out in Hokkaido, Japan, where artefacts from six sites were used to compile a comparative scale stretching back 20,000 years. Like bone analyses, the technique can be used to check contemporaneity of material from a single deposit, and to detect modern forgeries. On individual sites, the hydration rim thicknesses of large numbers of artefacts can be plotted on a graph; if the site was occupied continuously they should display a reasonably smooth progression with age, whilst discontinuities may represent periods of abandonment. In warm climates where hydration is rapid, obsidian is useful for quite recent centuries. On Easter Island in the Pacific, the layer formation rate has been calibrated by historical events, and allows a potential accuracy of around thirty-five years – impossibly precise for radiocarbon dating. This is however a special case, because of particularly fast hydration and the existence of historical dating to pin down the relative measure of time (Fleming, 1976, 158–9).

ABSOLUTE SCIENTIFIC DATING TECHNIQUES*

In order to give the study of prehistory a framework approaching the soundness of that used by historical archaeologists, a technique completely independent of the subjective observations of typology or the relativity of pollen or bone analysis was required. Fortunately, several techniques have been developed as a result of research into atomic physics and radioactivity, of which the most impressive and useful is radiocarbon dating, which has risen to prominence since the 1950s. However, two absolute techniques were developed much earlier – the study of varves and tree-rings.

Varves (Zeuner 1946)

Each year, the melting of a glacier washes heavy deposits of sediment into rivers and streams which are deposited on their beds or in lakes where the water moves more slowly. The sediment becomes sparser and finer as the year progresses and the flow is reduced, until winter freezing stops it again until the next summer. A section through an old lake-bed will therefore show a regular pattern of coarse and fine annual layers. Variations in climate produce different thickness of sediment in the build up of annual deposits, which allow comparisons to be made between deposits in separate lake beds (fig. 60). In Sweden, from 1905 onwards Baron de Geer traced overlapping sequences left by the retreat of the glaciers after the last Ice Age until a sequence of over 10,000 years was established down to the early medieval period. Not only was the end of the Ice Age dated, but the coarse deposits often contained pollen, and allowed the climatic sequence of vegetation to be dated absolutely. More recently, such material has also provided checks on radiocarbon dating.

Work on varves continues, particularly in

---

* Note: some writers prefer to use the term 'chronometric' rather than 'absolute' for dates which are not relative, but relate to a calendar of years; Oakley summarizes the objection to 'absolute dating' – 'Where it is possible to establish that two deposits in widely separated areas were formed contemporaneously (e.g. if they both contain the same fall of volcanic ash), they could be said to be of the same 'absolute' age even if their antiquity in *years* is unknown' (1969, 35). In the light of the problems of calibrating even the most accurate techniques, I feel that the distinction is rather academic.

60 Cores bored from sedimentary lake deposits in Sweden, showing the distinctive *varves*; each individual band of light to dark silt marks a single year's deposition of water-borne sediment. Varves may vary in thickness from a few millimetres to several metres; these average *c.* 2.5cm. *Photograph by courtesy of Dr D. Tarling, University of Newcastle upon Tyne*

North America, where eventually there may even be a possibility of tying the sequence of Scandinavian varves to some areas of the New World. Varves also contribute information to archaeomagnetic dating, for they contain a record of the Earth's magnetic field in their iron-rich clay particles (below, p. 121).

Tree rings (Bannister 1969)

Although some perceptive observations about annual growth rings in timber had been made since the late eighteenth century, tree-ring dating (or **dendrochronology**) was firmly linked to archaeology in the early 1930s, when A.E. Douglass examined timbers preserved in *pueblos*, prehistoric Indian sites in arid areas of Arizona and New Mexico (fig. 61). Trees grow annual rings which, like varves, are subject to seasonal variations affecting their thickness; again like varves, identical patterns of variation can be recognized in different samples of timber and establish contemporaneity (fig. 62). By collecting many samples, an overlapping series of rings has now been built up for the south-west of the United States stretching back to the first century AD, whilst the bristle cone pines of California provide a record of over 7000 years for radiocarbon comparisons. In Europe, many areas have sequences extending beyond the Roman period, as well as earlier 'floating' sequences which are roughly datable, but have not yet been linked to absolutely dated timbers. The latter can be used for relative dating, and on waterlogged sites the sequence of timber buildings can be examined in this way. At Charavines (Isère, France), a large scatter of stakes was found preserved on a submerged Neolithic village site, but no coherent plan was apparent.

61 Pueblo Bonito, in Chaco Canyon, New Mexico, is an extensive Indian site built mainly of stone with timber beams, lintels, roofs, etc. Its arid desert environment ensures the preservation of wood for hundreds of years, and therefore allows the use of tree-ring dating. Pueblo Bonito was in fact the first site ever to be systematically studied in this way, and the combination of dendrochronology and architectural analysis allowed a detailed picture of the development of the site (which dated to *c.* AD 900–1100) to be established (Judd 1964). The end of a large beam and a horizontal door lintel provide sources of dating for this part of the structure: their latest (outside) rings will give *termini post quos*; however, there is always a possibility that they have been re-used from an earlier phase of the building. Note also that the doorway was blocked at one stage, suggesting changes in the functions of these rooms.
Photograph by Neil Judd, 1926; copyright, National Geographic Society

Examination of the rings allowed two rectangular structures built in successive years to be isolated by plotting posts felled in the same year (Bocquet 1981).

There are problems in the direct application of dendrochronological dating. Not all tree species are sufficiently sensitive to display much variation in their ring characteristics, particularly when growing in temperate climates. Wood of course only survives on excavations under exceptionally wet or dry conditions; even when it does, large timbers are needed in order to provide enough rings for valid comparisons, which rely on distinctive patterns that accumulated over several decades. Timber used in buildings may well have been trimmed down, removing the evidence for the exact date of its felling. Even when complete, it may have been stored for many years before actual use in a structure. Worse, timbers may have been reused several times in repairs or reconstructions of wooden buildings – foundations rot long before roof timbers, which may well serve many times. Re-use is a particular problem on arid sites, where timbers do not easily decay. Therefore, a dendrochronological date from a building must only be considered as a *terminus post quem*, and the *latest* single date considered as the critical point after which the structure was erected.

Despite their problems, varves and tree-rings are perhaps the only truly absolute dating techniques, in that they are capable of providing exact dates in terms of a single year; they will never be universally applicable, however, because of the circumstances of their formation, and their regional and environmental limitations.

Radioactive decay

Several scientific dating techniques make use of the fact that many elements can occur in several different forms, or isotopes, with extra electrons which may be unstable; on decay, they may become more stable, or in the case of elements such as uranium, move along a protracted chain of existence as different elements until turning into a stable one (i.e. uranium→ lead). The dating of geological periods followed soon after

109

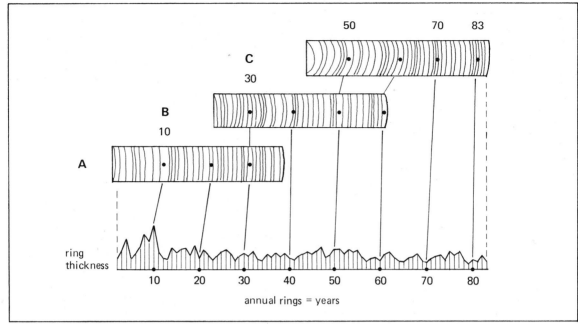

62 Dendrochronology: A, B, and C are three sections of tree-trunks showing the accumulation of annual growth rings; together, they cover a period of 83 years, from the innermost ring at the left of timber A to the outermost of C. The overlapping (contemporary) portions of the timbers are matched by similarities in the pattern of their rings, aided by any distinctive unusually wide or narrow rings reflecting particularly good or bad growing seasons for the trees. The graph records the average annual ring thickness for each year, allowing for the fact that outer rings are always narrower than inner because of their greater diameter – the same volume of wood is spread more thinly around a large trunk than a young sapling. Overlapping sequences from *dated* timbers can thus provide a reference against which individual undated samples can be compared. Thus, if this graph began in AD 1000, timber B was felled in AD 1060, which provides a *terminus post quem* for any structure into which it was incorporated: whether it was used straight away, or even re-used from an earlier structure, must be decided on archaeological grounds.

the discovery of radioactivity, and the age of rocks back to the Pre-Cambrian was assessed by measuring the proportions of uranium and lead or uranium and helium. Uranium could be used in this way because it remains radioactive for very long periods; elements with shorter decay periods are more useful for recent geological and archaeological dating. A term which describes this speed of activity is the **half-life** – the length of time that it takes for half of the radioactivity to decay. Half-lives can vary from seconds to millions of years; by the greatest good fortune, that of one isotope of carbon, an abundant element in organic matter, is 5730 ± 40 years – slow enough in its decay to include periods since the later Stone Age, but fast enough to be measured with some accuracy.

Radiocarbon dating (Willis 1969; fig. 63)
The most important thing about radiocarbon dating is that it is universal – radioactive decay is not influenced by environmental factors, and the rare isotope carbon-14 is formed throughout the atmosphere of the Earth. This radioactive isotope is produced by the effects of cosmic radiation on the atmosphere, and is

therefore forming and decaying continuously. An important factor is that the formation and decay seem to be in complete balance, and there has therefore not been a steady build-up of C-14 in the atmosphere. Thus, a fixed level of cosmic radiation should always have produced a fixed proportion of C-14 to the other isotopes of carbon, even though in fact it only makes up a minute fraction of carbon as a whole. Furthermore, all life-forms are carbon-based, and living organisms take in fresh carbon until their death; photosynthesis by plants is one mechanism. They therefore maintain the same proportion of C-14 as the atmosphere until their death, at which point it begins to decay. Thus, if a sample of ancient wood, charcoal or other organic matter is processed in the laboratory until pure carbon is isolated, the amount of radioactivity can be measured, and compared with the known half-life of the isotope; the older it is, the fewer emissions of beta-particles will occur in a period of observation. Five grammes of modern C-14 will produce 75 disintegrations per minute; five grammes giving only $37\frac{1}{2}$ counts would therefore be of the age of the half-life of

63 The counting of radioactive emissions from an archaeological sample requires sophisticated and highly accurate equipment if the margins of error are to be kept within reasonable bounds. Here, a sample is being placed into a counting chamber shielded from cosmic and other natural sources of radiation by massive steel and lead panels. It is ringed by Geiger counters to record the stray radiation which may penetrate the chamber, as well as the emissions actually derived from the sample. Cables convey the readings to automatic recording equipment during several separate prolonged periods of counting which may extend over several days. The older the sample, the less radioactive it will be, and the longer the counting period will have to be to provide useful results. *Centre de Datation et d'Analyses Isotopiques, Université Claude Bernard, Lyon* the isotope, around 5730 years. This description is simplified, of course, and does not do justice to the inspired hypothesis-formation and testing carried out by Willard F. Libby in Chicago in the later 1940s. He published his conclusions in 1949, but this was only a beginning, and not only has radiocarbon dating grown exponentially since then, but a variety of problems and inaccuracies have been isolated and examined, some of them leading to major adjustments of the results. Libby received a Nobel Prize in 1961 for his work; there are now over eighty radiocarbon laboratories all over the world, and upwards of 50,000 dates have been calculated. Despite problems, the dates have provided a framework for the prehistory of the world; for the first time, its study has become more like that of historical periods, and its emphasis has shifted away from chronology towards more fundamental social and economic factors. Some of these implications will be discussed in Chapter 6.

Several details of radiocarbon dating need to be examined more carefully to understand the way in which its results should be interpreted, particularly because the interpretation of individual dates has been revised since the technique began to be employed. Some of the basic assumptions have proved incorrect:

– **the half life** ($t\frac{1}{2}$) proposed by Libby has been shown by more accurate measurement to be too low by around 3%; it is now judged to be around 5730 years rather than 5568.

– **cosmic radiation** seems to have been subject to small fluctuations at all times, perhaps in relation to sunspot activity and the Earth's magnetic intensity. The formation of C-14 will have varied accordingly, producing misleadingly younger or older dates as more or less C-14 entered organic matter.

– **dendrochronology** has been used to provide dated samples of wood from annual tree-rings stretching back over 7000 years, thanks to the longevity of the bristlecone pines of the south west of the USA (several of which are still growing after more than 4000 years) and samples from even older

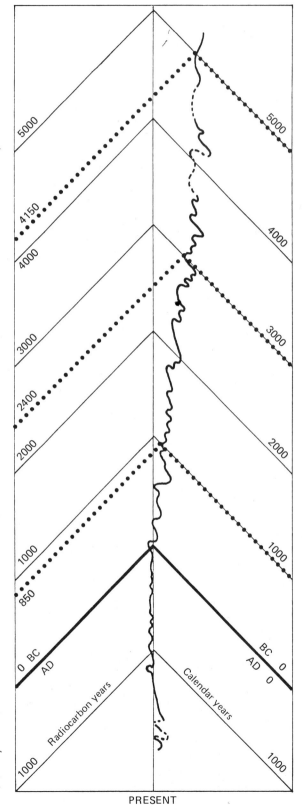

PRESENT

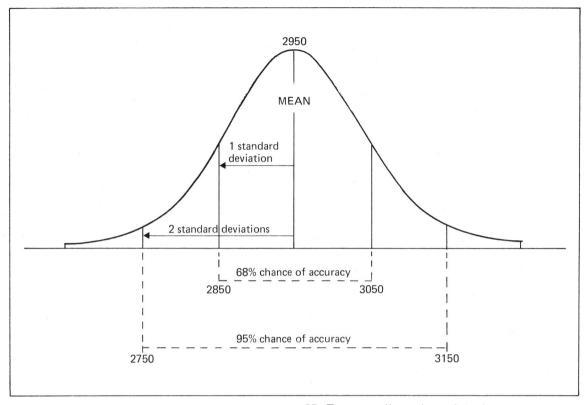

2950

MEAN

1 standard
deviation

2 standard deviations

68% chance of accuracy

2850   3050

95% chance of accuracy

2750   3150

64 Calibration curve for radiocarbon dates. The wavy line shows the effects of samples derived from dated tree-rings; it diverges progressively from 'real' or calendar years from around 2000 years ago. To convert a radiocarbon date of 850 bc into calendar years, follow the dotted line from the left scale across the centre axis until it meets the calibration curve, and then follow it down to the calendar scale on the right, where a 'real' date of 1000 BC is indicated. 4150 bc becomes 5000 BC in the same way – note that 'bc' denotes a raw date, 'BC' a calibrated date. The dotted line for 2400 bc could cross the curve in several places, giving dates from 3000 to 3400 BC!

65 Every radiocarbon date has a statistical margin of error, quoted in terms of one standard deviation – e.g. 2950 ± 100 bc. This graph shows how this should be interpreted: *one* standard deviation will give a 68 per cent probability of the true date lying within its 200-year bracket (and therefore a 32 per cent chance of it *not* doing so), whilst *two* standard deviations will increase the probability of accuracy to around 95 per cent.

trunks which have resisted decay in the semi-arid habitat of the tree. Not only does this study illustrate the short-term fluctuations in C-14 levels, but it also demonstrates a consistent and steadily increasing divergence between actual calendar years and 'radio-carbon years' before *c.* 1000 BC. This has led to the creation of a **calibration curve**, by which samples of 2000 years old or more are adjusted upwards – by as much as 500 to 1000 years where samples 5000–7000 years old are concerned (fig. 64). Some of the implications of these changes for the prehistory of Europe will be discussed in Chapter 6. There is no independent check on dates earlier than *c.* 5200 BC, for tree-rings cannot yet be extended further back in time.

— **standard deviations** are attached to all laboratory counts of radioactivity; the isotope decays are random, and only an extremely long (and therefore expensive) count would reduce this inherent statistical error. Several counting sessions of the same fixed length are normally carried out, and the range of differences between the separate results is conveyed by a figure preceded by '$\pm$' (known as the standard deviation) which follows the *mean* date. This allows limits of reliability for the mean date to be envisaged. Fig. 65 shows that there is a 68 per cent chance that the true date lies within 1 standard deviation *either side* of the given date; to increase confidence to nearly 100 per cent, three standard deviations would have to be considered, but this would produce an unacceptably wide date range if the standard deviation is large. It is best to think of radiocarbon dates as brackets containing a likely date, rather than in terms of the mean which is actually quoted, for two means which appear different cannot be considered separate dates if their 'brackets' overlap to any extent.

The interpretation of a given sample is therefore complex, but there are still further pitfalls because of the standardized way in which laboratories have agreed to present their results. Whenever a radiocarbon date is published in an archaeological report or article, the 'raw' uncalibrated date (with its laboratory identification number) should *always* be quoted, so that changing interpretations can be related to the situation at the time of its publication.

Interpreting a radiocarbon date

A radiocarbon date received from a laboratory might be:

$$4250 \pm 100 \text{ bp} \quad t\tfrac{1}{2} = 5568$$

This is a 'raw' date, and needs several stages of interpretation. 'bp' means 'before present', but the present is in fact standardised to 1950! It is therefore necessary to subtract 4250 from AD 1950; the half-life ($t\tfrac{1}{2}$) must also be adjusted from Libby's figure of 5568 to the more recently determined estimate of 5730. This is achieved by multiplying the date by a factor of 1.029. Our date will now read:

$$2367 \pm 100 \text{ bc} \quad t = 5730$$

The lower case 'small bc' indicates that the date has not yet been calibrated; consultation of a calibration curve derived from dated tree-ring samples transforms the date again, to a calendar date of:

$$2970 \pm 100 \text{ BC}$$

Note that BC is now written with capital letters, to show that 'real' rather than radiocarbon years are being presented.

The calibration curve most accessibly published and widely used by archaeologists is that provided by Clark in the periodical *Antiquity* (Clark 1975); there are others, however, and also many different ways of interpreting the mathematical problems of calibration. Having arrived at the calibrated date, it is now necessary to make allowance for the standard deviation.

At best, there is a 68 per cent chance that the true date lies between 2870 and 3070 BC; likewise, a 95 per cent chance that it lies between 2770 and 3170 BC. However, the tree-ring calibration curve is itself subject to statistical variation, so that the standard deviation should now be considered a *minimum* estimate of unreliability. Furthermore, two separate dates of 2875 ± 100 BC and 3025 ± 100 BC are not statistically separable, because their standard deviations overlap.

Most materials containing carbon are suitable for dating, but organic carbon is preferable; the higher the carbon content, the smaller the sample needs to be. Charcoal derived from the burning of wood is a common find on archaeological sites, and only small samples of around 10 grams dry weight are required, compared with around 350 grams of recent bone, or twice as much for bone more than 5000 years old. Many items can be tested, including cloth, flesh, pollen, and even iron, which almost always contains some carbon impurities. The collection of samples needs to be scrupulous, and their storage and handling must avoid contamination, even though they are subjected to a chemical 'laundry' process before being tested. From a purely archaeological point of view, an excavator must know exactly *what* is being sampled, and its stratigraphic relationship to the site. Most larger prehistoric sites now regularly produce dozens of samples, and the expense of the process (around £50 per sample at present) makes careful selection a high priority. The nature of charcoal and wood samples is important – twigs or nuts are ideal, because they are only likely to contain C-14 taken in during a short growing season, whereas the central portion of a large beam or post will obviously give a date decades earlier than the date of its use for fuel or construction.

Improvements in both the counting of radioactive emissions by computer-controlled apparatus (Hall and Hewson 1977), and the assessment of disturbing factors such as fluctuations in cosmic radiation continue; the standard deviation will never be eliminated, but it will be reduced, and greater precision in the composition of calibration curves is likely. The impact of this dating technique is hard to overestimate, however; it is without doubt the greatest single contribution to the development of archaeology since the rejection of the notion that the world was created in 4004 BC first freed prehistorians from the constraints of historical chronology. At least in outline, the major stages of human development from hunting through to

urbanization are now well dated over most of the world. Radiocarbon's half-life makes it possible to study periods back to around 50,000 BC, but the radioactive isotopes are so few by then that there are great problems in measuring the very small number of remaining particle emissions. The technique is therefore unsuitable for studying much of the Palaeolithic period, but fortunately a related method based on an isotope of potassium has been devised which allows the examination of early hominid developments.

Potassium-argon dating (Gentner and Lippolt 1969)

Potassium is an element which is abundant throughout minerals in the Earth's crust. Its isotopes include a small percentage of K-40, which decays into calcium-40 and argon-40. The latter is a gas; in volcanic rocks, it can escape during their formation, but as minerals crystallize, they trap new A-40 derived from the decay of K-40. The half life of K-40 is known, and compared with that of C-14 is staggeringly long: 1.3×10^9 years, covering most of the Earth's geological history. Its dating potential for geology has been known since the 1930s, and archaeological applications began in the 1950s. Dates are arrived at by measuring the amount of A-40 trapped in potassium-rich minerals in relation to that of K-40; the less there is, the more recent was the formation of the material involved. The wide range of the technique, and the inherent inaccuracies in measuring minute quantities of A-40 make it difficult to use right down to the comparatively recent upper limits of radiocarbon dating. However, it is ideal in connection with the early hominid fossils of East Africa, which occur in an area which was volcanically active at the time that the fossils were laid down; often, layers containing fossils can be found 'sandwiched' between deposits of volcanic ash and lava, which provide excellent samples of newly-formed minerals for measurement. The results cannot easily be independently assessed, but another radioactive decay technique, fission track dating, does give similar results. In periods of such long duration the significance of margins of error is of course very

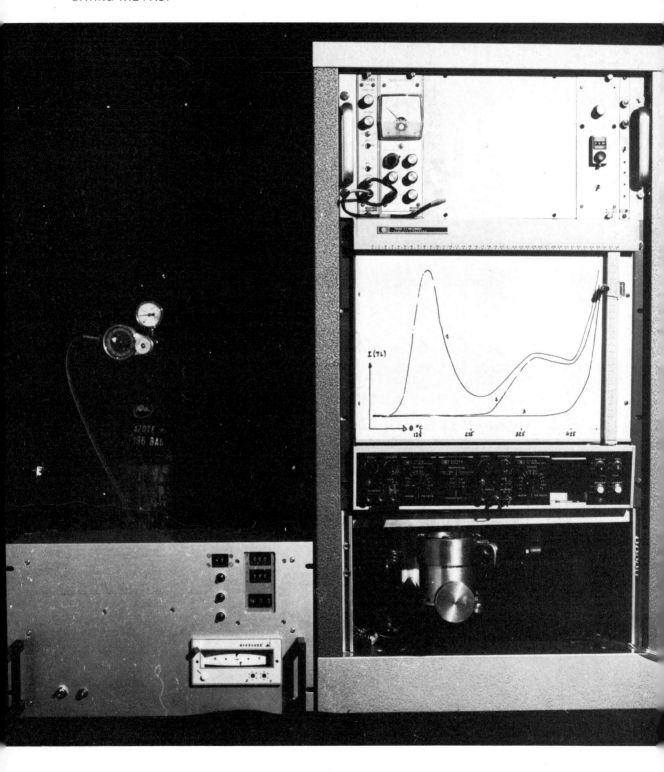

66–67 Thermoluminescence: apparatus for measuring the emission of light from ancient samples. A small sample is carefully prepared to separate out the particles from the clay most sensitive to the trapping of energy from radioactivity. It is placed in the small heating chamber in the recessed part of the equipment (bottom right: fig. 67) and heated intensely in an atmosphere of nitrogen supplied by the cylinder visible behind the heating control unit on the left. The emission of light is measured, and the results processed in relation to the rise in temperature of the sample by the control unit (top right) and plotted onto graph paper by a moving pen (centre right). *Centre de Recherche Interdisciplinaire d'Archéologie Analytique, Université de Bordeaux III*

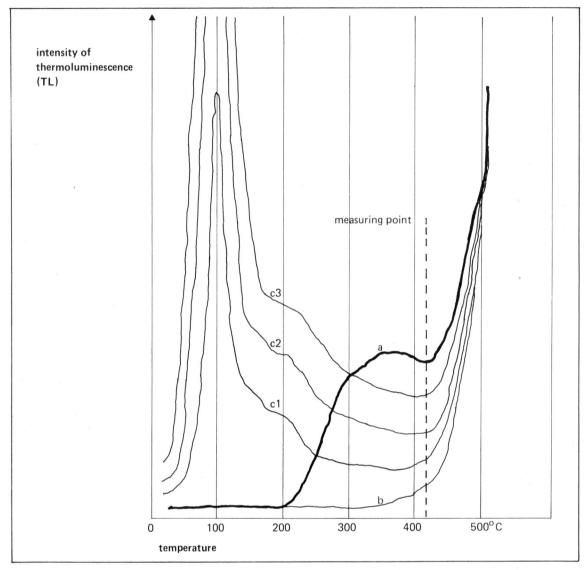

68 The apparatus illustrated in fig. 66 provides a graph of the light released at particular temperatures by a sample prepared from an ancient artefact (a), whilst a remeasurement of the same sample provides a graph for the natural glow of the same material (b). It can then be seen that the bulge in curve (a) between 300 and 400°C is the result of stored energy from the radioactive impurities. Curves (c) 1–3 are further measurements taken to study the amount of thermoluminescence produced by a series of exposures of the sample to known levels of radioactivity in order to study its sensitivity so as to help calibrate the ancient thermoluminescent glow. When further factors about the context of the find from which the sample has been taken are also considered, a date may be calculated.

slight compared with crucial time relationships between, say, the neolithic cultures of Europe. Work is proceeding on the dating of young samples, which may well bridge the gap with effective radiocarbon dating. One considerable problem is the nature of the material required for sampling; few areas in the world can provide archaeological remains stratigraphically related to sequences of undisturbed fresh volcanic material, containing crystallized minerals of the kinds best suited to measurement.

There are several other isotopes which can be used for geological dating, such as uranium-235, -238 or thorium-232. In addition, **fission track dating** (mentioned in connection with the confirmation of potassium-argon dates) involves the counting of minute damage trails in glassy minerals caused by particles emitted from radioactive isotopes.

Thermoluminescence (Aitken 1977; Fleming 1979)

This technique is based on the measurement of energy trapped in the imperfections of the crystals of minerals containing radioactive impurities. Over time the decay of these radioactive isotopes releases energy, some of which is dispersed, but some of which is retained in these imperfections. The technique derives its name from the fact that this energy is released as light when the crystals are strongly heated (figs 66–8). As soon as the heating is over, the same kind of energy begins to accumulate again, until such time as reheating to the same temperature occurs. The most important class of material to which this technique relates is fired clay, in particular pottery, which forms such an important part of the archaeological record in many parts of the world. Pots are fired well over the temperature required to release all of the energy stored in the minerals in their clay, and after their firing, the energy will have built up again until the present. If it can be released and measured, the pot should be datable; the older it is, the more energy should have accumulated since firing. Unfortunately, there are many problems connected with measurement. First of all, the stored energy does not only come from the (measurable) radioactivity within crystals incorporated into clay; it also comes from

cosmic radiation, and the radioactive content of the soil in which the potsherd has been buried. Different clays usually contain a variety of mixed minerals of differing particle size which also vary in their sensitivity, or ability to absorb radiation. All of these factors need to be weighed up individually in order to assess the date of each individual sample; they require elaborate preparation to separate out particles of the optimum size, and extremely sensitive equipment to record the very slight amounts of thermoluminescence emitted. No uniformity of approach has yet been developed, but many cases of plausible dates give some encouragement to hopes that this dating technique has much to contribute, particularly in situations where there are no suitable materials for radiocarbon dating, or when the age is over 40,000 years, when radiocarbon is of rapidly diminishing usefulness. While refinement of the dating of pottery proceeds, thermoluminescence dating is being extended to stones, and more important still to flint implements, which were burnt on a site to a high enough temperature to release their pre-existing stored energy. Both materials have recently been examined in relation to Palaeolithic France – flint tools from the coastal camp site at Terra Amata, Nice, and a burnt pebble found with pre-Neanderthal hominid remains from l'Abri Suard, where a date of around 126,000 years was obtained. In areas where volcanic materials suitable for potassium-argon dating are absent, this is an advance of great significance. However, the technique is not readily available; unlike radiocarbon dating, no commercial laboratories exist for routine use by excavators; most dating is carried out in the course of specific research projects.

All of the scientific dating methods so far described depend on radioactivity. The final technique to be discussed is based on magnetism, of the same form that is detected by the magnetometers described in Chapter 2. Unlike techniques based on radioactive emissions, which can be related to a known half-life, magnetic dating needs to be calibrated against other dating evidence before it can be used on its own.

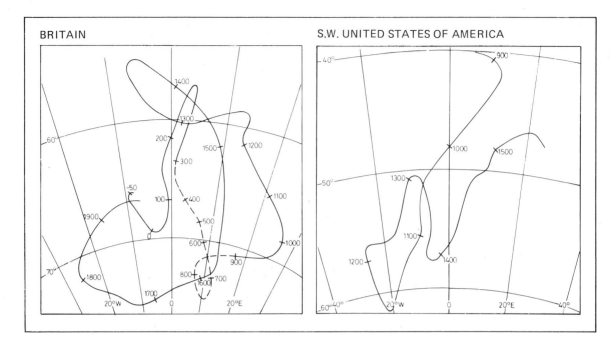

BRITAIN

S.W. UNITED STATES OF AMERICA

69 The movement of Magnetic North, measured from Britain and the south western USA; the graph shows the **declination** in degrees east or west of true north, and **inclination**, in degrees down from horizontal. The wandering lines are compiled from recent observations, and projected back into time with the help of samples from dated deposits or structures on archaeological sites. New samples from undated sites can then be measured in the laboratory and dated according to the curve established for their geographical area. Difficulties can occur, however – at around AD 1300 and 1600 on the British curve, Roman and late Saxon measurements are confusingly similar, and identical readings occur wherever the curve crosses itself. Independent measures of magnetic intensity might resolve these problems. *Redrawn from graphs supplied by Dr D Tarling*

Archaeomagnetic dating (Tarling 1975, 1983)

The iron oxides present in most minerals take on a fixed magnetic alignment in two main ways. **Thermo-remanent** magnetism is acquired when they are disoriented by heat over $675°C$., and then realign on cooling in accordance with the earth's magnetic field. Certain particle sizes are particularly stable, and can accurately record this field for hundreds of thousands of years. Magnetism can also be gained through **deposition** of sediments, for instance in lake beds, where particles may settle into alignment with the magnetic field. Magnetic alignment has two features – inclination or 'dip', and declination; magnetic north wanders at random around the North Pole (and has in fact reversed to the south on occasions) so that from any reference point, it can move up or down (inclination) and from side to side (declination), and these are the measurements which define its position (fig. 69). Contemporary records made by scientists only exist back to AD 1600 in Britain, and have begun much more recently elsewhere, so that archaeological and geological evidence is the only source for the reconstruction of past movements and positions. By the careful choice of dated evidence, the information for Britain has been extended back to the second century BC; geologists have also established a general pattern of major variations from magnetic rocks dated by the potassium-argon method.

To apply this technique to the dating of sites, it is necessary to find solid material which has not moved since becoming magnetized; kilns, hearths or burnt clay walls and floors are ideal. The positions of samples are carefully surveyed in relation to the present magnetic field, and their site alignment then duplicated in the laboratory, so that the difference between the ancient alignment and the present magnetic field can be measured. For calibration, one of the best sources of evidence has been found to be the varves (annual lake-bed deposits) described above (p. 107), which are magnetized during deposition, and could one day be to archaeomagnetic dating what tree rings are to radiocarbon – an annual series of deposits formed over a continuous period, allowing calibration with calendar years. Mud bricks from dated sites are also a potential source of precise information in the Near East.

Unfortunately, the earth's magnetic field varies from region to region, so that results from Scandinavian and American varves do not have the universality desirable in an absolute dating technique, and sediments are not as reliable as solid, fired structures such as kilns. Separate areas may eventually be tied together with the help of major anomalies such as pole reversals which can be dated in some areas, and then applied as checks to local series of observations elsewhere.

For portable fired objects such as bricks or pots, it is still possible to examine the 'dip' angle as long as an assumption can be made about the position in which they were fired.

A further aspect of archaeomagnetism is **magnetic intensity**, which reflects not the direction but the strength of the magnetic field. It is also thermo-remanent or acquired through deposition, as with varves; it also varies from area to area, and a dated reference series of measurements needs to be established for a region before it can be used as an independent dating method. Both the direction and intensity of the magnetic field are of an interest which extends beyond dating, for they probably influence climate and cosmic radiation. They are therefore of significance to environmental studies, and also the problem of the effects of fluctuating cosmic radiation upon the amount of carbon-14 which was being created in the atmosphere before tree-ring records allow independent calibration.

AUTHENTICITY OF ARTEFACTS

The fine art and museum world is inextricably bound up with commercial dealings in antiquities, and forgeries are widespread. Both thermoluminescence and archaeomagnetism provide useful checks on pottery, clay cores inside cast bronzes, and a variety of elaborate and highly priced ceramic sculptures such as Etruscan and South American terracottas (*Vie Mystérieuse* . . . 1980, 145–6). Precise dates may not be required, but direct comparisons between similar objects from a single area or culture. Only the most skilled forger could artificially create radioactive energy or past magnetic conditions at the precise levels which would elude these techniques. Dendrochronology and radioactive isotope measurement are similarly helpful in the study of wooden panels and pigments used in early paintings, and once again make the detection of recent fakes possible (*Vie Mystérieuse* . . . 1980, 69–71).

Thus, traditional archaeological dating has been immeasurably strengthened by the growth of scientific techniques, which, taken together with the range of other areas of archaeology to which they have contributed (Chapter 5) demonstrate the truly multi-disciplinary nature of modern archaeology. It must not be thought that traditional methods have been replaced, however; stratification, the sequence-defining aspect of excavation, still forms the basis for observations which may then be refined and made precise by the dating of material in laboratories. No amount of thermoluminescence dating of pottery or archaeomagnetic dating of the kilns can replace the typological classification of vessel and rim forms, or the morphology of kiln structures, for which the human eye and brain remain extremely powerful instruments. The dating techniques do of course add some precision, or allow specific hypotheses to be tested. The best of the old needs to accompany the best of the new.

HISTORICAL DATING (Dymond 1974)

Scientific dating techniques have received much attention in the last three decades, and their most spectacular successes have been related to prehistory, for example the destruction of the long accepted framework for Neolithic and Bronze Age Europe, or the addition of a million years to the estimated age of hominid remains from the Olduvai Gorge in Tanzania. However their use does not respect the compartmentalization of archaeology into prehistory and history (or text-free and text-hindered archaeology, as some have irreverently described them). The extent of documentation varies considerably in 'historical' cultures, and is limited by what people actually chose to write about in the past, as well as whether their successors preserved it, rewrote it in their own terms, summarized, misunderstood, or simply ignored it. In fact, for many areas visited infrequently by travellers from literate civilizations, written references may be little better than a scatter of radiocarbon dates in the amount of actual information they provide. Unlike prehistorians, however, most archaeologists working in a historical setting construct a framework from documentary sources, primarily of dates but also of cultural factors, and then proceed to incorporate archaeological evidence within it. Prehistorians normally worked in the opposite direction until radiocarbon dates provided the kind of established regional frameworks to which historians had long been accustomed.

Prehistorians may perhaps overestimate the accuracy and detail of historical frameworks. An attempt at objectivity is a very recent phenomenon in historical writing; in the past, history was normally written for a purpose, either to represent an individual or régime in a good or bad light (depending on the writer's viewpoint), or to convey a particular philosophical or religious point. A number of considerations have to be weighed up before a piece of information contained in a historical or biographical account is believed – the date and quality of the manuscripts in which the account has survived; the distance of the author from the events he describes, and his record of accuracy on other items which can be checked independently; the sources upon which he relied; and his personal bias and motives for writing.

Documents fall into two categories – those written with a clear historical purpose, and those whose historical value is a result of the attention of modern historians and archaeologists. The first category includes the great narrative historical works such as those of Tacitus, as well as biographies, and the barer chronicles maintained in many monasteries in medieval times. The second includes codes of laws and land-charters, poetry and drama, and miscellaneous letters or anything else written for use rather than posterity. In postmedieval and industrial archaeology, this kind of material is often preserved in archive offices, and of course it becomes more abundant as it decreases in age, until it includes company accounts, building designs, and detailed maps, any of which may potentially provide dates for events, sites or structures. Historical documents themselves may be discovered in archaeological excavations. Thousands of clay tablets with cuneiform inscriptions were found in Mesopotamia before Rawlinson deciphered their script, and the rubbish tips of Graeco-Roman cities in Egypt are full of fragments of papyrus on which everything from lost works by Greek poets to gossipy letters have been found. Inscriptions carved on stone are particularly recurrent in Egypt and the Greek and Roman world, ranging from terse dedications of buildings giving the date and builder's name through to lengthy texts of historical, religious, or legal material. Coins, too, are historical documents in as much as they often bear dates and short inscriptions about rulers and events which may not be recorded in surviving documents, and of course they are important in the dating of stratigraphy when found on excavations. The great importance of this general kind of historical evidence is that it consists of *primary* documents, which have not been copied out many times over the centuries by scribes who might introduce fresh errors at every stage in the transmission of a manuscript.

The ways in which dates derived from historical information are actually related to sites conform to the same basic methodology as those of all earlier periods. Sometimes direct associations can be established – coins in a stratified sequence, or inscriptions relating to phases of a building. Otherwise, there tends to be at least one remove between the evidence and the archaeology, whether it is the use of cross-dating by using dated finds from a historical culture in an undocumented area, or in identifying the remains of sites found by fieldwork with records of settlements named in texts. Local cross-dating is in fact extensively used in historical periods for the study of artefacts. The Roman frontier in Germany provides a good sequence of sites between the late first century BC and the later second century AD, resulting from gradual advances, retreats or modifications of the exact garrisoned line defending the Rhine-Danube frontier. Sites of the first century AD are particularly useful, for there were many changes, and the *Histories* and *Annals* written by Tacitus give very close dating. By the early twentieth century, German archaeologists had worked out detailed typologies for pottery and other artefacts found on these sites, which could then be applied to other areas where the same items were encountered. In fact, the famous use of cross-dating of Indian sites near Pondicherry by Mortimer Wheeler in 1945 used Italian tablewares (Arretine ware) which had first been classified and dated by their occurrence on Augustan sites in Germany (Wheeler, 1954, 119–25).

One of the dangers of historical dating is that dates have a mesmerising effect; if a site is excavated and found to contain a layer of burning and broken artefacts, there is a tendency to look at the historical framework for a reference to an invasion or warfare in the region, and to date the excavated context accordingly.

Unfortunately, even in the Roman period, the survival of historical information is uneven, and there may be unrecorded episodes which could equally well account for the remains found. Furthermore, buildings and even whole towns can burn down through purely accidental circumstances. The principal problem is that if a context on a site is *incorrectly* dated in this way, dates applied to similar artefacts found on other sites will also be wrong.

Scientific dating techniques are used widely in historical periods as well as in prehistory, although their rôle is a supporting one, where there is doubt over historical dates, or where gaps exist in the historical framework. It should not be forgotten that virtually all of the scientific techniques were first validated by using samples of known historical date. Libby used tree rings, and Egyptian wood dated by the recorded reigns of pharaohs to compile his first graphs to test the consistency of C-14 measurements. Radiocarbon dating is now extensive in the study of Viking period sites in Russia, Scandinavia, and Britain, where the historical framework is known, but not in sufficient detail to date the development of individual sites; it is frequently linked to dendrochronology where timbers survive. Later, the study of medieval carvings and roof timbers can confirm or refute traditional datings and building sequences; the large amounts of carbon-14 still present in recent timber allow narrow standard deviations to be defined, and little calibration is required. The same possibilities exist for thermoluminescence and archaeomagnetic dating where pottery and kilns are found, or earthenware bricks and tiles are used in construction. The whole procedure, as with other scientific approaches to archaeology, is founded on cooperation, and the increasingly complex methods of refining the accuracy of scientific dating techniques will demand still more cooperation between scientists, historians, prehistorians and excavators to produce results from which all may benefit in different ways.

Further reading

The appearance of various dating methods, traditional and technical, is charted in the historical surveys of archaeology by Glyn Daniel cited at the end of Chapter 1. An 'outsider's viewpoint' with plenty of biographical and circumstantial information is provided by a science journalist, David Wilson, in *Science and Archaeology* (1978; an earlier edition published in 1975 was titled *Atoms of Time Past*). The influence of changing dating methods on the interpretation of European pre-history is emphasized in the early chapters of Colin Renfrew's *Before Civilization*, 1973.

Scientific surveys of recently-developed dating procedures can be found in Stuart Fleming's *Dating in Archaeology: a Guide to Scientific Techniques*, 1976, or J.W. Michels' *Dating Methods in Archaeology*, 1973, as well as in briefer accounts in most general surveys of archaeology such as Brian Fagan's *In the Beginning*, 1978. Several individual chapters on specific techniques are included in *Science in Archaeology*, edited by D. Brothwell and E. Higgs (1969), whilst part 2 of volume 7 of the periodical *World Archaeology* (1975) is devoted to scientific dating techniques. New developments are frequently reported in other periodicals, principally *Archaeometry* and *Journal of Archaeological Science*, and dramatic advances may reach general science publications such as *Nature* or *Scientific American*.

A well-illustrated edition of *Les Dossiers de l'Archéologie* outlines many scientific dating methods (no. 39, November/December 1979 – 'Methodes de prospection et datation'), whilst an exhibition catalogue, *La Vie Mystérieuse des Chefs-d'Oeuvre: la Science au Service de l'Art* (Paris 1980), contains many interesting case-studies of their application.

5 The Sciences and Archaeology

Archaeology has borrowed concepts and techniques from many other fields throughout its development. The ravages of time have destroyed so much of the evidence left behind by past cultures that ever more refined methods are being employed to extract the maximum possible information from that which still survives. The impact of the sciences has been most dramatic in this connection; the radiocarbon revolution in dating relies completely on developments in nuclear physics, but is only a sideshoot from its central issues. The dating techniques and location devices such as magnetometers described in earlier chapters were rarely designed for archaeological research; their use relies on imaginative applications and modifications to archaeological situations, either by scientists who happen to be interested in archaeology, or by archaeologists who can understand their potential relevance to their own problems. The scientific contribution to dating is self-evident; less apparent but very significant is the way in which most of the basic questions which archaeologists ask about their sites and objects can now be explored with the assistance of the natural or biological sciences – indeed sometimes only by these methods.

An archaeological object, whether found casually or during a controlled excavation, immediately poses a range of straightforward questions which rely on little more than common sense or experience. What is it made of? how was it made? where was it made? where did the raw material come from? what was it used for? when was it made? All of these questions can be answered fairly satisfactorily at a superficial level for most objects, as any busy museum curator will know from visitors' enquiries. If we take the example of a polished stone axe, the material is obviously stone, probably flint or a volcanic rock hand-polished by careful abrasion. It was used for chopping, during a neolithic cultural stage, at a date depending upon the part of the world where it was found. However, to go any further would involve a whole range of specialist scientific knowledge – a geologist might be able to pinpoint a particular region or outcrop from which the stone had been quarried; microscopic examination of the surface might indicate the kind of abrasion and polishing employed, and reveal areas of subsequent wear resulting from cutting, and from its handle fittings. These observations would have to be matched against those made about similar objects, and elaborate experiments could be designed to explore the methods of manufacture and use more precisely; an axe can be an agricultural tool or a weapon of war – which use could produce the observed patterns of wear, and what form of handle would have been most efficient? Mathematical study of the dimensions of the axe could help to compare it with previous finds, and might show it to belong to a type characteristic of a particular region or period. If the axe came from an excavation, scientific dating methods would probably be used on other materials found in order to provide a closer date within the cultural phase to which it belonged. The stone axe is a simple example; hardly any aspects of a modern excavation or its finds would not respond to this kind of examination, which not only answers some questions, but often raises new and unexpected ones.

The relationship between science and archaeology is a double one; first, there are scientific techniques which can be applied more or less directly to sites or finds; second, there is an

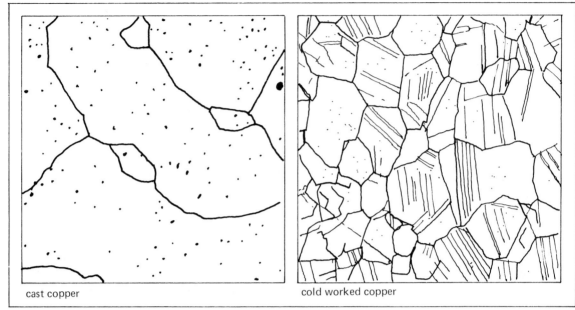

cast copper

cold worked copper

70 Microscopic examination of metal artefacts can reveal many technical details to a metallurgist. The large crystals of cast copper are shown, and it can be seen that their even structure is distorted by hammering into a finished artefact (these traces can, however, be removed by reheating the object – the process is called **annealing**). Scale of magnification: × 1000. *After Brothwell and Higgs 1969, pl. 25*

attitude of mind which demands critical observation, the formulation of hypotheses, and the designing of means of testing their validity. Archaeology is neither 'art' nor 'science' – it is a blend of the best features of both; in the ideal archaeologist the humanist exercises creative thinking, interpretation, and expounds the results in human terms, whilst the scientist ensures that the evidence upon which they are based is gathered in strictly controlled conditions and subjected to the most critical examination available, in order to extract the maximum possible relevant and accurate information.

METALLURGY (Tylecote 1976; Oddy 1977)

The purpose of the analysis of metal artefacts is to establish three things: the materials from

which they were made, the relative quantities of the various constituents present, and the techniques involved in their manufacture. The metal objects of Europe's Bronze Age provide a good example of the kinds of information to be gained, and their implications for the understanding of the changing societies which existed during the thousand years between the end of the New Stone Age and the beginning of the Iron Age. Bronze usually consists of copper alloyed with tin, and varying percentages of other metals. It was realized long ago that before bronze was made, unalloyed copper was utilized, because (like gold) it occurs naturally, and can be worked to a certain extent without smelting. However, all but the simplest artefacts required the metal to be poured molten into a mould. Their shape usually makes it clear if this happened, but a metallurgist can often determine the kind of mould used (metal, stone or clay) and distinguish cold-worked from cast objects by examining their cross-section microscopically – the crystalline structure of cold-worked objects is severely distorted and flattened by hammering (fig. 70). To check that an artefact is indeed made of copper requires more complicated analysis, usually by *spectrometry* (Härke 1978). A sample of the metal is vapourized in a flame or laser, or subjected to radiation; each element emits light or radiation of a different wavelength which is carefully recorded. The presence or absence of elements can thus be detected, and furthermore the actual quantity of each can be measured from the amount of light recorded. There are always very small quantities of various impurities present; the question which arises is whether these 'trace elements' were already in the ore used to make the metal, or added to the alloy intentionally in order to improve the properties of the finished article. Because most of the first rich sources of ore have been quarried away, we may never know in many cases, but detailed work by Austrian and Swiss analysts has gone some way towards identifying the areas from which ores came by analyzing both the ores and the products to find typical trace-elements. It is only when several thousand results are available for careful statistical comparison that any confidence is possible, and they do not exist in many areas. However, it was normal practice to use scrap objects as a source of bronze as well as the quarried or mined ores, and the results of such mixtures could conceivably confuse attempts to pinpoint the source of the metal. Programmes of analysis of finished objects have however been carried out in various parts of Europe with a

71 Inflation and debasement in the Roman Empire is reflected by the accelerating fall in the silver content of the *denarius* from the late second to the late third century AD. Each time the State issued new coins with a reduced silver content, a profit was made, for they cost less to make than previous issues; that the population in general would not accept them as equal in value to purer coins led to the hoarding and melting down of older issues in order to avoid exchanging them for new debased coins, and undoubtedly contributed to the rampant price-inflation and political instability of the period. *Silver content after Kent 1978, 357*

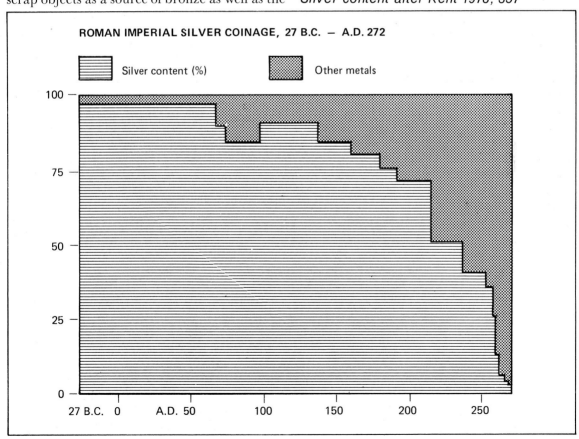

ROMAN IMPERIAL SILVER COINAGE, 27 B.C. — A.D. 272

Silver content (%)   Other metals

good measure of success since the 1930s (e.g. Junghans *et al.* 1974); the general pattern which has emerged is that the use of pure copper or arsenical copper was soon replaced by bronze made with around 10 per cent tin added to it, and that this change was accompanied by the use of more sophisticated moulds which required less further working after casting. Lead was also included as a major constituent in some areas at various dates; this shows some sophistication in the understanding of metallurgy, as a balance had to be achieved between two conflicting factors – the lead may make the metal easier to cast into long elaborate swords and hollow socketed axes, but it can also make it weaker in actual use. This conflict had presumably to be overcome by the bronzesmith through a compromise between easier casting and the acceptability of his products to customers.

Such analyses do not only provide information for prehistory; Roman metallurgy has been extensively studied through similar examinations of ores, ingots and manufactured objects, and it is evident that alloys could be prepared very accurately in order to match the properties of the metal to the function of the end product. Of particular interest is the way in which the Roman silver coin, the *denarius*, gradually lost its content of silver as successive Emperors debased the metal in a desperate attempt to outstrip inflation. Under Augustus (27 BC–AD 14) this coin was as pure as it could be made, containing 98 per cent silver; by the middle of the third century AD when inflation and political chaos reigned, it had fallen to 2–3 per cent and the coins left the mint with a thin silver coating which soon wore off in use, leaving a coin which only size could differentiate from contemporary bronze issues. The extremes are obvious to the eye, but analysis has charted the details of the decline, which have clear implications for any consideration of the contemporary economy and the political problems of the rulers who authorized such debasement (fig. 71).

PETROLOGY

The study of Bronze Age metalwork or Roman

5 cm

coins relies on techniques derived from metallurgy; geology also has much to offer to archaeology, particularly in cultures relying heavily on the use of stone. The techniques employed in the identification and analysis of stone are closely related to those of metallurgy, whether microscopic examination of sections cut through objects, or the spectrographic identification of elements or minerals. The same techniques can be extended to pottery, which of course includes distinctive features related to the geology of the areas from which clay has been taken for its manufacture (Peacock 1977).

One kind of stone which has attracted considerable attention is a volcanically-formed glass, *obsidian*, which has excellent properties, like flint, for chipping, flaking, and grinding into tools with sharp cutting edges (fig. 72). The raw material is found in both the New and Old Worlds, and has received considerable attention, particularly around the Mediterranean, in order to be able to identify the sources from which ancient sites were supplied – with obvious implications for prehistoric trade. In some parts of the world, such as New Zealand, straightforward techniques of microscopic examination or even visual appearance have proved sufficient to separate the different sources, but around the Mediterranean and the American cordillera there are several varieties of obsidian, which require more subtle differentiation. The method used is trace-element analysis; instead of quantifying the principal constituents of the mineral (which contains more than 65 per cent silica), attention is focused upon rarer elements, such as barium and zirconium. Elements can be detected and measured down to a few parts per

72 Obsidian, a natural volcanic glass, formed an important raw material for tool production in many parts of the world, and was often traded over long distances. Its sources are rarely identifiable by the eye, however, and petrological analysis is required to study the distribution of obsidian from different sources. *Flake of semi-translucent obsidian from Greece; flake, core, and two arrowheads from Patagonia: Hancock Museum, University of Newcastle upon Tyne*

million by spectrographic means similar to those used in the analysis of bronze objects. They can be plotted against each other on graphs until it is established that certain proportions of elements found at one source are significantly different from those at all others (fig. 73). This process is called 'characterization' and aims to provide individual 'fingerprints' which can be looked for when new samples of unknown origin are tested. Hundreds of specimens known to have come from definite sources need to have been analyzed before artefacts found on sites can be tested for their origin, and not all sources have yet been fully characterized, but a picture has emerged of the distribution patterns of many, which provides remarkable new information on the wide trade connections which existed between early Neolithic sites in the Near East as early as the seventh and sixth millennia BC (Cann, Dixon & Renfrew 1969). In these undocumented cultures, it is difficult to envisage any way in which such information could have been gained other than by the use of such scientific techniques; but the problems of interpreting the human factors involved in the distribution and use of obsidian are still a purely archaeological matter. Geology can tell where obsidian has come from, but it is up to the archaeologist to speculate why a particular site should have received its raw material from that source rather than another, and to discover whether the artefacts arrived already worked, or if blocks of obsidian were broken up and fashioned on each site – the characteristic waste material and flakes chipped off during the manufacturing process can only be recognized by an experienced observer.

The two most basic functions of chemical or physical analysis are illustrated by the study of bronze and obsidian: The first is the basic qualitative assessment: what is an object made of? The second is a more refined quantitative examination of the exact quantities of an object's constituents, particularly the significant rare trace-elements which may help to distinguish between different sources. For obsidian, this is not the end of the story; the weathering of the stone after working into an implement produces a thin 'hydration layer' which increases

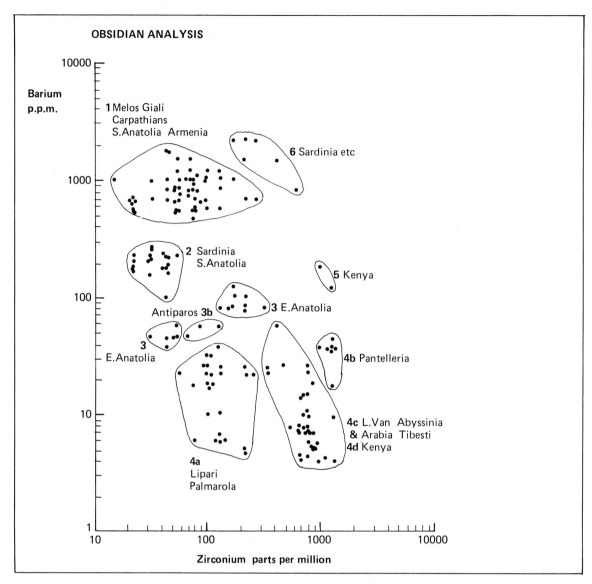

OBSIDIAN ANALYSIS

73 Sources of obsidian in the Near East and Mediterranean: samples from known sources have been analysed, and the results processed in order to find trace elements which differ significantly. In this diagram, barium and zirconium are plotted against each other on a logarithmic scale, to form clusters of results against which artefacts from sites can be tested to determine the origin of the raw material from which they were manufactured. Some clusters are more convincing than others; several different relationships between a range of trace elements may be needed to improve the characterization of each source. The techniques of source characterization seen here have also been used in the study of pottery and other kinds of stone. *After Cann* et al. *1969* with time, and can be used as a dating technique (described in Chapter 4).

Geological examination remains important in historical archaeology right up to recent times; the identification of the sources of building stone, whether in Roman villas, medieval cathedrals, or nineteenth century town halls can provide insights into the technical skills, communications, and prosperity of the societies and individuals who created them.

CONSERVATION (Dowman 1970)

The excavation of ancient objects in poor condition and the preservation of historic or archaeological sites present considerable problems for museums and antiquities services all over the world. No excavation is complete without at least 'first aid' facilities for preventing the further decay of delicate finds until they can be handed over to fully-equipped laboratories for long-term preservation; at the other end of the spectrum, large commercial companies run research programmes devoted to finding methods of preserving ancient stonework which is being eroded by air pollution.

The first problem to be overcome in conservation is the exact identification of what an object is, what it is made of, and how it was made. A combination of visual microscopic and X-ray study can achieve an understanding of its structure (figs 74–6), but analysis of some kind may well be necessary to establish what exact alloys or substances are involved, for these will influence the treatment which is employed. The most important task is to neutralize decay, whether the corrosion of metals or the rotting of organic matter, and only a detailed knowledge of chemistry can provide the correct answers. The next stage is to stabilize the object so that decay will not start up again – often, it will be impregnated with some substance which will seal it from the air and moisture, but even in the best cases, objects which are intended for museum display will have to remain in closely monitored conditions in order to maintain their stability. There are ethical problems involved in conservation – it is irresponsible for an archaeologist to excavate without facilities to preserve his finds, for many artefacts such as waterlogged or dessicated wood are reasonably stable until removed from their sites. Excavated structures soon suffer from exposure, and will need permanent supervision if they are to be left on display, otherwise wind, rain, frost, plant growth and human erosion (by visitors or vandals) will soon destroy even quite sound-looking masonry structures. Further ethical issues are involved in restoration – on a site, display quality and consequently tourist attraction can be enhanced by rebuilding ruined structures, but this is only acceptable where a clear visual distinction is made between original and restored work. Rather more sensitive is the restoration of artefacts; a badly corroded or damaged object may have little commercial value, but cleaning, stabilization and repair will not only improve its display quality for a museum, but increase its market value in the antiquities trade; the borderline between a heavily-restored genuine artefact and a fake is sometimes difficult to draw. Ethics aside, the scientific background of conservation is perhaps one of the most crucial aspects of archaeology experienced by visitors to sites and museums; sadly, it is certainly the most easily overlooked.

THE ENVIRONMENT (Evans 1978; Shackley 1981)

Archaeology began by studying sites and objects as part of the range of phenomena to be encountered in the landscape, but in the

74–76 Conservation of archaeological finds and their presentation for archaeological display involves many scientific and practical skills. These heavily-corroded objects from a Frankish grave of the seventh century AD at Olk in Germany were shown by X-ray examination to bear 'tausia' decoration – an inlay of silver hammered into the surface of the iron harness equipment. Careful cleaning of the surface exposed the intricate decoration, and the objects were finally displayed on modern leather straps to illustrate their original layout and function. *Rheinisches Landesmuseum, Trier; Wihr 1973*

cm

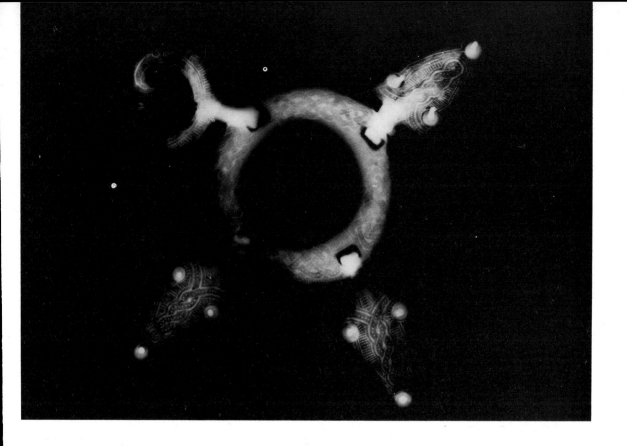

nineteenth and twentieth centuries specialized studies of particular cultures or civilizations, art, architecture, typology, etc. led the discipline away from the biological sciences until recent decades. The later the period in question, the truer this is; Old Stone Age studies are hardly feasible without detailed reference to the plant and animal resources available to hunter/gatherer societies, together with the prevailing climatic conditions. Excavations of sites of this period – right back to the early nineteenth century – paid close attention to animal and plant remains as well as human bones and artefacts. In Roman and medieval studies, however, it is only in the last few years that environmental factors have been taken sufficiently seriously in the interpretation of sites and general history. To the outsider, it may seem ludicrous that the archaeology of Roman villas has been debated in terms of ground-plans, wall paintings, mosaics, and dates of occupation with little reference to the agriculture that was the basis of their prosperity. Only rarely has excavation extended beyond the principal dwelling house to its barns and animal sheds, let alone to a full examination of animal bones and plant remains. New World archaeology has been more closely interested in environmental and anthropological aspects of sites, because of the particular ways in which its cultures developed, with a very close dependence on food crops such as maize. The superb preservation of some Basket-maker and Pueblo sites in the south-west of the United States in arid desert conditions also made the observation and examination of environmental evidence a much more obvious part of archaeology than on European sites, where most organic remains have disappeared through decay.

Environmental archaeology is now almost a separate discipline embracing a variety of specialist skills from many fields, particularly anatomy, botany, ecology, geology and geography. Its strength lies in the unchallengeable assumption that man, his sites and his artefacts can only be understood properly if full account is taken of their surrounding landscape, climate, plants and animals, together with factors such as diet, physical condition and life expectancy. All provide a constant supply of new information on old problems, and often indicate others which had not previously been considered, thus improving the range of information which archaeologists can take into account in their attempts to explain the past.

BONES AND SHELLS

On most archaeological sites, bones are found in prodigious numbers, with the addition of shells near coasts. However there is one basic weakness in this form of evidence; soil conditions must be favourable to their preservation. Damp, acid-soiled sites may completely destroy everything except burnt bone. Alkaline subsoils, well-drained sands or gravels, and arid or completely waterlogged conditions are most helpful. Rather different questions tend to be asked about human and animal bones, relying on the skills of the pathologist and anatomist for the former and the zoologist for the latter. Shells fall into two categories – those brought to a site for food, mostly from the sea, and the much greater number of species of snails which actually lived on the site; many of the latter are extremely small and can only be separated from samples of soil under laboratory conditions. It has only recently become common practice for special 'flotation' techniques to be employed on sites (fig. 77) which greatly increase the chances

77 Dr John Collis of Sheffield University with flotation equipment on his excavation at Aulnat in central France. Samples of soil are placed in water with a frothing agent in the square tank, and air is pumped through the pipe at the bottom, which mixes the sample and causes materials such as seeds or small bones to float in the bubbly surface layer, while heavier soil particles sink to the bottom. This layer can be drained off into a separate container for further study through the pipe visible near the top of the tank. Combined with preliminary sieving to isolate small artefacts and bones, this equipment allows a very high recovery rate for environmental evidence. *Photograph by courtesy of Dr R. Dennell*

of recovery of very small bones of rodents, birds, reptiles, fish and small shells, as well as insect and plant remains, all of which may have significance for the final interpretation of a site, its environment and resources.

Animal bones (Chaplin 1971)

The first task of a zoologist confronted with bones from an excavation is to sort them out into their appropriate species and to estimate the number of animals involved. Neither is straight-forward; the older the site, the more the animals are likely to differ from their present counter-parts, and closely-related animals like sheep and goats are difficult to separate from each other. It is not sufficient simply to count the bones, as some animals may be represented by just one bone, whilst others have left most of their skeletons; it is possible to estimate the minimum and maximum number of individuals which could be present by counting specific kinds of bones. As with all such calculations, the larger the collection available, the more accurate they will be. Further observations can be made. What meat-poundage could be gained from the different animals found? Were the animals but-chered on site, or do certain bones (such as ribs or leg bones) occur more plentifully, suggesting that the carcasses were cut up elsewhere and jointed before reaching the site? Factors such as these need to be weighed up carefully before any deductions about diet can begin to be made.

A key issue studied by zoologists is the domestication of wild species, and the changes caused by selective breeding for characteristics suitable for animal husbandry rather than survival in the wild. On the earliest sites where domestication was practised, only the relative numbers of different species illustrate the phenomenon, as the domesticated varieties did not yet differ from the wild; hunting should present a cross-section of available animals, whereas selective domestication will increase the proportion of those animals which are being specially exploited by herding. Before long the very different life-styles of wild and captive animals led to differences in size and other characteristics which allow a clear division to be made. When species have been separated, the

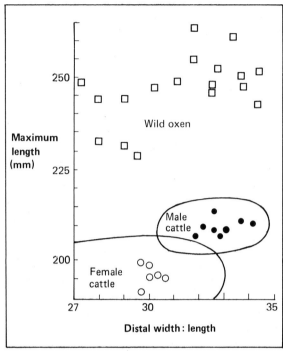

78 Detailed measurements of animal bones at Troldebjerg, Denmark, revealed differences between wild and domesticated cattle, and separate sex groups within the latter. Like the trace elements used in the characterization of obsidian (fig. 73), significant measurements or ratios between measurements need to be carefully selected to reveal these differences clearly. *After Evans 1978, 41, fig. 16*

approximate ages of the animals can be es-tablished by examining the state of ossification of particular bone structures, and the amount of wear on teeth. The sex of animals is more difficult to establish, but can be determined by careful statistical studies of bone sizes (some bones being more helpful than others) to divide them into size groups of which the smaller is likely to represent females (fig. 78). Again, this relies on the presence of large samples, of similar date, otherwise results are likely to be insignificant.

When species, age and sex have been es-tablished, it may be possible to make certain deductions about animal husbandry. A case which has received considerable attention is a Neolithic site at Troldebjerg (Langeland, Denmark), where cattle bones were exhaustively examined, in particular the shin and foot bones of the front legs, and the jaws, which were most likely to provide evidence of sex and age (Higham and Message 1969). The interpretation shed very complimentary light upon the skill of the farmers involved. The site probably lasted no more than fifty years, as its cornfields utilized freshly cleared forest whose soil would soon have become impoverished, causing the settlement to move on to new areas. The cattle bones indicated that 96 per cent of the animals survived their first winter, and 60 per cent still survived their third; the provision of winter foodstuffs was obviously well organized. The male animals (mostly castrated steers, it seems) were killed at around three to four years, the age at which 90 per cent of their full body weight would have been attained, but the earliest age that they would have become useful for pulling carts and ploughs. The implication is clearly that it was meat, not traction, that was wanted. Of the animals which lived beyond $3\frac{1}{2}$–4 years, 80 per cent were females, obviously intended for milk and breeding; the number of bulls required for breeding would be fairly small, and some of the mature males may have been (castrated) oxen used for draught purposes, although these cannot be distinguished by their bones. The husbandry involved was confident; although both male and female animals were killed young, presumably to provide meat and to weed out unsatisfactory stock, later killing was clearly aimed at maximising the meat production of male cattle whilst preserving females for milk and breeding. Such confidence was presumably based on the competence shown in preserving animals through the winters. Once again, it is up to the archaeologist to assess the full implications of such findings, but it is difficult to think of any way in which such a clear insight into the Neolithic farming practices of Denmark could have been gained other than by resorting to such a searching application of zoological inquiry. There will always be unknown factors however; a cautionary tale is provided by an American site, the eighteenth-century British Fort Ligonier, where excavated bones could actually be compared with the documented history of the fort. The bones found indicated only enough animals to feed the occupants for a single day, whereas a garrison of varying strength was in fact in occupation for eight years – living principally on a diet of boneless salt pork (Guilday 1970)!

Human bones (Brothwell and Higgs 1969, 429–512; Wells 1964)

The circumstances of discovery of human bones are normally rather different from those of animals, which are usually found in domestic rubbish. Most human societies have paid special attention to the disposal of their dead, and this factor adds a further complication to the survival of bone material in different soil conditions. In many cases, complete bodies were buried (often with accompanying 'grave goods' which may help to date the burial and denote its social status and, where soil conditions allow, whole skeletons can be recovered intact for study. In others, the body may have been burnt, and the surviving fragments of bone crushed and placed in an urn or other container. In extreme cases, the dead could be disposed of in ways that left no trace, such as throwing their bodies into rivers or scattering their cremated ashes. Multiple burials are common, where bodies are jumbled together in collective tombs used over long periods, or cremated bones might be simply emptied out into burial chambers in irretrievable confusion. To complicate matters further, bodies were frequently buried incomplete after the corpse had been exposed to the elements and scavenging birds and mammals – a practice well-known amongst American Indians and contemporary inhabitants of New Guinea, as well as on excavated prehistoric sites.

Given reasonably well-preserved remains, the kind of questions which human bones can answer are not unlike those asked of animal remains and many of the same techniques are employed in answering them. Age can be estimated from a number of osteological developments, and the growth of teeth. Sex can be determined with some difficulty from a number

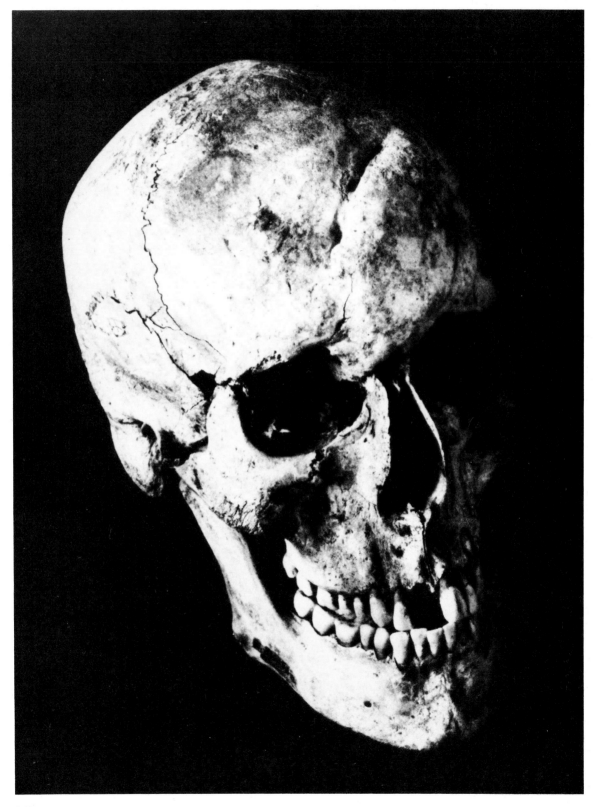

of parts of the skeleton, and stature postulated by comparisons with observations made from large numbers of modern people, although discrepancies of several centimetres exist between two different but widely-used systems of measurement. Pathologists can examine such features as injuries, whether healed or fatal, deformities, and evidence of disease ranging from malnutrition, arthritis, and dental decay to the erosion of bone through leprosy (fig. 79). Work is progressing on the identification of blood groups from bones, which might prove useful in charting ethnic continuity or change over periods when artefacts seem to indicate the arrival of external influences which could have either resulted from peaceful contact and exchange, or represent the equipment of invaders and settlers.

The evidence provided by the examination of human bones needs particularly close scrutiny from archaeologists, and the most difficult deduction to make is the general age-structure and physical well-being (or otherwise) of the population involved. Were primitive peoples tall healthy 'Noble Savages' or diseased, shortlived, and stunted people for whom life was 'nasty, brutish, and short'? The underlying problem is not easily solved; do the burials recovered from a particular culture (assuming that soil conditions allow their preservation in the first place) represent the dead of *all* levels of society, or simply a wealthy or social élite? Roman gravestones frequently commemorate individuals of advanced age, but they were pre-sumably only erected by those with some social standing, whose life-style was likely to be above average and to favour longevity. From a technical point of view, graves with elaborate stones or rich grave-goods are much more likely to have been explored by looters or archaeologists than simple unaccompanied burials, which might escape notice completely if discovered accidentally. However, both excavated remains and tombstones confirm the general impression that few individuals lived to a great age in earlier times, while infant mortality was high, and that many young women died in childbirth or as a result of it.

Other animal remains

Waterlogged, arid, or frozen conditions are favourable to the preservation of other animal material as well as bones; whole bodies have been preserved in many parts of the world – Egyptian mummies are the most widely known, and few museum collections do not possess at least one, often bought by travellers in the nineteenth century. Even more striking are the bog bodies found in Denmark, which include 'Tollund Man', an individual who met a particularly grisly end as a sacrificial victim of the Iron Age, complete with his clothing, and remains of a last meal in his stomach (Glob 1969). The studies of such bodies and mummies is like an excavation itself; X-ray examination, dissection, and the study of all of the materials encountered, whether fibres of clothing, skin tissues, or food remains (David 1979). From Siberian graves have come frozen human bodies upon whose skin the details of elaborate tatooed patterns can still be seen.

Leather and textiles (some made from animal hair, others from plant fibres) were such important raw materials in the past that their absence from most sites makes the study of those which have survived particularly significant if a proper understanding of the exploitation of the environment is to be achieved. In the arid south west of the USA, the Basket-maker culture is defined by a particular use of an organic raw material; it is a sobering thought that under European climatic conditions such a description would be unthinkable, as basketwork would have perished on all but exceptional sites. Every

79 Skull of a Frankish warrior from a cemetery at Köln-Müngersdorf near Cologne, Germany, *c.* AD 700. He was buried with many weapons and other grave goods of high social status, having died in his forties. Across his forehead can be seen a severe injury, probably caused by a sword, which had however healed. His teeth are in good condition compared to those from Roman burials in the same region or modern teeth, thanks to the lack of refined and sweet foods in his diet. Human bones can shed much light upon ancient society through such observations.

archaeologist should regularly visit a museum of ethnology or folk-life and count the number of items which would survive on a normal archaeological site; different styles of hair, body paint, head-dresses and costume play such an important role in the identity of cultures and personal status within them (even in contemporary urban civilization) that it is impossible to have too many reminders of their general loss from the past.

Shells (Brothwell and Higgs 1969, 395–427)

A distinction must be drawn between the shells found on sites which were brought there and discarded after their contents had been eaten, and those of molluscs which actually lived on the site. The former are informative about diet and the exploitation of natural resources; the latter give details of the local environment.

Many coasts bear evidence of extensive seashell exploitation in the form of large mounds of discarded shells; for some societies it was the central activity of their lifestyle, for others it was a seasonal occurrence. The former, known as 'strandloopers', survived until recent times on the South African coast, and similar mounds or 'middens' occur at various dates all over the world. The food potential of shells is fairly simple to calculate, but deeper insights can be gained by more detailed observations. The size and shape of common species such as limpets can show whether they were collected at random, or whether particularly large examples were chosen at low tide (the shape of the limpet shell varies in relation to the distance it lived from the high water mark). The latter would obviously imply a more planned exploitation than random collection, perhaps indicating a greater dependence on shellfish than other food sources. The collecting of shells all year round or seasonally can be examined by measuring the oxygen isotopes present in the edges of shells (fig. 80): these vary according to the prevailing temperature, so that summer camps should show the same isotope proportions, whilst permanent camps would contain the range found in a whole year. On deeply stratified sites, such isotope analysis can also document general fluctuations in average temperature, which can be checked against the presence or absence of species which are sensitive to temperature conditions; an increase in the proportion of warmloving species would obviously be expected if a warmer climate existed. Sea shells are not always evidence of diet, particularly when found inland – large examples can act as containers, spoons, and even tools. The Mediterranean *murex* provides purple dye; and more exotic uses such as charms, jewellery, and even ceremonial trumpets have been recorded by archaeologists and ethnologists. Once again, the skills of marine biologists can only be used to identify shell species and subject them to available forms of analysis, but as with all other such technical information, it requires careful interpretation by archaeologists.

Land molluscs, mainly snails (Evans 1973), vary in size from large edible species down to minute forms only visible and identifiable with the use of a microscope. On a general level the species recovered from geological deposits reflect the changes in temperature and vegetation involved in the variation of the climate during successive Ice Ages and warmer periods; their present habitats can be compared with their past distributions in exactly the same manner as animal species such as lions and elephants. On a much smaller scale (more relevant to archaeology) is the recognition of the fact that hundreds of small shells can be recovered from layers of soil encountered during excavations. If the habitat of each species is known, samples can be sorted into types preferring grassland or woodland, open or shaded localities, damp or dry conditions, etc. Thus, if a structure such as a rampart or burial mound is excavated, the snail species found in the ground surface buried beneath it should clearly indicate whether it was erected on open heathland or freshly cleared forest. A particulary gruesome illustration of the technique may be cited from the Roman city of Cirencester, Gloucestershire, where several corpses were excavated, lying in a roadside ditch within the city. The snails found inside a skull indicated that the body had not been buried, but had rotted in the overgrown ditch, for the species in question enjoyed a damp dark environment, but not an underground one. The

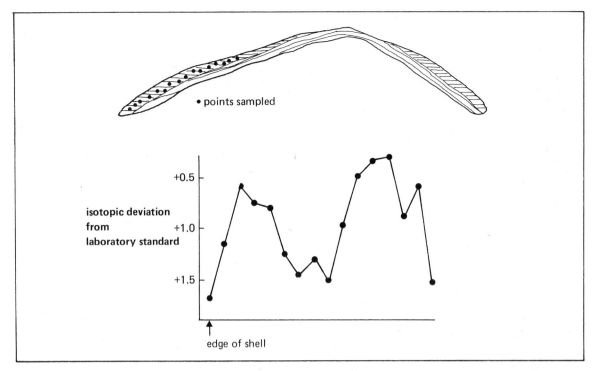

• points sampled

isotopic deviation
from
laboratory standard

+0.5

+1.0

+1.5

edge of shell

implications for the decline in civic life are clear, and it has been suggested that the bodies were victims of a plague which led to the desertion of the city in the fifth century AD. This is a further example of an archaeological explanation based on scientific evidence which would have been very difficult to hypothesize without it (Wacher 1974, 313).

A further advantage of land snails is that they survive well on calcareous soils which are unfavourable to pollen preservation, and go some way to rectifying this loss. In fact, they reflect a much more local environment than pollen, which is scattered over many miles by wind. Ideally, both sources of evidence can be examined to establish both the general and immediate surroundings of a site.

PLANTS (Dimbleby 1978; Renfrew, J., 1973)
As with bones, various plant remains can be preserved or destroyed according to the particular conditions prevailing on sites, and even individual soil deposits on them. In arid conditions, and their opposite, complete waterlogging, wood is well preserved, as are pips, seeds, and the fibrous matter from leaves, stalks, etc.

80 Molluscs can provide information on sea temperatures; the balance between different oxygen isotopes incorporated into this limpet during its growth shows fluctuations which reflect the temperature of the sea over two years. The peaks of the graph indicate summer; this shell stopped growing in winter. Studies of large numbers of shells from human occupation sites can therefore show whether they were harvested all year round or in one particular season. *After Evans 1978, 63, fig. 26*

Such conditions are geographically limited to areas of extreme climate; such as the deserts of Arizona and Egypt, the peat-bogs of Ireland and Scandinavia, or the frozen tundra of Siberia. On sites with ordinary soils, however, a surprising amount of information can still be gained. Burning can convert plants into charcoal under the right conditions, and species of wood, grain, and other plant material can be identified from such burnt remains. Indirectly preserved by burning are impressions of grain on pottery; when damp clay vessels were stood to dry before firing, their bases frequently

141

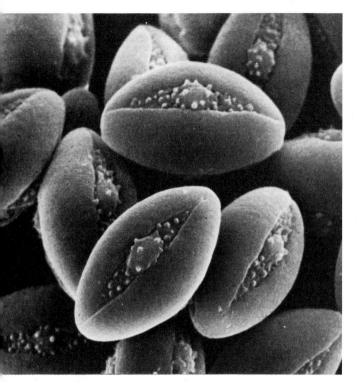

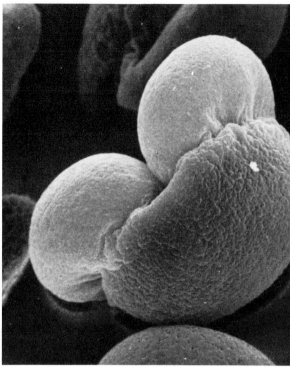

81 Pollen grains seen by electron scanning microscope, which allows a three-dimensional view of microscopic objects and reveals surface detail with remarkable clarity (the same technique is used to study microscopic wear on stone tools). Different plant species have distinctive pollen grains which can be identified by specialists after their separation from soil samples in the laboratory. These grains belong to the horse chestnut (left) and Scots pine (right). *School of Botany, University of Cambridge*

picked up straw and grain (which may have been laid out intentionally to prevent them sticking). Such organic matter burnt out completely during the firing process, leaving hollow voids which can be used as 'moulds' to recreate their form with latex or plaster. These 'casts' can then be examined microscopically to identify the species present. Once more, the larger the sample, the more reliable the results are likely to be, and they must be considered in conjunction with all other available plant evidence from the site. Such identifications are time consuming and expensive and require botanical training, but are extremely important to the interpretation of any site. However, perhaps the most productive skill which has been applied to archaeological plant remains is **palynology** – the study of pollen.

Pollen analysis (Dimbleby 1969; Shackley 1981)

As hay fever sufferers know, the air is full of pollen during the summer months, transported by the wind. The advantage to the archaeologist is that each minute grain of pollen has a tough outer shell, which is of a different shape for each species. The shells are not only preserved under the kinds of conditions already described as favourable for other plant material, but also in acid soils, where the acidity reduces the bacterial activity which would cause them to decay. The loss of pollen from chalklands (in England and northern France for instance) is unfortunate, but their soils are favourable to the survival of molluscs, which can go some way towards repairing the loss. The toughness of the pollen grains allows them to be fairly easily separated from samples of soil collected on sites by straightforward laboratory methods, but they must then be painstakingly identified and counted under a microscope by an experienced palynologist; it must be emphasized that most grains are under 100 thousandths of an inch in diameter, and many are under 50 (fig. 81). Their abundance makes counting a tedious procedure but has the advantage that statistically significant quantities are easily obtained from small samples of soil.

On a single period site, the intention of pollen analysis would be to create a picture of the plant population of the surrounding area – most pollen is deposited within a few miles of its source. A broad division is made into 'TP' and 'NTP' – tree-pollen and non-tree pollen. A site which occupied a small clearing in a forest would have a high proportion of TP to NTP, whereas a farm in open country would show the reverse. The TP and NTP can also be examined in terms of individual species or groups of related plants; the NTP may show different proportions of grasses and cereals which will indicate the relative importance of grazing and grain production in the economy of the site in question, whilst crops such as legumes, flax and hemp may indicate other specializations in the production of food and materials. Samples of pollen taken from soil buried beneath this hypothetical single-period site can tell the archaeologist whether the land was forested or covered with scrub before its occupation, and soil overlying the excavated structures which formed after their abandonment may show if the land returned to scrub and then forest, or perhaps remained open, as part of the farmland of another settlement in the vicinity. Further questions of direct relevance to an excavator can be answered by palynology. Mounds or ramparts on a site can be examined to see if their material was dug from the subsoil, and thus contain a mixture of contemporary and very old fossil pollen, or whether they were formed by scraping up surface turf or topsoil; on a complex site, this kind of information may help in the interpretation of ditches, pits, etc., and their relationship to the construction of such raised features.

Palynology has a much wider application than the study of the contexts from which soil has been sampled on an individual excavation; it can monitor general changes in climate and vegetation over long periods which are of considerable interest to climatologists, ecologists, botanists and geographers as well as to archaeologists. Sample cores can be bored from deep peat bogs or lake sediments, which are particularly favourable to pollen preservation and whose dampness traps and preserves large quantities of local pollen; such samples are stratified, with the earliest part lying deepest. The counting of pollen grains from regular intervals through the entire thickness of a deposit which has formed over thousands of years can build up a picture of overall changes from tundra to forest or from forest to farmland, and indicate fluctuations in the prominence of individual plant species (fig. 82). Such analyses have been made in many places all over the world, to the extent that a fairly clear picture of the major changes of vegetation since the last Ice Age and 'zones' of different climatic conditions have been defined since well before the last war. These formed a basis for relative dating (as described in Chapter 4), before they were themselves dated absolutely by radiocarbon since the 1950s. The importance of these vegetational zones is that they provide a general context into which to place man's activities, whether the open tundra hunting of the Old Stone Age, or forest hunting and gathering in the Mesolithic period before settled agriculture began. When a picture of the vegetation is added to the evidence of animal bones, the possibilities for the correct interpretation of past economies and the likely functions of tools and weapons can be greatly increased.

Perhaps the key issue which can be studied from this kind of pollen analysis is the appearance of Neolithic culture – the first settled farming communities, which represent such a momentous stage in human development in terms of the exploitation of the environment and social organization. The Neolithic economy necessitated the building of permanent structures and the clearance of land for grazing and arable land, with a consequent destruction of

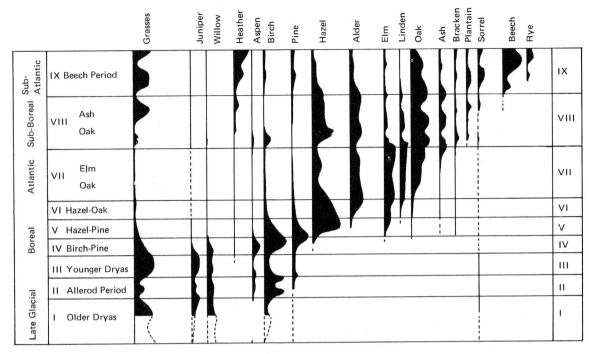

82 Pollen diagrams are at first sight difficult to interpret; the results from several samples are presented on this diagram of vegetation in Jutland, Denmark. In stages I–III, grasses and small hardy trees (birch, willow, juniper) dominated the cold landscape which followed the retreat of the last Ice Age. From V, a number of more temperate tree species colonized the area as warmer conditions developed; grasses consequently declined. Soon after the beginning of VIII the actions of Man appear to have an effect, as forest was cleared to supply fuel, timber, and areas for cultivation and grazing. Grasses are once more common, and cereals or 'weeds of cultivation' such as plantain appear for the first time. The form of the diagram is similar to seriation (fig. 57); the thickness of the line for each individual species reflects its relative importance; also similar to seriation is the way in which new samples could be set in their correct relative place in the sequence according to their proportions of different species. This was an important relative dating technique until the development of radiocarbon dating in the 1950s. This diagram covers over 12,000 years, and is based on research by Dr J. Iversen. (*Dimbleby 1969, 169*)

woodland which clearly influences the ratio of tree-pollen to non-tree-pollen in stratified deposits. Thus, even if no Neolithic sites have been actually discovered in a particular region, the pollen record may indicate their existence; as the TP declines, the NTP rises, and tell-tale species of grasses and cereals appear, together with 'weeds of cultivation' which thrived in the new conditions. With the assistance of radiocarbon dating, the appearance of this new economy can be accurately charted even before actual sites have been found, and such information may provide a spur to fieldwork which can attempt to locate the relevant settlements.

The application of palynology is worldwide; it is not only restricted to prehistoric times, but can be used to examine the environment of individual sites or their general regional settings in any circumstances before written documentation and land-surveys provide such information in sufficient detail to render it unnecessary. Environmental approaches to historical phenomena are in their infancy, but have vast potential. To take a single example, the desertion of land and decline of farming so often linked with the end of the Roman Empire by both ancient and modern historians could be examined by a careful examination of suitable pollen deposits from all around the Mediterranean and surrounding provinces. Such a decline should be reflected by a regeneration of scrub and forest, and the species involved might also reflect any changes in climate which might have contributed to the situation. Palynology illustrates the ideal state of science and archaeology; each contributes information which is vital to the interpretation of the other. A prominent environmental archaeologist, G.W. Dimbleby, has remarked that 'a proper understanding of the place of man in his environment, at all stages of his history, is as vital to the student of the environment as it is to the student of man. The two disciplines meet fully in pollen analysis.'

The study of coprolites (Brothwell and Higgs 1969, 235–250)

A notable feature of American and Canadian research on the natural resources available to man has been the study of coprolites (solid human excreta) preserved on arid sites belonging to Indian cultures in the south western United States, Mexico, and South America. The importance of these sites to dendrochronological dating because of the survival of their timber has already been discussed in chapter 4; the conditions which ensured its preservation apply to many other materials, including the fibrous matter which passes through the human digestive system. This includes fragments of bone, skin, scales, hair, feathers, and meat from animals, fish and birds; pieces of insects and parasites and their eggs; the fibres and seeds of many plants, and microscopic pollen and 'plant opals' (crystals of silica of distinctive shapes formed by some plants). With careful processing and sieving of the re-hydrated remains even soft tissues of plants and animals can be extracted and identified. Where large collections have been recovered from latrine deposits, detailed surveys can be made of the diet of the occupants of a site; when deposits of different dates are available from a particular site or area, changes of diet can be charted which presumably reflect variations in the relative availability of foodstuffs.

GEOLOGY AND SOIL SCIENCE
(Limbrey 1975)

The contribution of geological techniques to the analysis of stone artefacts and the origin of their raw materials has already been described. The wider application of geology to the formation of the present landscape, and more important, its past configuration, changes in sea level, erosion of land masses, and the deposition of new land by sedimentation or volcanic activity influence not only the concepts we may form about past cultures, but technical factors such as the likelihood of finding sites and artefacts of various dates in particular areas. The significance of early finds of bones and flint tools in deep gravel beds was only fully appreciated when geologists had studied their formation and the timescale involved, and devised the principles of stratification – upon which the details of archaeological excavation are still firmly based. The earlier the period of archaeology that is being studied, the more important that geology is likely to be, particularly in the phases related to Ice Ages.

For many questions of direct relevance to the interpretation of excavated sites, the special skills of **pedology** (soil science) are frequently required. Soils of greatly differing colours, textures and other characteristics are formed by the activity of nature and man, and in some instances natural discolourations are difficult to distinguish from genuine archaeological features. Some straightforward examples of soil examination indicate the value of this science clearly. Archaeological structures often bury earlier surfaces (which are important for their content of pollen and/or molluscs, as described above), which may occasionally be clearly visible to the experienced eye, but are frequently rather ambiguous; the examination of humus content (decomposed organic matter and minerals found near a natural soil surface)

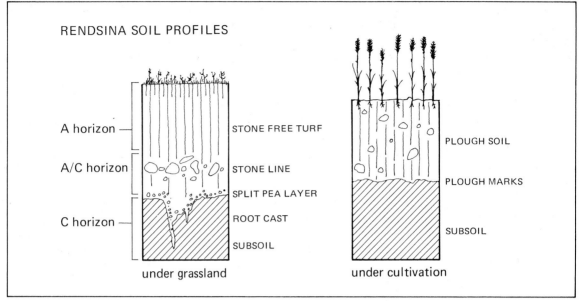

RENDSINA SOIL PROFILES

A horizon — STONE FREE TURF

A/C horizon — STONE LINE

SPLIT PEA LAYER

C horizon — ROOT CAST

SUBSOIL

under grassland

PLOUGH SOIL

PLOUGH MARKS

SUBSOIL

under cultivation

83 There is a clear structure to the profile of rendsina soil (found on chalk, limestone, or gravel) under permanent pasture (left), where earthworm activity has caused stones to sink to a distinct layer which will also contain any large artefacts such as coins or pottery which have been deposited in the soil at any date. Ploughing disturbs this soil structure (right), which will take a considerable time to reform when cultivation ceases; soils buried by ancient earthworks can thus be examined to see what kind of agriculture was responsible for their formation. *After Evans 1978, 75, fig. 29*

can clarify the nature of a suspected buried surface. A high phosphate content in soil generally results from human or animal occupation, and samples taken systematically over an area can help to define the limits of a settlement without extensive excavation; this has been carried out on the early medieval farming complex at Vallhagar, in Sweden (fig. 25). Measurement of the level of acidity in a soil is a useful guide to the likelihood of the survival pollen and molluscan evidence; if unfavourable, time spent on the fruitless collection and processing of samples can be saved.

Soils have been divided into a number of principal types, which can provide interesting

insights into the effect of man upon the environment. A good example is provided by the 'podsols' characteristic of heath and moorland, which have a thin surface layer of vegetation, below which occurs a layer of soil from which iron and humus have been removed by rainwater washing them down to accumulate on the surface of the subsoil. However, when areas of soil are found buried under prehistoric earthworks on moorland they are frequently found to be 'brownearths' typical of woodland, not podsols. Brownearths are stable when covered by trees, but when such land is cleared, they deteriorate into poorer podsols. Thus, the open moorlands of much of upland Britain, with their harsh, inhospitable, soil conditions are a direct result of human interference during a short occupation which rendered them exhausted and uninhabitable for later farmers. A similar process is likely to result from the destruction of the Amazon forests in the twentieth century, as the stable recycling of nutrients by trees is brought to end, and wet and dry alternations break down the structure of the soil.

On chalk, limestone, or sands and gravels derived from them, a soil called 'rendsina' is found, rich in humus and earthworm activity which results in the sinking of stone particles to the bottom of the turf layer, as the worms continually deposit fine soil upwards. The advantage to the archaeologist is that ploughing or similar human disturbance mixed the stones back into the whole soil profile; thus, if a buried rendsina is encountered beneath a later structure, it can be determined at a glance whether the land had been under arable cultivation or not – an important factor in assessing a site's economy, and its reliance on grown crops or grazing animals (fig. 83). Soils can also provide evidence of past climates; extreme heat can produce distinctive colouration, and soils deposited by water during damp stages, or conversely wind-blown material deposited during periods of low rainfall can be identified by the techniques of pedology, as these natural processes influence the size and shape of soil particles in recognizable ways.

COMPUTERS, STATISTICS, AND ARCHAEOLOGY (Doran and Hodson 1975; Brothwell and Higgs 1969, 635–80)

The principal purpose of computers in any situation is to record, store, retrieve, and process large quantities of information. Most of the scientific techniques used in the dating and discovery of sites and the analysis of artefacts employ computers, which can be linked directly to the appropriate apparatus in order to record results. This is not only an important way of saving the time of skilled laboratory staff, but is faster and more reliable. However, computers cannot tell the archaeologist anything about their materials without a full understanding of the kind of uses for which they can be programmed. Information needs to be presented in a form suitable for feeding into the memory system, with a clear idea of what questions are going to be asked; the archaeologist must be aware of these factors while actually recording the features of the sites or artefacts in question. For instance, the details of a complex excavation may be suitable for computer study. The presence and absence of a long list of attributes must be recorded for every layer of soil, post hole, wall, or whatever else is encountered – dimensions, location, soil colour and texture, any finds, relationship by stratigraphy to adjacent features, etc. This recording stage will be tedious and time consuming, but the attributes can easily be simplified into number or letter codes to be fed into a computer to create a file of data. When the excavator comes to study the site in order to write his report, such recording is rewarded. It may appear that post-holes filled with brown, stony soil have some particular significance; in a few minutes, the computer can be instructed to print out a list of all such features. This list could then be refined by selecting all features which contained pottery or similar material suitable for dating. It may be suspected that the post-holes formed patterns representing the plans of buildings, but they may be so numerous that they appear meaningless to the eye on a plan; a computer with suitable graphic hardware can print out information in map or plan form. Thus the hypothetical archaeologist could obtain plans incorporating specified attributes, such as square post-holes, or those of a certain depth; assuming that a building has similar posts used in its construction, this may go a long way towards establishing the plans of individual houses or other buildings. If as a result we imagine that the archaeologist has before him a convincing plan of a building, all of its constituent parts could be tested for their relationship with other plans or individual features so that a stratigraphical sequence might be established. Having established that a particular building dates to a particular period, it would be an easy step to call up information on all other features of the site which contained material of the same date; contemporary rubbish pits, fences, hearths, etc., could thus be plotted by this technique.

The advantages of computer-coded recording become particularly obvious if its alternatives are considered – card-indexes, masses of site plans, photographs, notebooks, and perhaps only the memory of the excavator for some details. The time involved in the manual sifting through all of these records again and again even to provide the information demanded by each stage of the straightforward enquiry outlined above would obviously be enormous, and the boredom it could generate might seriously affect the accuracy and completeness of the process. For small sites, the cost and availability of computer time and expertise would be unnecessary, but no excavator of a large, complex site can afford to ignore the potential of such procedures.

The applications of computers extend far beyond the simple storing and selective retrieval of information, however; they make it easy to carry out statistical tests on the observations which are drawn, in order to test their validity. Again, such tests can be carried out manually, but many programmes already exist for testing data in the natural and social sciences which can be applied to archaeological problems if the information has been recorded in the appropriate way. Most archaeologists look at maps and plans of sites, or artefacts (or illustrations of them), and are often struck by similarities or patterns; settlement sites on a map may seem to cluster around certain focal points in one period, but be more evenly scattered in others; axes, pots, or brooches apparently fall into separate classes because of differences in size and shape, or similarities of style and decoration. In both cases, these intuitive observations are based on the observation of factors which can easily be measured. To take the distribution of sites, a simple statistical analysis can measure how easily the clusters which struck the observer could have been the result of chance, and the level of significance of the results; most sciences take a probability level of at least 0.05 as meaningful – it means that the situation observed has only a 1 in 20 likelihood of occurring by chance. To take the case a step further, other tests can examine whether two different distribution patterns are in fact significantly different from each other, and again, the level of probability can be clearly defined and stated in a publication of the results.

The classification of artefacts is a more complicated example of the application of statistics, usually requiring computer processing. Like features encountered during an excavation, artefacts can usually be reduced to a fairly finite number of attributes, such as dimensions, decoration, raw material, etc. An archaeologist (or for that matter, anyone else) looking at a selection of objects subconsciously weighs up most of these attributes, but individuals give widely differing prominence to them. Thus two people given the same dozen stone axes may classify them in completely different ways – one according to their length, another according to the width of their cutting edge, for instance. A study of the classification of European Iron Age brooches has been made in which a number of computer programmes used in zoological and botanical classification were tested, which essentially attempted to measure objectively the degree of similarity between the brooches (Hodson 1969). At one extreme, all are the same, namely brooches; at the other extreme, all are different, as even mass-produced brooches made by the same craftsmen on the same day will have subtle differences. The brooches in question were examined for the presence or absence of a clearly-defined list of attributes, and the computer programme employed compared the degree of similarity between each brooch and all of the others, and placed those with most in common together. In the case of these brooches, there was an independent check on the data, as they had been found in a cemetery at Münsingen, Switzerland, which had gradually spread away from a settlement along a narrow ridge. The classes defined by the computer's analysis correlated well with groups of finds from particular areas of the cemetery which seemed likely to be of approximately the same date. Further analysis of these brooches was attempted by which the computer was programmed to place the brooches in a single general line of development from early examples to late; the direction of the development could be checked from the cemetery in question and other dated finds. Several of the various computer programmes tested produced much more consistent results than four archaeologists and an anatomist who were given the same brooches and objectives!

The use of computers or seemingly complicated statistical procedures can be dangerous if their results are accepted uncritically. The answers which they produce are only as good as the evidence upon which they are based, and the suitability of the programmes and tests which have been employed. Their great advantage (aside from the time-saving and convenience already emphasized) is the way in which they require careful and thoughtful collection and recording of evidence, and their statement in objective terms of the mathematical levels of probability of certain hypotheses which would otherwise depend largely on intuition. Where the classification of artefacts is concerned, the bias of the individual observer is largely removed; given the figures and programmes, exactly the same criteria can be applied to different collections of objects, and valid comparisons can be made between them. Newly-discovered artefacts can be slotted into their appropriate places in the system of classification only when its basis is clearly defined; when statistical approaches are being employed, this will have been at an early stage. Above all, a computer analysis can take a mass of confusing detail into account and weigh it up absolutely consistently, without the preconceptions which any archaeologist will inevitably possess. But the archaeologist has to remain the final judge of findings of mathematical procedures, and the problems of interpretation are just as human and individual as they always have been; as with all other scientific techniques, the principal benefit to interpretation is that the available information is more abundant, better defined, and more accurate than it would otherwise be.

EXPERIMENTAL ARCHAEOLOGY
(Coles 1979)

An indirect effect of the scientific outlook on archaeological methods has been the increasing tendency to design practical experiments to test hypotheses. These can range from one-off tests of individual ideas to long-term programmes observing a whole range of problems. The strict definition of an 'experiment' in the scientific world involves essentials like replicability and the control and measurement of variables which are frequently absent from much 'experimental' archaeology. Many examples are simply demonstrations or simulations rather than true experiments. However, the idea of doing them at all can only be beneficial.

Artefacts can be studied profitably by experimental archaeology, making full use of inform-

ation gained by methods of scientific analysis; technology has been widely explored by reconstructions of primitive metal casting, pottery making and firing, and stoneworking. There are two drawbacks to such work – they rely on assumptions about technical processes which are often themselves hypothetical; and their results, if successful, can only suggest that certain methods *could* have been used in the past, and not that they actually were. This is why a strictly scientific approach is important; a single demonstration of one technique for firing ancient pottery is virtually worthless until dozens of firings have been carried out (with detailed records) using different fuels, kiln structures, methods of arranging the pots in the kiln, etc., etc. It will never be proved that the most effective technique revealed in this way was actually employed, but some unsatisfactory techniques may be ruled out, and the possibilities of gross error thus reduced. It goes without saying that only techniques and equipment known to have been in use in the relevant society may be used. The function and efficiency of tools have frequently been examined – stone axes, primitive ploughs, weapons of various kinds. Related to these experiments is the question of manpower; the speed with which a Neolithic axe will cut through trees of various kinds and thicknesses is obviously fundamental to the understanding of the process of forest clearance associated with agricultural settlement. But even here, there is a possibility of making elaborate calculations which are meaningless if forests were mainly burnt, not cut down, and if the axes were in fact weapons In addition, a twentieth-century archaeologist will never possess the physical fitness and experience of the original user of an artefact.

Large-scale structures and sites can also be subjected to simulation studies, by the attempted reconstruction of excavated evidence. At a basic level, such an exercise can test whether a postulated structure could actually have stood up; beyond this, estimates of man-hours involved in construction, and the amount and source of the necessary raw materials are worthwhile questions. Experience has shown on many occasions that the chief advantage of

84 A long-term archaeological experiment: Morden Bog experimental earthwork, Dorset (Evans & Limbrey 1974). Two similar banks and ditches were constructed in the early 1960s on different subsoils, in order to study the ways in which they weathered and changed shape. Excavations are carried out at intervals to examine the bank and ditch sections, and to retrieve objects buried at precise locations when the earthworks were constructed. Comparisons with the original profiles show exactly how fast the banks have settled and eroded, and how the ditches have silted up; the movement and decay of the various artefacts and organic materials should also contribute to a better understanding of the excavated remains of ancient earthworks and their associated artefacts. One drawback to this experiment is that unlike most ancient sites, there is no continuous human occupation or maintenance and repair of the structures. This photograph was taken by the author in 1969, six years after the construction of the earthwork; the bank had already been lowered 25cm by settling and erosion.

simulation studies is that they demand a much closer analysis of excavated traces than might otherwise be carried out; if it is found that an imaginative reconstruction of an excavated ground plan is unsound or even impossible, an excavator will be forced to review his evidence, and to look again for hitherto unnoticed features. In contrast, some excavated traces which have proved difficult to explain may be clarified. Scattered post-holes around a structure may well have supported scaffolding or temporary props for a building during construction, for instance. Again, what is found feasible can only be accepted as one possible solution, not a definite answer.

When archaeologists examine sites, they are excavating decayed remains, from which original forms have to be postulated. The study of the processes of decay is therefore fundamental to such interpretations, and a number of experiments have been designed to explore this area. The most dramatic have been carried out in Denmark, where reconstructed timber buildings have been burnt down and then re-excavated to establish the way in which the remains reflect the superstructure, to facilitate the excavation of ancient burnt remains on other sites. In England long-term studies of the erosion of earthworks were begun in the early 1960s which will be monitored well into the next century; at Overton Down, Wilts, a bank and ditch were constructed on a chalk subsoil, and near Wareham, Dorset, a similar structure was created on sand (fig. 84). Not only were the earthworks constructed to exact measurements, but a range of objects and materials, organic and inorganic, were buried at precisely recorded locations. Thus erosion, settlement, decay, and the movement of objects by earthworms and other disturbances of the soil can be charted by the periodic re-excavation of small sections of the earthworks. It could be said that the conditions are too well controlled; access to the sites is strictly limited, and the effects of human erosion by trampling which would have affected any structure in actual use have therefore been excluded. Furthermore, most structures in the past were probably carefully maintained until obsolete, and not allowed to deteriorate from the minute they were finished. These problems illustrate the basic weakness of experimental archaeology; experiments require controls, but past human activity need rarely have been rational or consistent – tabus and traditions may have been as influential as efficiency in the design of tools and structures, and we are in constant danger of applying twentieth-century ideals of technology and progress to inappropriate situations. It may be suggested that anthropology has more to offer to the interpretation of many of the problems explored by experimental archaeology than some of the approaches at present in use.

The range of scientific methods employed more or less directly in archaeological research is increasing every year, and their results will impinge upon a growing number of areas within the subject. However, the relationship between archaeology and science is clear; science only forms a part of archaeology, and mainly supplies new or better information upon which interpretations can be based. Furthermore, the use of scientific evidence can improve the precision of archaeological research, both in its design and in the gathering of information. No archaeologist or historian engaged in the study of the past can afford to be ignorant of the scientific evidence about the environment and resources which contributed so much towards the development of particular lifestyles and social behaviour of mankind.

Further reading

There is now a wealth of archaeological literature on scientific techniques of research, much of it highly technical; some has already been cited at the end of Chapter 4.

The most convenient collection of short reports on scientific studies is undoubtedly *Science in Archaeology*, edited by D. Brothwell and E. Higgs (1969), which contains many individual chapters by scientists working in many of the fields included in this chapter. Rather older but less technical is E. Pyddoke's smaller collection of papers entitled *The Scientist and Archaeology*, 1963. General texts are few compared with books on specific sciences, but *Archaeological Site Science* by F.H. Goodyear (1971) or M.S. Tite's *Methods of Physical Examination in Archaeology*, 1972, may be suggested.

The scientific study of the environment is particularly well provided with fairly basic texts, perfectly comprehensible to the nonspecialist; John Evans' *An Introduction to Environmental Archaeology*, 1978, is a good starting point, whilst more detail is contained in Myra Shackley's *Environmental Archaeology*, 1981; comprehensive references to more specialised publications are attached to each chapter of the latter. For numerical procedures, J. Doran and F. Hodson's *Mathematics and Computers in Archaeology*, 1975, is very technical but includes many detailed case studies; Clive Orton's *Mathematics in Archaeology*, 1980, is more accessible to the general reader. *Experimental Archaeology* by John Coles (1979) is a comprehensive survey of its subject, whilst a specific project is described in Peter Reynolds' *Iron-Age Farm: the Butser Experiment*, 1979.

For readers of French, there is an excellent edition of the popular series *Dossiers de l'Archéologie*, no. 42, March/April 1980, (*L'analyse des objets archéologiques et les procédés statistiques d'interprétation*), and a superbly illustrated catalogue of an exhibition, *La Vie Mystérieuse des Chefs-d'Oeuvre: la Science au Service de l'Art*, Paris, 1980, which contains numerous case-studies.

6 Making Sense of the Past

In recent decades, almost every subject in the humanities and sciences has undergone an 'information explosion'. Librarians are particularly aware of this, as the number and thickness of periodicals of learned societies have increased, and as alternatives to the printed page are being sought through microfiches, computerized databases, and other technologically advanced information storage and retrieval systems. It has become steadily more difficult for specialists in a subject to keep up to date in anything more than their own narrow field of research, or for reliable 'over-views' or syntheses to be presented to the public. Archaeology is a comparatively small field compared to most of the major sciences, but there has been rapid growth on several fronts since the Second World War. It has become a popular part of education at both school and university levels, because of its variety of practical and theoretical work, its mixture of scientific and aesthetic approaches, and its concern with everyday objects and structures as well as the higher social élites upon which history has traditionally tended to concentrate. Mobility and leisure have increased commensurately; tourism now regularly includes ancient sites and museums, and archaeology in general receives extensive publicity through television, popular writing and journalism. Museum displays are now aimed at the general visitor rather than the specialist, and well-documented eye-catching visual effects have replaced the former dull rows of pots with terse and undersized type-written labels (fig. 85).

At the time of the establishment of the Antiquity of Man in the middle of the last century, the academic world was small and international, and by no means confined to universities and museums. John Evans, who visited Boucher de Perthes and witnessed the stratigraphic position of Palaeolithic artefacts at Amiens in 1859, was a busy paper-mill manager, and published articles and books on geology, pre-Roman coins, and bronze implements as well as flints in his spare time. As President of the Royal Society in London, he not only rubbed shoulders with most of the prominent geologists, physicists, biologists and other scientists of his day, but was accepted amongst them on equal terms. The breadth of the cross-fertilization of information and concepts between figures such as Evans, Lyell, and Darwin that lay behind that exciting phase in the development of archaeological thinking would be impossible today; the kind of cooperation between different disciplines which exists now tends to be directed towards more specific research projects.

As the amount of information produced by excavation, fieldwork, and other research has increased, so too have the expectations of its quality and detail, with the unwelcome result that the rich variety of supporting techniques and sources of specialist information make it more difficult rather than easier for a report on an excavation or fieldwork project to be completed. The size and complexity of the end product, if it is indeed completed, may be unwieldy, costly to publish, and difficult for non-specialists to digest. An extra burden is thus thrown onto its author – the ability to communicate in simple terms which do not oversimplify, and to present the findings in an form accessible to the public. Otherwise, what is the purpose of archaeological research? An archaeologist needs to reflect upon who is his paymaster (usually a taxpayer) and his justifi-

153

85 The 'democratisation' of archaeology: the Römisch-Germanisches Museum, Cologne, is one of the most lavish examples of the modern style of presentation of archaeology to a large and increasingly well-informed public. Displays are now aimed at the ordinary rather than the academic visitor, and at Cologne the striking displays are backed by audio-visual aids to provide extra information on a range of topics at the press of a button. Critics of current display methods feel that the artefacts are subordinated to the overall design, and that some museums have the atmosphere of a supermarket rather than a place of learning. *Römisch-Germanisches Museum/Rheinisches Bildarchiv*

cation for adding yet more detail to the complicated analysis of the material remains of the past.

Some of these factors have produced a situation where academic archaeology has become fragmented in a number of ways – into periods, geographical areas, and philosophies of its study. More seriously, the difficulties that exist in communicating its results in an intelligible form have undoubtedly contributed to the flourishing of the writers such as Erich von Däniken who take a particular delight in deriding the inability of 'experts' to find expla-

nations. Although the tradition of finding supernatural, mystical or extra-terrestrial connections with antiquities is not new (as Stukeley's Druids demonstrate), never before have they been so widely disseminated. How many of the 'experts' have sold as many paperbacks as von Däniken?

FRAMEWORKS FOR THE PAST

A recurrent aspect of archaeology has been the attempt to establish a satisfactory conceptual framework into which to slot the surviving remains; it is in fact a prerequisite of serious

32.2ᵈ Kits Coty house 15 Oct. 1722. The N.E. Prospect.

The View

The Groundplot

Stukeley delin

The lower Coty house

E Kirkall sculp.

research. Frameworks have come and gone, according to the progress of research or sometimes mere taste, and the hottest area of debate in contemporary archaeology is between traditional and 'new' archaeology, and the applicability of various theoretical approaches and their resultant frameworks. An excellent example of a complete break in the manner of interpretation is provided by the study of megalithic tombs, and the impact of radiocarbon dating.

Megalithic tombs

These are large stone constructions which are found all around the coastal fringes of western Europe, as well as in southern Scandinavia and north Germany (fig. 90). They usually contain one or more stone-lined chambers (some with long entrance passageways) under an earth or stone mound, which has subsequently disappeared in many cases to leave the uprights and capstones so often illustrated by early engravers of antiquarian books (fig. 86). Where the contents of the chambers survive, they are usually found to contain the remains of large numbers

86 A characteristic view of a megalithic tomb; the mound which originally covered the stone burial chamber has eroded away leaving the stonework exposed. It is not surprising that megaliths were among the first antiquities to attract attention and illustration, and that their size gave rise to many tales of construction by giants. This engraving of Kits Coty House in Kent was made from a drawing by Stukeley and included in his *Itinerarium Curiosum* (1776, II, pl. 32)

of skeletons or cremated bones, known as collective burials. Some are architecturally sophisticated, with enormous stones or elaborate vaulting (fig. 87), and they may be decorated with geometric or curvilinear carving. Many thousands still survive today, so it is not surprising to find that they have received considerable comment in the past. Underlying almost all discussions of them was the tacit assumption that they were exotic, and too sophisticated to have sprung up around the fringes of Europe without outside stimulus. The first monumental

stone architecture appeared in Egypt in the early second millennium BC, and soon reached remarkable sophistication in early monuments such as Zoser's step pyramid and its courtyard walls at Saqqara, c. 2650 BC. Close parallels for tombs with stone passageways and vaulted chambers exist in the East Aegean area around 1600 BC. European scholarship had been haunted by the civilizations of the Mediterranean and Near East ever since the medieval period, and there was no logical inconsistency in assuming that all impulses towards progress should have emanated from those areas, particularly when Mesopotamia and Egypt became better known in the nineteenth century. This assumption became firmly rooted in twentieth-century archaeology, whether in a rational manner with Montelius or Childe, or to the extreme extent of Eliot Smith, who extended the influence of Egyptian pyramids and embalming techniques to South America. This particular framework is known as **diffusionism**, and upon it were erected many of the detailed inter-relationships of European prehistory, according to cross-dating by Montelius and others (fig. 88). As late as 1965, Stuart Piggott summarized the main themes of the diffusionist interpretation of megalithic tombs, which had survived the first impact of the newly-developed radiocarbon dating technique:

Radio-carbon dates imply that as early as 3000 BC or slightly before, peoples of early Neolithic cultures in France were also building monumental collective stone-chambered tombs . . . scattered from the western Mediterranean to the Shetlands and south Scandinavia. . . . Their distribution poses a problem: what likely set of circumstances in antiquity can

87 A megalithic tomb at Barnenez, Brittany; the corbelled *tholos* and the passage were uncovered when the mound was quarried for road building in 1954–5; fortunately not all of the eleven chambers and passageways in the same mound were damaged (Giot 1958). Several radiocarbon dates place Barnenez back beyond 4000 BC after calibration (Renfrew 1973, 99), far earlier than the supposed Aegean antecedents for this form of construction. *Photograph by courtesy of Colin Burgess*

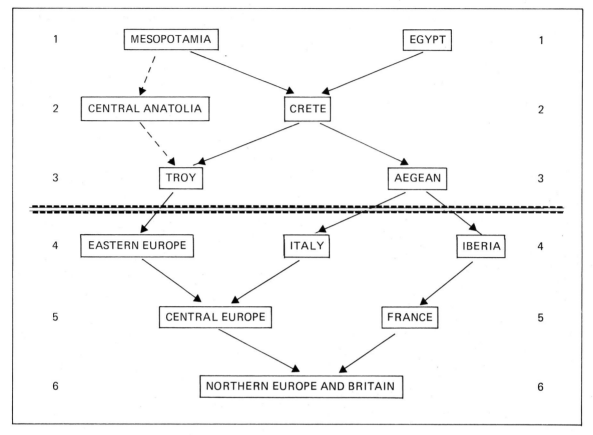

88 Diffusionism: the spread of influence and improvements in European prehistory from the civilizations of the Near East as envisaged by archaeologists like Oscar Montelius or Gordon Childe, based upon supposed connections between typologies of artefacts in the various regions involved. The advent of radiocarbon dating broke the links between stages 3 and 4, and caused reconsideration of the origins of such phenomena as megalithic tombs and the development of metallurgy (Renfrew 1973).

cause a group of specialized ritual structures to be built over such a sweep of territory? It is not, I think, inapposite to consider these monuments in the same terms as one would the churches of Christendom or the mosques of Islam. . . . Creeds and beliefs can be transmitted in many ways; conquest or evangelism, fanaticism or fashion, by saints or merchants. . . . An eastern Mediterranean origin seems inherently likely, but is difficult to document with any precision. The corbelled or false-vaulted burial chamber, re-

current in the west from perhaps the beginning and certainly the middle of the third millennium BC, first appears in this fully stone-vaulted form in the Aegean around 1600 BC, where it is usually thought to be derived from the earlier circular, but not unambiguously stone-vaulted, tombs (Piggott, 1965, 60).

There are already several undertones of doubt in this passage, particularly the embarrassingly late date for the supposed prototype in the Aegean, and the early dates emerging through radiocarbon dating – rather earlier than the Egyptian stone architecture which had been so convenient when megaliths were placed around 2000–1500 BC. However, the early dates came from France, rather than Spain, which was theoretically earlier in the process of diffusion, and possible errors were suspected in the French radiocarbon dates. The diffusionist view survived into the second edition of the authoritative *World Prehistory* by Grahame Clark (1969), but in its third edition (1977), there is a new categorical statement:

Despite . . . variations which were commonly favoured in particular regions, the occurrence of collective tombs in most cases of megalithic construction over so great an extent of the Atlantic seaboard has often been attributed exclusively to seaborne diffusion. On the other hand the notion that burial in collective tombs of monumental construction originated in the east Mediterranean has recently been disproved by radiocarbon dating (*op. cit.* 135).

Clark gives a rather more prosaic explanation than most earlier writers of why such tombs should have spread around the coastal fringes – fishermen following hake and mackerel are proposed, rather than priests or trader/prospectors. The full implications of the reinterpretation were brought home by the recalibration of radiocarbon dates according to the tree-ring correction curve derived from bristlecone pines in California (fig. 64), and the nettle was firmly grasped by Colin Renfrew, who wrote one of the most readable popular explanations of complex archaeological issues ever written – *Before Civilization* (1973), a book brimming over with excitement about the new possibilities for reshaping the prehistory of Europe (but not without its defects and critics, e.g. Coles and Orme 1974). Many new dates for megaliths were now available, and several from Brittany could be set back before 4000 BC when recalibrated, confirming that they did indeed antedate the supposedly earlier Spanish tombs (*op cit.*, tables on pp. 90–1). Renfrew summarized the new position in outspoken terms:

The implications are altogether clear: passage graves, some with corbelled vaults, were already being built in these regions before 2500 b.c. in radiocarbon years, and thus by 3300 BC in calendar years. Quite obviously, if they have their ultimate origin in the Aegean, this must have been a long time before 3000 BC Yet there are no collective built tombs in the Aegean until after this date. The Breton dates, even without calibration, make nonsense of the diffusionist case. If there are earlier passage graves in Brittany, why derive the Iberian ones from the east Mediterranean? (*op. cit.*, 89–90).

It should also be mentioned that not only are megaliths affected by recalibrated radiocarbon dates, but also a whole range of diffusionist connections between the Aegean area and the Balkans, western and northern Europe, with the same effect of placing supposed 'derivations' earlier than the cultures, artefacts or sites from which they were supposed to have 'diffused'; for instance, phase III of Stonehenge, previously assumed to have been inspired by Mycenean architecture, is now around 500 years too early.

The main challenge of reinterpreting the megaliths or any of these other new aspects of prehistory is to find an alternative to the diffusionist account – which was undeniably intellectually satisfying and methodologically sound for a long period. A key word which comes into play is **explanation**, for this whole issue has arisen at a time when many archaeologists are looking at rather different approaches to the past, and trying to replace the preoccupation with chronology, artefacts, and a narrative account of cultural developments by something more fundamental; some would claim to go as far as seeking general laws of human behaviour by which to explain cultures and the processes of cultural change. This will be examined before the reinterpretation of the megaliths is discussed.

Social evolution

Before looking at the so-called 'new' archaeology (how many movements have later regretted being dubbed 'new' when hindsight allows their place in a mainstream of development to be seen?), it is necessary to look back at early examples of the use of anthropology or even abstract political philosophy to provide frameworks for the interpretation of the past. At the most basic level, the drawing of analogies between New and Old World artefacts by early antiquaries is an obvious example of the kind of informative interaction that is possible between the observation of existing primitive cultures and those of the past (fig. 11). Stuart Piggott has drawn attention to the sociological approach of some French and Scottish (but not English) thinkers of the eighteenth century, of whom Rousseau is the most widely known; several different schemes were proposed for the development of human society through, for instance, hunting and fishing, pasturage, agriculture, and commerce (Piggott, 1976, 153).

The Antiquity of Man and Darwinian evolution became widely accepted in learned circles in the 1860s, and several books combined this sociological approach with more informed anthropological and archaeological observations, together with a concept of social evolution which was of course given greater credibility by the biological concepts of Darwin. Its clearest expression came in the American anthropologist Lewis Morgan's *Ancient Society* (1877), where the stages of development were further elaborated through the author's own knowledge of the American Indians. The book was subsequently raised to a dogmatic level by Friedrich Engels, who took over and completed some of Karl Marx's writings which it had inspired; Engels summarized Morgan's main stages in a work published in German in 1884:

Savagery – the period in which man's appropriation of products in their natural states predominates; the products of human art are chiefly instruments which assist this appropriation. Barbarism – the period during which man learns to breed domestic animals and to practise agriculture, and acquires methods of increasing the supply of natural products by human agency. Civilization – the period in which man learns a more advanced application of work to the products of nature, the period of industry proper and art.

A combination of concepts such as these with the Three-Age System's approach to the typology of artefacts did much to form the framework of many twentieth-century archaeological works, such as those of the Australian Marxist prehistorian V. Gordon Childe, in particular his popular work *What Happened in History* published in 1942, which has chapter headings such as 'Palaeolithic Savagery' and 'The Higher Barbarism of the Copper Age'. Childe was nevertheless immersed in a basically historical account of the past, through which diffusionism supplied a connecting thread; for prehistoric times, he defined recurrent groups of related artefacts and settlements as *cultures*, assuming that they represented a distinct ethnic or social reality. Historical archaeology provided a respectable antecedent for this view; many of the various peoples such as Huns or Goths who took part in the complex movements of the Migration Period in Europe in the late Roman period and its succeeding centuries could be matched with distinctive brooches, buckles, etc., from cemeteries found in areas where they were historically attested by contemporary historians (fig. 89).

In Europe, it was obvious that history gradually receded back into the unknown undocumented past, and it was very difficult to prevent the intrusion of concepts of nationalism into early times. A variant on Montelius' or Childe's diffusionism from the East was proposed by Gustav Kossina, who traced all major European developments from Germany – an idea taken up with enthusiasm after his death in 1931, because it gave a welcome pedigree to Nazi claims for the superiority of the Aryan race. American archaeologists were at a great advantage in this respect; their indigenous peoples and their predecessors were entirely unconnected with the Old World, and large numbers survived in various conditions in both North and South America, still following non-European lifestyles. The possibility for integrated anthropological and archaeological study was therefore apparent, working back from surviving peoples into the past; lessons for the Old World were also promising, as New World agriculture and civilization had developed independently, except in the minds of a few 'hyperdiffusionists' who claimed that they had resulted from contacts with Egypt, the Lost Tribe of Israel or other exotic cultures (the list still grows to this day). New World archaeology, particularly that of North America, had been largely ignored by European archaeologists. In the post-war decades, it has become a vigorous debating ground for new approaches to archaeological study, some of which have spilled out into the thinking of the rest of the world. Much of the discussion is conducted at a philosophical level, full of scientific or sociological terminology which makes it inaccessible to outsiders without a considerable effort.

PROCESSUALIST ARCHAEOLOGY

The best-known exponent of the 'new' archaeology is Lewis R. Binford, Professor of Anthro-

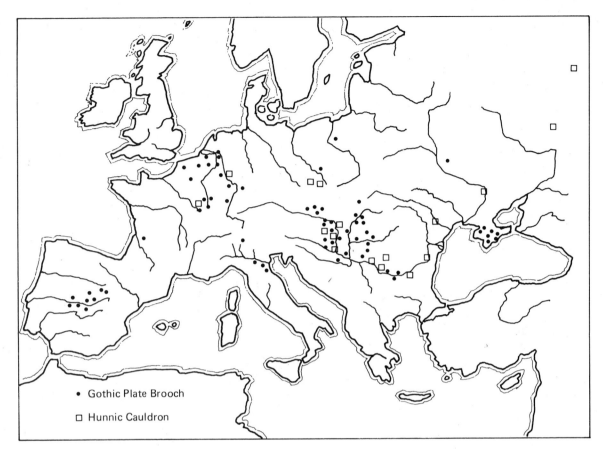

● Gothic Plate Brooch

□ Hunnic Cauldron

89 Do artefacts reflect people? Gordon Childe's concept of 'cultures' assumed that a recurrent assemblage of types represented some social, political or ethnic reality, conveniently called a culture in accordance with anthropological usage. The Migration Period in Europe (*c.* AD 400–700) allows some interesting comparisons to be made between historically documented invasions, migrations and settlements by known barbarian tribes. The successive settlement by the Goths of South Russia, Roumania/Hungary, Italy, and Spain are well illustrated by their distinctive plate-brooches, buried in the graves of women – but an important Gothic kingdom in south-west France is not revealed, whilst finds from between the Seine and Rhine would suggest substantial settlement there. In fact, the latter come from Frankish graves, having been adopted from the Gothic style of dress. More closely related to their historical situation are the bronze cauldrons of the Huns, an Asiatic nomad people who briefly dominated the whole of eastern and central Europe in the mid-fifth century AD, from eastern France to the Caucasus. *After Dixon 1976, 14*

pology at the University of New Mexico. In 1972 he published a collection of his own papers to illustrate various themes which he felt were particularly important, together with an amusing (if rather egocentric) autobiographical introduction in which he traced the influences –

evil or benign – of his university teachers. What emerges is his dissatisfaction with the chosen restrictions of traditional archaeology and anthropology, combined with a passion for precise scientific thinking, and 'theory' as a conscious working process. It is dangerous to attempt to summarize Binford, but some elements recur in his writings in a way which reflects his almost evangelist desire to propagate better modes of thought. 'Explanation' and 'process' are keywords; archaeology can provide a depth of information back into the past which anthropologists studying present societies cannot hope to achieve – none of them live long enough to see the unfolding of a major process. Unlike most traditional archaeologists, Binford does not find the small amount of archaeological evidence which actually survives and is recovered an inhibition:

It is highly improbable that the multiple, independent variables which determined the form of any item or the distribution of items should be restricted to only one component of a cultural system. This means that data relevant to most, if not all, the components of past sociocultural system *are* preserved in the archaeological record (*op. cit.*, 95).

From this follows the ability, and necessity, to examine social systems and processes through archaeological remains; but Binford goes further:

In our search for explanations of differences and similarities in the archaeological record, our ultimate goal is the formulation of laws of cultural dynamics (*op. cit.*, 100).

Process, as I understand it, refers to the dynamic relationships (causes and effects) operative among the components of a system or between systematic components and the environment. In order to deal with process we must seek explanations for observed phenomena, and it is only through explanations of our observations that we gain any knowledge of the past. *Explanation begins for the archaeologist when observations made of the archaeological record are linked through laws of cultural or behavioural functioning to past conditions or events.* Successful explanation and the understanding of process are synonymous, and both proceed dialectically – by the formulation of hypotheses (potential laws on the relationships between two or more variables) and the testing of their validity against empirical data. Hypotheses about cause and effect must be explicitly formulated and then tested. Only when this is done are we in a position to judge what facts might be relevant, only then can we objectively evaluate the implicit propositions which underly 'plausible' historical interpretations of archaeological data (*op. cit*, 117).

Most of the elements of the 'new' archaeology are encapsulated in this passage – process, system, explanation, laws, hypotheses, testing. **Systems theory** provides a useful way of studying the interactions between various parts of a society and its environment – they can be linked together in a diagram rather like that used for electrical circuits, including the concept of 'feedback', where an interaction actually changes part of the system. **Hypothesis formulation and testing** reflects the interest in scientific theory and the use of statistics; it is a development of traditional methods of reaching conclusions intuitively. The greatest sticking point is the question of **laws**, and the acceptance of the assumption that such laws not only exist but can be detected archaeologically is fundamental to the embracing of 'new' archaeology. Many would question whether any of its features are 'new'; in the view of Braidwood (who had come in for particularly acrimonious comment in Binford's autobiographical notes, right down to the weave of his tie and pattern of his shirt) it simply represents 'the obstreporous spirit of . . . the unrest of the Vietnam years. These people belonged to the "don't trust anybody over thirty" generation' (Braidwood 1981, 25).

A modified form of this view is found in Glyn Daniel's latest consideration of the history of archaeology:

The new archaeologists of the 1960s and their present followers in Britain and Scandinavia will become the disillusioned men of the 1980s and 1990s, realizing that man's past is something to be recorded, described, appreciated and understood, but that the hope of discovering laws of cultural dynamics in archaeology and anthropology is probably a vain one doomed to failure. I may be proved wrong, however; the history of archaeology is full of false assumptions and predictions' (1981, 192).

I share Glyn Daniel's suspicion of the pursuit of laws, but most archaeologists agree that the new archaeology has greatly improved the quality of information in some areas of archaeology, and has produced a better framework for seeking explanations for that very reason. It is in many ways similar to the demands made by Edward de Bono in the general field of problem solving by lateral thinking, in which a number of techniques are used to generate hypotheses, many of which may prove irrelevant, but the very act of thinking about them usually improves the conclusions which are reached (De Bono 1970).

New interpretations of megalithic tombs

Let us return to megalithic tombs to see what alternative to diffusion has been proposed by Renfrew, using the methods of new archaeology. He emphasizes that the **process** is as important as anything else:

... we are no longer obliged to see the tombs as the result of a single movement, whether it originated in Iberia or in Brittany (as one could now argue, on the basis of the new dates). Instead our task is to create some social model, some simple picture of how it all came about (1973, 124).

Renfrew then divides the area where megaliths are found into four or possibly five regions where an independent local origin could be claimed, rightly stressing that the tombs may be the only thing which their individual cultures have in common (fig. 90). He stresses that even the most magnificent tombs could have been built by a few hundred men from simple farming communities, using simple technology – a fact easily overlooked in our technological age. This is a good example of the setting-up of a hypothesis in the manner demanded by Binford; it is not the *result* of detailed research, but a stage within it:

What is argued ... is that the generation of inferences regarding the fact should not be the end-product of the archaeologist's work ... once a proposition has been advanced – no matter by what means it was reached – the next task is to deduce a series of testable hypotheses which, if verified against independent empirical data, would tend to verify the proposition (Binford, 1972, 90).

What Renfrew did was to examine two islands in different parts of Scotland (Arran and Rousay) where the survival of tombs was good, and to divide them up into hypothetical 'territories' around each tomb (fig. 91). Each was found to have a fairly consistent amount of potential farmland in its vicinity: 'The easiest

explanation, although perhaps not the only possible one, is that the nearby land was occupied by a single farming community' (*op. cit.*, 134). It is likely that at this period villages shifted regularly as land became exhausted, and the tombs might therefore have an added significance through their very permanence. Renfrew then proceeded to an important variable, population, and used modern ethnographic observations to arrive at figures of between 25 and 70 people for each of the 'territories' on the two islands in question – assuming that all of the tombs were in simultaneous use, a view reinforced by their even spacing. Further ethnographic parallels suggested a tribal social system of a fairly egalitarian nature, and other observations indicated that such tombs could be built in thirty days or more by around twenty able-bodied occupants of their territory. However, observations from a surviving 'megalithic' culture in Borneo suggested the possibility of communal efforts by neighbouring groups, with the social distinction denoted by a grand tomb as an incentive rather than a purely religious motivation. The culture in Borneo held an enormous feast to which local groups were invited, followed by a large combined building effort; an old man without heirs gave an exceptionally large feast which led to the construction of a particularly grand structure, clearly indicating that large tombs do not necessarily indicate high social status, but disposable resources. A further implication is that such monuments would continue to act as a focus not simply for burials, but also for the various feasts and ceremonies which were so important in the social interactions of these agricultural communities.

The hypothesis that such tombs were the products of small farming groups was thus tested against the geography of two islands, and information was fed in from ethnographic analogy, with the result that the phenomenon was demonstrated to be possible, although not of course proven. Further analogies, or new fieldwork and excavation on the islands concerned or others might produce counter-hypotheses which would need to be tested in similar ways. Binford would say that:

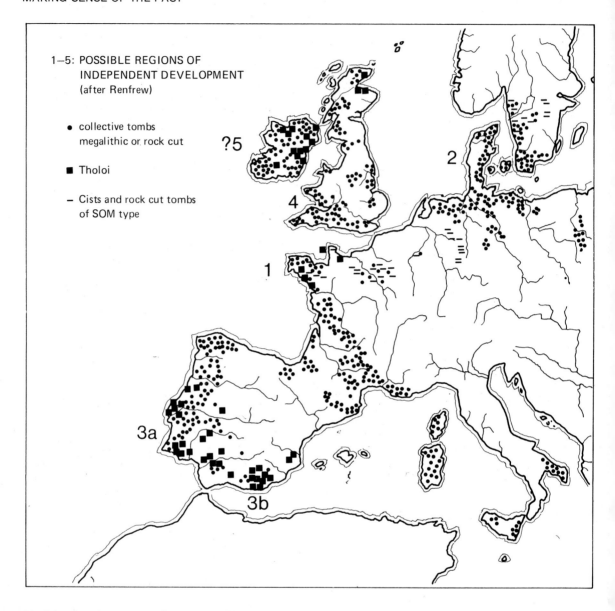

90 Distribution map of megalithic tombs; the *tholoi* are corbelled tomb chambers which it had been supposed were derived from examples in the Aegean area, but which are now known to be much earlier. Radiocarbon dates suggest that the earliest megalithic tombs are in Britanny, but rather than simply changing the origin of their diffusion to there, Renfrew has proposed five possible regions in which they may have developed *independently*. *After Fox 1959, fig. 7*

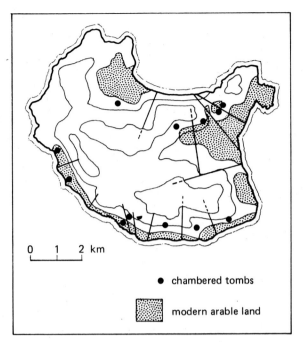

91 The island of Rousay in the Orkneys provides a case-study for the analysis of the inter-relationship of megalithic tombs; the island is small, with a high chance that all of the tombs there are known. Renfrew has proposed that the size of the hypothetical territories of each tomb (marked by lines) would be appropriate for a single farming community. *After Renfrew 1973, 136, fig. 30, with modifications from Renfrew 1979, fig. 4, 14*

As far as the truth value of any given proposition is concerned, the presence of equally defensible alternative propositions does not in any way diminish the potential truth value of any of the alternatives. The only method available . . . is to test them against relevant materials from the archaeological record (1972, 53).

From this attitude, a much more open-minded view of new evidence will proceed, for interpretations will not be so full of the personal or emotional commitment that can result from the development of a single interpretation based on traditional intuition.

Renfrew did not stop at the individual demonstration of the feasibility of local construction of megaliths; he also tackled the problem of

general explanation – why should similar monuments develop in as many as five different parts of the fringes of Europe (but nowhere else) at around the same time? The diffusionist explanation did at least have a single straightforward idea of missionaries from the Near East, or some related concept. Here, Renfrew's words have some echoes of the establishment of 'laws':

To make the coincidence understandable, all we have to do is show that the development of monumental building in this way was, in the special circumstances of each individual area, the natural result of intelligible processes operating more generally (*op. cit.*, 142).

He proposed (very tentatively) that the general process resulted from population pressures which developed as farming communities reached the coastal limits of Europe, combined with the influence of the indigenous local hunter-fisher peoples – in other words, similar circumstances producing similar results in separate but comparable areas. But whatever the ultimate truth:

. . . we can now begin to talk about these monuments in human terms, as a product of living communities, and to give full credit to their builders, the world's first architects in stone, without any longer appealing by way of explanation to the convenient arrival of wise men from the east (*op. cit.*, 146).

I have discussed the question of megaliths in some detail, because it demonstrates many features of the problem of making sense of the past. First, the impact of radiocarbon dates and their calibration into earlier calendar years shows just how quickly any long accepted interpretation of the past can come crashing down in ruins when one prop is removed. Secondly, this happened at just the time when new approaches and preoccupations were emerging from the United States. The re-interpretation of the megalithic tombs by Renfrew indicates how the theory can be applied in a real situation, and illustrates how important anthropological analogies can be in formulating hypotheses in archaeology which can then be tested. The greatest mistake to make now would be to

accept Renfrew's interpretation as the replacement for the diffusionist analysis; what makes the 'new' archaeology so important is its built-in recognition that a constant reshaping and even rejection of hypotheses is necessary. Any interpretation that reaches the fixed printed page is only a progress report; the rate of change is likely to increase rather than decline. Although good for archaeology itself, this is one of the factors which contributes to the growing difficulty that archaeologists find in communicating anything comprehensible to the public without over-simplification.

ETHNOARCHAEOLOGY (Hodder 1982a)

One important side-effect of the 'new' archaeology has been to revive the close relationship which existed in the nineteenth century between archaeology and anthropology. Both for the setting-up of hypotheses about the past and for seeking explanations, anthropology is an obvious source of information. It can provide a general background of how an activity such as trade, agriculture, or burial is carried out in different societies with varying social structures, religions, and resources; it can likewise provide a source of potential explanations for artefacts, sites or 'cultures' defined by archaeology – the use of observations from Borneo in the understanding of megaliths by Renfrew is a good example of the latter.

A more specific result of attempts to study past society and human behaviour has been the development of **ethnoarchaeology**. If anthropological observations are to be applied to archaeology, it is felt necessary to understand the nature of archaeological evidence more fully, and fieldwork has been carried out in several parts of the world in order to examine ways in which archaeological deposits are formed. Binford has made detailed studies of

92 Ethnoarchaeology; postgraduate students from Cambridge University observing a smith of the Tugen tribe (Barengo district, Kenya) making an iron spear. Studies of the physical traces left by such activities may help to elucidate Iron Age sites in other parts of the world. *Photograph by courtesy of Dr Ian Hodder*

Eskimos in Canada (Binford 1978), and Hodder has instigated several investigations in different parts of Africa (Hodder 1982b; fig. 92). Such studies are a matter of urgency, of course, for the number and range of primitive lifestyles still available for observation is rapidly diminishing. The results are not always encouraging, for many important social and economic activities can take place without leaving any helpful physical traces, but such difficulties must be faced if archaeology is to progress. In historically documented societies the problem can be approached through the study of sites and cultures about which literary accounts exist.

On the whole, closer contact between archaeology and anthropology is to be welcomed; a recent study concluded:

. . . anthropology's greatest potential contribution to the interpretation of archaeological evidence . . . (is) . . . not the identification of odd artefacts, nor the provision of information about any single aspect of human activity . . . but the provision of a framework for human action that shows us when the past has not been satisfactorily explained. If we are fortunate, the study of anthropology may also prompt new avenues of interpretation (Orme 1981, 284).

SPATIAL ARCHAEOLOGY AND THE LANDSCAPE

Both 'new' and 'traditional' archaeologists have taken a much broader interpretation of their sites and artefacts in recent decades. The study of the environment through animal species had of course formed an important part of Stone Age studies since the 1870s, when Lartet had divided the upper Palaeolithic according to its phases of species, such as the Cave Bear period or the Woolly Mammoth and Rhinoceros period. In the 1920s, pollen analysis allowed an elaborate sequence of climatic phases to be marked by the changing vegetation patterns. The mapping of archaeological finds, particularly when related to topography, and the general settings of sites visible on high-level aerial photographs all contributed to a stronger appreciation of the essential integration of finds, sites, and their natural setting, and the relationships which these implied. In recent decades this has resulted in increased research in two rather

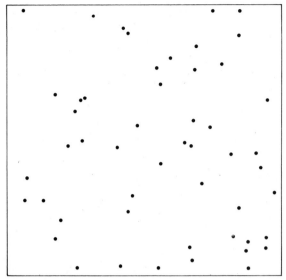

93 When is a distribution random? The human eye is very good at discerning patterns, and there appear to be clusters and centres of gravity in the points in this square, although the dots have been distributed in a mathematically random manner. Statistical tests can be applied to archaeological distributions of sites or artefacts to test whether they are significantly clustered or regularly spaced.

different directions – the general relationships between things, and the detailed development of the landscape. The former – **spatial archaeology** – is very much a product of 'new' archaeology and its methods, whilst the latter is more widely found amongst historical archaeologists; both have been influenced by recent developments in geography.

Spatial archaeology operates in a number of ways. It can examine different levels of information, from wide regional studies down to the positions of artefacts within a single building. Underlying the whole process is an elaborate battery of statistical techniques which attempt to establish basic considerations, such as whether a given scatter of points on a plan or map is random or has some structure, such as clusters or a regular spacing (fig. 93). The human eye is rather unreliable in this situation, and can often impose patterns on to random points without justification. When more than one kind of

artefact or settlement is mapped, comparisons between them may be made to establish the likelihood of a connection between them. Results are expressed in terms of probability rather than 'yes' or 'no', and of course are affected by the quality of both the information being used and the appropriateness of the statistical techniques employed. A consciousness of these problems is a positive factor, however:

It is important that most of the techniques . . . demand good data. Although bodies of reliable information are beginning to be collected and many have been used . . . , it is to be hoped that archaeologists will be stimulated by the possibilities offered by the techniques to collect in the future more data of high standard (Hodder and Orton, 1976, 238).

Settlement patterns are frequently studied, employing much theory and statistical techniques used by geographers; the relationship between large towns and smaller centres (fig. 94), the effects of the spacing of markets, the fall-off of traded goods as distance increases from their place of manufacture, can all be subjected to detailed study. Like other areas of 'new' archaeology, explanations can be sought through analogies drawn from historically documented societies or ethnographic observations. For instance, the realization that markets operating in a supply-and-demand manner are a fairly recent phenomenon has been instructive. Many early forms of trade were based on exchanges with strong social significance, such as the giving of lavish gifts in order to demonstrate wealth and power. Similarly, in the Near East, storehouse economies existed in which agricultural and other products were all collected by the royal or religious authorities and then redistributed down the social chain from warehouses (whose complicated recording systems gave a stimulus to the development of writing). Obviously, the processes of distribution will give rise to different patterns of site finds. Therefore, better mapping which shows information by means of a variety of symbols representing quantities as well as mere findspots, and negative symbols to show where items do *not* occur, should all make archaeological information clearer.

Landscape archaeology

This is closely related to the fieldwork techniques described in Chapter 2. Although it has no chronological limits, the availability of evidence in the field and in archives increases in recent centuries. The objectives are succinctly presented in a recent manual of techniques:

The landscape is a palimpsest on to which each generation inscribes its own impressions and removes some of the marks of earlier generations. Constructions of one age are often overlain, modified or erased by the work of another. The present patchwork nature of settlement and patterns of agriculture has evolved as a result of thousands of years of human endeavour, producing a landscape which possesses not only a beauty associated with long and slow development, but an inexhaustible store of information about many kinds of human activities in the past. The landscape archaeologist needs to develop an eye and a feeling for patterns in town and country and, even more important, to recognize anomalies in, for instance, the large isolated medieval church of the deserted medieval village; the straight stretch of stream channelled by monks in the thirteenth century; the regular eighteenth century Parliamentary enclosure hedge lying across medieval ridge and furrow; the lumpy ground next to the church, marking the site of an old settlement; and even a fine Jacobean building in an otherwise apparently poor area, indicating a former prosperity linked to a long-forgotten trade or industry. Ideally it should be possible to look at any feature in the landscape, know why it is there in that form, and understand its relation to other features (Aston and Rowley 1974, 14–15).

The process sounds almost mystical to the uninitiated, but is of course based on informed fieldwork and documentary research. When done properly, the results are suitable for subjection to some of the mathematical techniques of spatial analysis. It is also valuable in providing a background to the interpretation of aerial photographs, indicating the land-use at various periods which will have influenced the survival of surface features or created suitable conditions for the observation of crop-marks (above, pp. 45–8). The same considerations also help to explain the nature of any data, whether sites or artefacts, which is being subjected to statistical treatment; if half of an area has been farmed

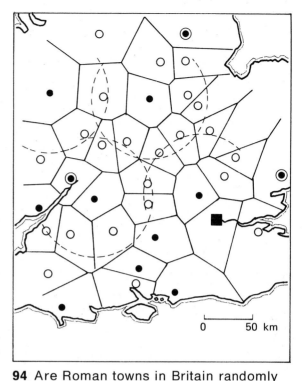

94 Are Roman towns in Britain randomly spaced? This study shows the hypothetical 'territories' of the towns by constructing Thiessen polygons around them in the manner already seen in the case of megalithic tombs on Rousay (fig. 91); their areas do not vary greatly. When circles are drawn centred upon four of the major tribal/regional capitals (filled circles), it can be seen that the lesser walled towns lie close to the perimeters of the circles, as geographical theory would predict. Different roles are implied for the *colonia* (ringed filled circles) and London (square). The obvious conclusion is that the towns of Roman Britain were *not* randomly spaced: the use of a 'model' derived from geography allows distributions of centres of varying sizes to be compared with an idealized theoretical distribution. If serious departures from a theoretical situation are encountered, further research is obviously required. *Hodder and Hassall, 1971*

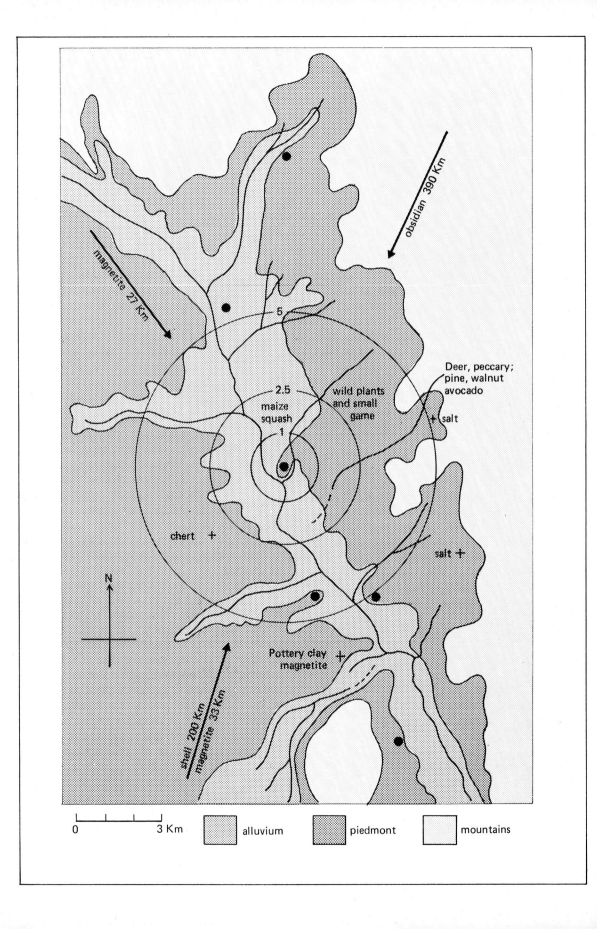

obsidian 390 Km

magnetite 27 Km

5

2.5
maize
squash

1

wild plants
and small
game

Deer, peccary;
pine, walnut
avocado

+ salt

chert +

salt +

N

Pottery clay +
magnetite

shell 200 Km
magnetite 33 Km

0   3 Km   alluvium   piedmont   mountains

consistently and the other half has been masked by woodland, casual finds of artefacts such as stone axes or pottery will be very different, for reasons which are artificial, and unrelated to the objects themselves. Such disturbing factors form an important level of information which can be added to distribution maps in order to clarify them.

Landscape archaeology is also essentially related to geology, in particular the nature of soils and surface deposits which influence agriculture and other resources for food-production or minerals. Given a free choice, a settlement is likely to be located where there is the optimum access to all the necessary parts of its economic system. This has given rise to **site catchment analysis**, a technique by which the potential resources within a day's walking distance of a site are surveyed. An arbitrary circle can be drawn around the site, or a more distorted territory constructed to take account of the actual terrain. Although this technique sounds rather mechanical, it does at least allow a clear perception of a site's potential, which can be compared with finds from its excavation; furthermore, a standardized measuring system such as an arbitrary 10km circle allows valid statistical comparisons to be made between sites. In Mexico, Flannery varied the catchment analysis by looking first at the items recovered on a site at San José Mogote, whose date centred on 1000 BC, and examining how large a catchment area would be necessary to acquire them (fig. 95). Essential agricultural needs would be fulfilled within 2.5km, and all but the more exotic materials within 5km; the 2.5km circle was then found to be the average 'territory' surrounding other local sites, without overlapping (Flannery, 1976).

95 Site catchment analysis: circles can be drawn around any site in order to study the resources theoretically available to its inhabitants, and the proportions of different kinds of agricultural land. This technique also allows separate sites to be compared. In this valley in Mexico, it can be seen that the sites are fairly evenly spaced at 5km intervals. *After Flannery 1976*

In Britain, interesting comparisons have been drawn between the kinds of farmland available to Roman villas and native sites of the same period, also compared with pre-Roman and Anglo-Saxon settlements; the villas, as expected, proved to draw upon the best balance of agricultural potential, reflecting their wealth and specialized economy (fig. 96). In addition, it has been observed that many medieval parishes perpetuate the boundaries of Anglo-Saxon estates, and show a fairly even distribution of arable and grazing land; this has the virtue of being a fairly 'natural' situation without circles or polygons imposed by landscape or spatial archaeologists – as well as giving some confidence in the validity of their approach. As the techniques of 'new' archaeology are applied more widely, beyond prehistory and primitive societies, it may well be found that some of the best testing situations lie within historical settings, where landscapes and documents have already been thoroughly examined and integrated.

'ASTRO-ARCHAEOLOGY'

One field of archaeology in which public interest has been sustained despite the advances of scientific terminology and mathematical techniques has been the relationship between ancient sites and astronomy. Part of the reason is the spectacular nature of Stonehenge and the religious associations of the sun and moon in many cultures. However, the subject also attracts the greatest number of those who roam what Glyn Daniel has called 'the wilder shores of archaeology', and astronomy is inevitably linked with space-gods, who are devoured by an eager public in terms of visitors from space who affected various aspects of past human culture.

It is evident from the history of archaeology that people often find reflections of the present in the past, and their preoccupations change in relation to the interests of their time. Thus, Napoleon was inspired to launch a great academic research team as well as an army on Egypt in 1798; similarly, Mussolini both invaded and studied the past of areas of north Africa, and restored and imitated Imperial Roman buildings there and in Italy. In the

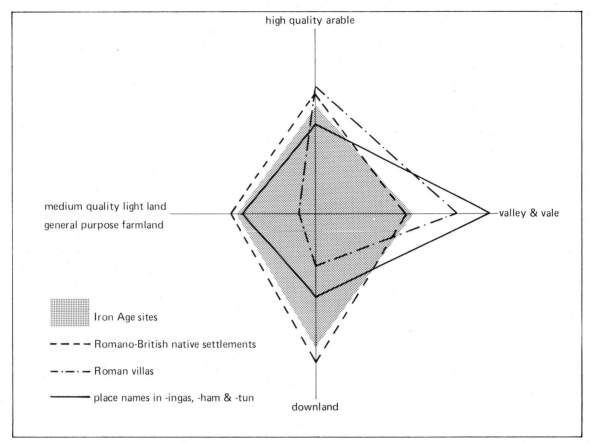

96 Direct comparisons between the catchments of sites of different types and dates in a single area can reveal different emphases in their agricultural resources. In this study of sites in southern England, pre-Roman Iron Age sites have an even balance of arable and grazing land when their catchment is assessed according to present land-classification; Roman native settlements show a similar catchment, which is not surprising, as most were probably farmed by descendants of the Iron Age population of the area. The specialized agriculture of Roman villas is clearly visible, with a greater proportion of valley and vale soils and high-quality arable rather than the less productive downland or medium-grade land. Anglo-Saxon sites deducible from place names return to a more even distribution, but have a greater emphasis on low-lying land. A further benefit of such studies is the economical way in which such complex information can be summarised in diagrammatic form. *Ellison and Harris 1972*

nineteenth century, 'Gothic' tastes of the Romantic movement favoured picturesque locations, and preferred prehistoric and medieval antiquities to those of the Greek or Roman period, which had been favoured by their Neo-Classical predecessors; country houses lost their columns and porticos, and gained battlements and turrets. Later, the industrial revolution led to an interest in technology and society; John Evans worked on new machinery for his paper mill by day, and classified bronze implements by night. Underlying such studies of artefacts or the evolution of society lay a confident assumption of progress and improvement.

On some occasions, the past has become a refuge from the present, or at least a lost ideal; European philosophers praised the life of the primitive 'noble savage' in the eighteenth century, as had Tacitus in the first century AD, whilst in both cases their governments conducted fierce conquests of such people for colonization and slavery. A similar reaction can be found in our time – alternative (i.e. simple) technology, self-sufficiency, and, I suppose, much of the general interest in the past, and prehistory in particular. An extension of these feelings is to claim that lost understanding and powers are somehow represented by ancient monuments. These ideas are commonly foisted onto megaliths, which at all times have been obvious and visible recipients of such attentions; Stukeley's Druids are not alone. A further element in such current interests is the idea of 'extraordinary' technical skills. Stonehenge is not only built of stones too heavy to lift, but it is a sophisticated computer! In the light of previous movements, it is not surprising that a reflection of the age of the computer, space flight and high technology should be sought in the past. How comforting for an anti-nuclear lobby to read of a veritable National Grid of 'lines of force' connecting monuments, which harnessed some lost source of power (which, presumably, did not have adverse environmental effects!).

What archaeologists find offensive in this kind of thinking – apart from the very naivety of any concept of a Golden Age fabricated as a reaction to or against the present – is that it seriously underestimates the abilities and aspir-

ations of early Man: astronomical calculations *were* important in an agricultural community, as any modern gardening calendar will show, and people *could* build impressive structures through brute force, organization, co-operation, and the desire to honour their dead, their gods, or their society. If extra-terrestrial beings did not build medieval cathedrals, why demand their influence in earlier societies?

Academic argument is often useless against such modes of thought, just as conventional theology is powerless against the Moonies; emotional commitment rather than reason is the driving force. Even on film, Erich von Däniken's public lectures look more emotionally satisfying than many a church service. All that archaeologists can do is to persevere in presenting their findings, however abstruse, in a clear and intelligible form, without evading the key issues or uncertainties. Surely continuing research and detailed evidence is just as potentially interesting as the easy answers and garbled information of the average astro-archaeologist?

Scholars make things very easy for themselves. They stick a couple of old potsherds together, search for one or two adjacent cultures, stick a label on the restored find and – hey presto! – once again everything fits splendidly into the approved pattern of thought. This method is obviously very much simpler than chancing the idea that an embarrassing technical skill might have existed or the thought of space travellers in the distant past. That would be complicating matters unnecessarily (Erich von Däniken, *Chariots of the Gods?* 1971, 37).

CONCLUSIONS
The interpretation of the past from archaeological remains has come a long way since antiquarians first managed to disprove Samuel Johnson's depressing contention that 'We can known no more than what old writers have told us'. More and more determined attempts were made to utilize physical traces of the past to reconstruct prehistoric times or to fill out the bare bones of poorly-documented historical periods. Some, like John Frere, hardly dared to countenance the great antiquity of man implied by stone implements found in deeply stratified

geological deposits (p. 15–19); others, such as Thomsen and Montelius, used common-sense observations about the technological development of artefacts to subdivide, classify, and even to attempt to date the great depths of prehistoric time (p. 31–4). Some wished for more vivid re-creations of the past, whether they involved the romantic Druids of William Stukeley (p. 26–7) or the inexorable stages of social development seen by the more anthropologically- and politically-minded Morgan or Childe (p. 160). In their own ways, von Däniken and Binford represent styles of interpretation which have an unbroken history of development stretching back at least to the eighteenth century. The terminology and preoccupations do of course change, but the objectives and attitudes to the evidence (not to mention the disputes with opponents) have a familiar ring. One of the great benefits of the retrospective study of archaeology is to appreciate this point, and to take a more detached view of any school of thought which claims to be new or to have sole possession of the truth.

An open-minded attitude is required not only in relation to changing fashions in archaeological interpretation, but to the subject as a whole. The lesson to be learnt from the rapid advance of scientific techniques in the last few decades is that new and revolutionary evidence may appear at any moment from a completely unsuspected source. My personal commitment to the subject is greatly enhanced by this aspect, for any discipline which incorporates so much uncertainty and so many different but valid academic approaches, and ignores the conventional boundaries between the sciences and the humanities, is well worth studying at school, university, or as a leisure pursuit. If my book has conveyed any of this feeling to its readers, I will consider its purpose to have been successfully achieved.

Further reading

Glyn Daniel's historical studies of archaeology discuss the changing concepts which influenced the study of the past, whilst a transatlantic perspective on the emergence and impact of the 'new' archaeology is very clearly presented by Brian Fagan's *In the Beginning*, 1979, chapter 3. Lewis Binford's *An Archaeological Perspective*, 1972, blends a semi-autobiographical commentary with a selection of the author's publications, which allow his theoretical approach to be seen at work on a variety of archaeological problems. The most important British contribution to 'new' archaeology is the massive *Analytical Archaeology* by David Clarke (1968: rather more accessible to the reader in its second edition, 1978).

Readers who wish to delve deeper into the 'new' archaeology may like to tackle Michael Schiffer's *Behavioral Archeology*, 1976, which sets up a theoretical strategy and then subjects an individual excavation to it, or Stanley South's *Method and Theory in Historical Archaeology*, 1977, to examine the impact of this kind of approach on historical sites of recent centuries in America.

Spatial analysis is comprehensively presented in Ian Hodder and Clive Orton's *Spatial Analysis in Archaeology*, 1976, and more simply in parts of *Mathematics and Archaeology* by Clive Orton, 1980. Landscape archaeology, its aims and methods of study are clearly presented in M. Aston and T. Rowley's *Landscape Archaeology: an Introduction to Fieldwork Techniques on Post Roman Landscapes*, (1974). From a more scientific point of view, Claudio Vita-Finzi's *Archaeological Sites in their Setting*, 1978, or Oliver Rackham's *Trees and Woodlands in the British Landscape*, 1976, show the contribution of specialist studies (see also Chapter 5).

Anthropology and ethnoarchaeology in archaeology can be studied through Ian Hodder's *The Present Past: an Introduction to Anthropology for Archaeologists*, 1982, or R.A. Gould's *Living Archaeology*, 1980; case-studies from Africa are presented in Ian Hodder's *Symbols in Action: Ethnoarchaeological Studies in Material Culture*, 1982.

The tricky subject of astroarchaeology ranges from serious mathematical studies such as

Douglas Heggie's *Megalithic Science: Ancient Mathematics and Astronomy in Northwest Europe* (1981) through harmless pursuits, for instance *The Ley Hunters' Companion* by P. Devereux and I. Thompson, 1979, to the unreason of Erich von Däniken (*Chariots of the Gods?: Unsolved Mysteries of the Past*, 1969, and its many sequels), whose popularity seems to known no bounds despite 'hatchet jobs' such as R. Story's *The Space Gods Revealed*, 1976.

Bibliography

AGACHE, R., *Détection Aérienne de Vestiges Protohistoriques, Gallo-Romaines et Médiévaux*, Amiens, 1970 (= Bull Soc. Préhist. Nord, 7)

AITKEN, M., 'Thermoluminescence and the archaeologist', *Antiquity*, 51 (1977), 11–19

ALCOCK, L., *By South Cadbury is that Camelot: the Excavation of Cadbury Castle 1966–1970*, London, 1972

ALEXANDER, J., *The Directing of Archaeological Excavations*, 1970

ASTON, M., & ROWLEY, T., *Landscape Archaeology: An Introduction to Fieldwork Techniques on Post-Roman Landscapes*, Newton Abbot, 1974

BACON, E., *The Great Archaeologists*, London, 1976

BANNISTER, B., 'Dendrochronology', in Brothwell & Higgs 1969, 191–205

BARKER, P., *Techniques of Excavation*, 1977

BERSU, G., 'Excavations at Little Woodbury, Wiltshire', *Proc. Prehist. Soc.*, 6 (1940), 30–111

BIDDLE, M., 'Excavations at Winchester, 1969: eighth interim report', *Antiq. J.*, 50 (1970), 277–326

BINFORD, L.R., *An Archaeological Perspective*, 1972

BINFORD, L.R., *Nunamiut Ethnoarchaeology*, 1978

BIRLEY, E., 'Excavations at Corstopitum, 1906–58', *Archaeologia Aeliana*, 37 (1959), 1–32

BIRLEY, E., & RICHMOND, I.A., 'Excavations at Corbridge, 1936–1938', *Archaeologia Aeliana* 15 (1938), 243–94

BOCQUET, A., 'L'histoire d'un village par la dendrochronologie', in *Vie Mystérieuse . . .*, 1980, 179–80

BOUCHER DE PERTHES, J. DE C., *Antiquités celtiques et antédiluviennes*, 2 vols., Paris, 1847–57

BRAIDWOOD, R.J., 'Archaeological retrospect 2', *Antiquity*, 55 (1981), 19–26

BROTHWELL, D., & HIGGS, E., ed., *Science in Archaeology*, 2nd ed., 1969.

BRUCE-MITFORD, R.L.S., ed., *Recent Archaeological Excavations in Europe*, London, 1975

BRUCE-MITFORD, R.L.S., *The Sutton Hoo Ship Burial: a Handbook*, London, 1979

CANN, J.R., DIXON, J.E., & RENFREW, C., 'Obsidian analysis and the obsidian trade', in Brothwell & Higgs 1969, 578–91

CASSON, S., *The Discovery of Man*, London, 1939

CHAMPION, S., *Dictionary of Terms and Techniques in Archaeology*, Oxford, 1980.

CHAPLIN, R.E., *The Study of Animal Bones from Archaeological Sites*, 1971

CHILDE, V.G., *What Happened in History*, Harmondsworth, 1942

CHRISTIE, H., 'Lom Stave church', *World Archaeol.*, 10 (1978–9), 192–203

CLARK, G.D., *World Prehistory: a New Outline*, Cambridge, 1969

CLARK, J.G.D., *World Prehistory in New Perspective*, Cambridge, 1977

CLARK, R.M., 'A calibration curve for radiocarbon dates', *Antiquity*, 49 (1975), 251–66

CLARKE, D.L., ed., *Models in Archaeology*, London 1972

CLARKE, D.L., *Analytical Archaeology*, 2nd ed. (revised by Bob Chapman), London, 1978

COLES, J.M., *Experimental Archaeology*, London, 1979

COLES, J.M., and ORME, B., review of Renfrew 1973, *Proc. Prehist. Soc.*, 40 (1974), 223–4

CRASTER, H.H.E., *A History of Northumberland, X, The Parish of Corbridge*, Newcastle, 1914

CRAWFORD, O.G.S., *Air-Photography for Archaeologists*, London, 1929

CUNLIFFE, B.W., *Fishbourne: a Roman Palace and its Garden*, London, 1971

DANIEL, G., *The Origins and Growth of Archaeology*, Harmondsworth, 1967

DANIEL, G., *150 Years of Archaeology*, 1975

DANIEL, G., *A Short History of Archaeology*, London, 1981

DARWIN, C., *The Origin of Species by Means of Natural Selection*, London, 1859

DAVID, R., *The Manchester Museum Mummy Project: Multidisciplinary Research on Ancient Egyptian Mummified Remains*, Manchester, 1979

DE BONO, E., *Lateral Thinking: a Textbook of Creativity*, London, 1970

DE LUMLEY, H., 'A palaeolithic camp at Nice', *Scientific American*, May 1969, 42–50

DEUEL, L., *Flights into Yesterday: the Story of Aerial Archaeology*, London, 1971

DEVEREUX, P., and THOMSON, I., *The Ley Hunter's Companion*, London 1979

DIMBLEBY, G.W., 'Pollen Analysis', in Brothwell & Higgs 1969, 167–77

DIMBLEBY, G.W., *Plants and Archaeology*, 2nd ed., London, 1978

DIXON, P., *Barbarian Europe*, Oxford, 1976

DORAN, J. and HODSON, F.R., *Mathematics and Computers in Archaeology*, Edinburgh, 1975

DOWMAN, E.A., *Conservation in Field Archaeology*, London, 1970

DYMOND, D.P., *Archaeology and History: a Plea for Reconciliation*, London, 1974

ELLISON, A., & HARRIS, J., 'Settlement and land use in the prehistory and early history of southern England', in Clarke 1972, 910–62

EVANS, A.J., 'Knossos I. The Palace', *Ann. Brit. School Athens*, 6 (1899–1900), 3–70

EVANS, A., *The Palace of Minos at Knossos, I: the Neolithic and Early and Middle Minoan Ages*, London, 1921

EVANS, J., 'On the occurrence of flint implements in undisturbed beds of gravel, sand, and clay', *Archaeologia*, 38 (1860), 280–307

EVANS, J., *Ancient Stone Implements*, London, 1872

EVANS, J., *Ancient Bronze Implements*, London, 1881

EVANS, JOAN, *A History of the Society of Antiquaries*, Oxford, 1956

EVANS, J.G., *Land Snails in Archaeology*, London, 1973

EVANS, J.G., *An Introduction to Environmental Archaeology*, 1978

EVANS, J.G., and LIMBREY, S., 'The experimental earthwork on Morden Bog, Wareham, Dorset, England: 1963 to 1972', *Proc. Prehist. Soc.*, 40 (1974), 170–202

FAGAN, B., *Elusive Treasure: the Story of Early Archaeologists in the Americas*, 1972

FISHER, C.S., *Excavations at Nippur: I, The Topography and City Walls*, Philadelphia, 1905

FLANNERY, K., *The Early Mesoamerican Village*, New York, 1976

FLEMING, S., *Dating in Archaeology: a Guide to Scientific Techniques*, 1976

FLEMING, S.J., *Thermoluminescence Techniques in Archaeology*, Oxford, 1979

FORSTER, R.H., & KNOWLES, W.H., 'Corstopitum: report on the excavations in 1914', *Archaeologia Aeliana*, 12 (1915), 226–86

FOWLES, J., ed., & LEGG, R., annot., *John Aubrey's Monumenta Britannica, Parts 1 and 2*, Sherborne, 1980

FOX, C., *The Personality of Britain*, 4th edn., Cardiff, 1959

FRERE, J., 'Account of flint weapons discovered at Hoxne in Suffolk', *Archaeologia*, 13 (1800), 204–5

FRIEDMAN, I., SMITH, R.L., & CLARK, D., 'Obsidian dating', in Brothwell & Higgs 1969, 62–75

FUNK, R.E., *Recent Contributions to Hudson Valley Prehistory*, New York, 1976

GENTNER, W., and LIPPOLT, H.J., 'The potassium-argon dating of Upper Tertiary and Pleistocene deposits', in Brothwell & Higgs 1969, 88–100

GIOT, P.-R., 'The chambered barrow of Barnenez in Finistère', *Antiquity*, 32 (1958), 149–53

GLOB, P.V., *The Bog People: Iron Age Man Preserved*, London, 1969

GOODYEAR, F.H., *Archaeological Site Science*, 1971

GOUGH, R. (trans. and ed.), *Britannia*, by William Camden, 3 vols. London, 1789

GOULD, R.A., *Living Archaeology*, Cambridge, 1980

GRAHAM-CAMPBELL, J., *The Viking World*, London, 1980

GREENE, J.P., & GREENE, K.T., 'A Trial Excavation on a Romano-British site at Clanacombe, Thurlestone, 1969', *Proc. Devon Archaeol. Soc.*, 28 (1970), 130–136

GUILDAY, J.E., 'Animal remains from archaeological excavations at Fort Ligonier', *Ann. Carnegie Mus.*, 42 (1970), 177–86

HAARNAGEL, W., *Die Grabungen Feddersen-Wierde*, 2 vols., 1979

HALL, J.A., & HEWSON, A.D., 'On-line computing and radiocarbon dating at the British Museum', *J. Archaeol. Sci.*, 4 (1977), 89–94

HANSON, W.S., DANIELS, C.M., DORE, J.N., & GILLAM, J.P., 'The Agricolan supply base at Red House, Corbridge', *Archaeologia Aeliana*, 7 (1979), 1–97

HÄRKE, H., 'Probleme der optischen Emissionsspektralanalyse in der Urgeschichtsforschung. Technische Möglichkeiten und methodische Fragestellungen', *Prähist. Z.*, 53 (1978), 165–276. (English summary 257–61)

HARRIS, E.C., 'Units of archaeological stratification', *Norweg. Archaeol. Rev.*, 10, 1977, 84–94

HARRIS, E.C., *Principles of Archaeological Stratigraphy*, 1979

HATT, G., *Nørre Fjand, an Early Iron Age Village in West Jutland*, Copenhagen, 1957

HAWKES, J., *Mortimer Wheeler: Adventurer in Archaeology*, London, 1982

HEGGIE, D.C., *Megalithic Science: Ancient Mathematics in North-West Europe*, London, 1981

HIGHAM, C.F.W., & MESSAGE, M.A., 'An assessment of a prehistoric technique of bovine husbandry', in Brothwell & Higgs 1969, 315–30

HODDER, I., *The Present Past: an Introduction to Anthropology for Archaeologists*, London, 1982

HODDER, I., *Symbols in Action: Ethnoarchaeological Studies of Material Culture*, Cambridge, 1982

HODDER, I., & HASSALL, M., 'The non-random spacing of Romano-British walled towns', *Man*, 6 (1971), 391–407

HODDER, I., & ORTON, C., *Spatial Analysis in Archaeology*, Cambridge, 1976

HODSON, R.F., 'Classification by computer', in Brothwell & Higgs 1969, 649–60

HOLE, F., FLANNERY, K.V., & NEELY, J., *Prehistory and Human Ecology of the Deh Luran Plain*, Ann Arbor, 1969

HOLM, B., & REID, B., *Indian Art of the Northwest Coast: a Dialogue on Craftsmanship and Aesthetics*, Washington, 1979

HORSLEY, J., *Britannia Romana*, London, 1732

JUDD, N.M., *The Architecture of Pueblo Bonito*, Washington, 1964

JUNGHANS, S., SANGMEISTER, E., & SCHRÖDER, M., *Kupfer und Bronze in der frühen Metallzeit Europas*, Berlin, 1974

KENT, J.P.C., *Roman Coins*, London, 1978

KLINDT-JENSEN, O., *A History of Scandinavian Archaeology*, London, 1975

KNOWLES, W.H., & FORSTER, R.H., *The Romano-British Site at Corstopitum: an Account of the Excavations during 1909*, London & Newcastle upon Tyne, 1910

LANE-FOX, A., 'On the evolution of culture', *Notices Proc. Roy. Inst. Grt. Brit.*, 7 (1875), 496–520

LANGDON, S., *Die neubabylonischen Königinschriften*, 1912

LEAKEY, R.E., & LEWIN, R., *Origins*, London 1977

LÉVA, C., & HUS, J.J., 'Recent archaeological discoveries in Belgium by low-level aerial photography and geophysical survey', in Wilson 1975, 81–102

LIMBREY, S., *Soil Science and Archaeology*, 1975

LYELL, C., *Principles of Geology*, 3 vols., London, 1830, 1832, 1833

LYELL, C., *The Geological Evidences of the Antiquity of Man*, London, 1863

MANNING, W.H., *Report on the Excavations at Usk 1965–1976: the Fortress Excavations 1968–1971*, Cardiff, 1981

MATTINGLY, H., (trans.), *Tacitus on Britain and Germany*, Harmondsworth, 1948

MERCER, E., *English Vernacular Houses*, London, 1975

MEYER, K.E., *The Plundered Past*, 1973

MICHELS, J.W., *Dating Methods in Archaeology*, 1973

MILLON, R., 'Teotihuacan', *Scientific American*, June 1967, 38–48

MODDERMAN, P., 'Elsloo, a neolithic farming community in the Netherlands', in Bruce-Mitford 1975, 260–86

MONTELIUS, O., *Die typologische Methode. Die ältere Kulturperioden im Orient und in Europa*, Stockholm 1903

MORGAN, L.H., *Ancient Society: or Researches in the Lines of Human Progress from Savagery through Barbarism to Civilization*, 1877

MOORE, P.D., & WEBB, J.A., *An Illustrated Guide to Pollen Analysis*, 1978

MUELLER, J.W., ed., *Sampling in Archaeology*, Tucson, 1975

NORMAN, E.R., & ST. JOSEPH, J.K., *The Early Development of Irish Society*, Cambridge, 1969

OAKLEY, K.P., 'Analytical methods of dating bones', in Brothwell & Higgs 1969, 35–45

OATES, D. & J., *The Rise of Civilization*, Oxford, 1976

ODDY, W.A., ed., *Aspects of Early Metallurgy*, London, 1977

ORME, B., *Anthropology for Archaeologists*, London, 1981

ORTON, C., *Mathematics in Archaeology*, London, 1980

PEACOCK, D.P.S., *Pottery and Early Commerce: Characterization and Trade in Roman and Later Ceramics*, London, 1977

PETRIE, W.M.F., 'Sequences in prehistoric remains', *J. Royal Anthr. Inst.*, 29 (1899), 295–301

PETRIE, W.F., *Prehistoric Egypt*, London, 1920

PIGGOTT, S., *Ancient Europe from the Beginnings of Agriculture to Classical Antiquity*, Edinburgh, 1965

PIGGOTT, S., *Antiquity Depicted: Aspects of Archaeological Illustration*, London, 1979

PIGGOTT, S., *Ruins in a Landscape: Essays in Antiquarianism*, Edinburgh, 1976

PITT-RIVERS, GENERAL, *Excavations in Cranborne Chase*, 4 vols., 1887–1898

PRESTWICH, J., 'On the occurrence of flint implements, associated with the remains of extinct mammalia, in undisturbed beds of a late geological period', *Proc. Royal Soc. London*, 10 (1860), 59–9

PYDDOKE, E., ed., *The Scientist and Archaeology*, London, 1963

RACKHAM, O., *Trees and Woodland in the British Landscape*, London, 1976

RENFREW, C., ed., *British Prehistory: a New Outline*, London, 1974

RENFREW, C., *Investigations in Orkney*, Rep. Res. Comm. Soc. Antiq. London, 38, London, 1979

RENFREW, C., *Before Civilization: the Radiocarbon Revolution and Prehistoric Europe*, 1973

RENFREW, J., *Palaeoethnobotany: the Prehistoric Food Plants of the Near East and Europe*, New York, 1973

REYNOLDS, P.J., *Iron-Age Farm: The Butser Experiment*, London, 1979

RODWELL, W., *The Archaeology of the English Church*, London, 1982

ST. JOSEPH, J.K., 'Air reconnaissance: recent results, 26', *Antiquity*, 45 (1971), 298–9

SCHIFFER, M. B., *Behavioral Archeology*, New York, 1976

SCHLIEMANN, H., *Ilios: the City and Country of the Trojans*, 1880

SCHÖNBERGER, H., 'The Roman frontier in Germany: an archaeological survey', *J. Rom. Stud.*, 59 (1969), 144–97

SCIENTIFIC AMERICAN. *Avenues to Antiquity* (readings from *Scientific American*), San Francisco, 1976

SHACKLEY, M., *Environmental Archaeology*, London, 1982

SHERRATT, A., ed., *The Cambridge Encyclopedia of Archaeology*, Cambridge, 1980

SMITH, R.A., *A Guide to the Antiquities of the Bronze Age*, 2nd ed., London, 1920

SOUTH, S., *Method and Theory in Historical Archaeology*, New York, 1977

STENBERGER, M., ed., *Vallhagar, a Migration Period Settlement on Gotland, Sweden*, Copenhagen & Stockholm, 1955

STORY, R., *The Space Gods Revealed*, New York, 1976

STUART, J. & REVETT, N., *The Antiquities of Athens*, I, 1762; II, 1787; III, 1794; IV, 1816; V, 1830

STUKELEY, W., *Itinerarium Curiosum*, London, 1776

TARLING, D.H., 'Archaeomagnetism: the dating of archaeological materials by their magnetic properties', *World Archaeol.*, 7 (1975), 185–197

TARLING, D., *Palaeomagnetism: Principles and Applications in Geology, Geophysics, and Archaeology*, London, 1983

TAYLOR, C., *Fieldwork in Medieval Archaeology*, 1974

THOMPSON, F.H., 'Three Surrey hillforts: excavations at Anstiebury, Holmbury, and Hascombe, 1972–1977', *Antiq. J.*, 59 (1979), 245–318

THOMSON, M.W., *General Pitt-Rivers: Evolution and Archaeology in the Nineteenth Century*, Bradford on Avon, 1977

TITE, M.S., *Methods of Physical Examination in Archaeology*, 1972

TYLECOTE, R.F., *A History of Metallurgy*, London, 1976

VIE MYSTERIEUSE.. . , *La Vie Mystérieuse des Chefs-d'Oeuvre: la Science au Service de l'Art*, Paris, 1980 (Catalogue of an exhibition held at the Grand Palais, Paris, 1980–1)

VITA-FINZI, C., *Archaeological Sites in their Setting*, London, 1978

VON DÄNIKEN, E., *Chariots of the Gods?*, London, 1969

WACHER, J.S., *The Towns of Roman Britain*, London, 1974

WELLS, C., *Bones, Bodies and Disease*, 1964

WHEELER, R.E.M., & WHEELER, T.V., *Verulamium: a Belgic and two Roman Cities*, Rep. Res. Comm. Soc. Antiq. Lond., 11, Oxford, 1936

WHEELER, R.E.M., *Archaeology from the Earth*, London, 1954

WHEELER, R.E.M., *The Stanwick Fortifications*, Rep. Res. Comm. Soc. Antiq. Lond., 17, Oxford, 1954

WHEELER, R.E.M., *Still Digging*, London, 1955

WIHR, R., 'Konservierung und Restaurierung des silbertauschierten Pferdegeschirrs von Olk, Krs. Trier-Saarburg', *Trier. Z.*, 33 (1973), 277–291

WILLIS, E.H., 'Radiocarbon dating', in Brothwell & Higgs 1969, 46–57

WILSON, D., *Science and Archaeology*, Harmondsworth, 1978

WILSON, D.R. (ed.), *Aerial Reconnaissance for Archaeology*, Council Brit. Archaeol, Res. Rep., 12, 1975

WILSON, D.R., *Air Photo Interpretation for Archaeologists*, London, 1982

WINKELMANN, W., 'Eine westfälische Siedlung des 8 Jahrhunderts bei Warendorf, Kr. Warendorf', *Germania*, 32 (1954), 189–213

WOOD, J.T., *Discoveries at Ephesus*, 1877

WOOLLEY, L, 'Corstopitum: provisional report of the excavations in 1906', *Archaeologia Aeliana*, 3 (1907), 161–86

WOOLLEY, SIR L., *Spadework*, London, 1953

WORSAAE, J.J.A., *Primeval Antiquities of Denmark*, (trans. W.J. Thoms) London, 1849

ZEUNER, F.E., *Dating the Past: an Introduction to Geochronology*, London, 1946

Glossary

Absolute date A date which, unlike a relative date, can be expressed in calendar years

Adobe Sun-dried mud brick

Anthropology The study of man as an animal: social anthropology concentrates on patterns of behaviour and institutions

Archaeology The study of the past through its physical remains

Archaeomagnetic dating A method exploiting changes in the direction and intensity of the earth's magnetic field

Artefact An object made or used by man

Assemblage A range of objects found associated together

Astroarchaeology The study of the astronomical relationships of ancient sites, or interpretations of the past involving intervention by 'space gods'

Brownearth The soil type resulting from prolonged forest conditions

Classification An essential stage in the sorting and description of artefacts or sites; it may be based on form, material, or complex mathematical considerations. See also Typology

Coprolites Human or animal faeces preserved in arid or frozen conditions

Crop marks Indications of buried sites revealed by the abnormal growth of overlying crops

Cross dating The extrapolation of dates from one area or culture to another, often through finds of historically-dated artefacts exported into an adjacent undocumented area

Culture Archaeologically, a recurrent assemblage of sites and artefacts; in anthropology, the term has a wider significance including behaviour and beliefs as well as physical objects

Cumulative section A record of a stratigraphic sequence in which each layer is drawn and then removed, rather than left standing as a reference and drawn in its entirety at the end of the excavation

Cuneiform Writing system developed in Mesopotamia, using combinations of wedge-shaped impressions on clay tablets

Dendrochronology Dating timber by counting annual growth rings

Diffusionism A concept of the spread of technology or civilization through the diffusion of improvements from a single centre; an alternative concept is that similar developments may occur independently in similar social or environmental conditions

Environmental archaeology The study of any aspects of the environment of man in the past, whether biological, botanical, or geographical

Ethnoarchaeology The study of living societies in order to elucidate the formation and interpretation of physical traces encountered on ancient sites

Experimental archaeology The study of artefacts, structures, etc. through scientifically controlled experiments and simulations

Feature Any man-made pit, post hole or other disturbance encountered in an excavation; it is a useful neutral term for the initial stages of site recording before more precise interpretations are given

Fieldwalking Systematic exploration of an area by teams of walkers, collecting and recording surface artefacts or noting earthworks and other phenomena

Fieldwork Any form of archaeological research carried out beyond the confines of a museum or office – excavation, surveying, fieldwalking, etc.

Fission track dating A technique in which microscopic damage-trails resulting from the decay of radioactive impurities in glass or glassy minerals are counted

Flotation The recovery of small seeds, bones, etc., using a machine which agitates a sample of soil in water, causing these items to separate from heavier soil particles and to float on the surface in a frothing agent which can be skimmed off

Foundation trench Trench dug into the subsoil to accommodate hardcore or walling to provide support for the superstructure of a building

Geophysical prospecting The location and recording of buried sites by means of variations in the magnetic properties or resistance to an electrical current of the soil

Grid system Excavation trenches laid out according to a regular grid, leaving unexcavated baulks between them; also known as a box system

Harris matrix Methods of summarizing the vertical and horizontal interrelationships of all of the layers and features on a site in a diagrammatic form

Hunter-gatherer Member of a group subsisting from the hunting of animals and collection of wild plants rather than settled agriculture

Hydration rim Surface layer on obsidian artefacts which can be measured as a dating technique

Interface The point of contact between two layers or features in an excavation; it need not have any physical existence, but is stratigraphically important, such as the interface between the fill of a buried ditch and the soil through which it was dug

Isotope A form of an element with a specific number of electrons; many (such as carbon 14 or potassium 40) are unstable, and decay into different elements, releasing their surplus electrons. Radiocarbon, potassium-argon, fission track and thermoluminescence dating all rely on this phenomenon in different ways

Magnetometer Machine used in geophysical surveying to measure the strength of the local magnetic field at regular intervals over a buried site

Megaliths Tombs and other structures built from very large stones, principally during the later stone and early bronze ages

Mesopotamia The area containing the valleys of the Tigris and Euphrates rivers, largely contained in present-day Iraq

Methodology Working concepts or approach, whether consciously adopted or otherwise acquired

Midden Rubbish deposit, usually from cooking

Mud brick Unfired, sun dried construction medium commonly used in the dry climates of the Near East and Mesoamerica from antiquity to the present

New archaeology A movement which began in America in the 1960s, aimed towards consciously scientific studies of the past, and explanations based on carefully designed models of human behaviour; its novelty and scientific pretensions are hotly disputed

Obsidian Naturally-occurring volcanic glass, valued for the manufacture of stone tools

Palisade Continuous wall of upright posts, usually set side by side in a continuous foundation trench

Palynology The study of pollen

Pedology The study of soils

Petrology The identification of stone, usually by microscopic or spectrographic analysis (see Spectrometry)

Podsol A soil type characteristic of heath or moorland

Pollen analysis The identification and interpretation of pollen grains recovered from soil or peat samples

Post hole A cavity or soil-filled indication of a timber upright; more precisely, a post pipe marks the position of a post in a pit dug to accommodate it and any packing added to increase its stability

Potassium argon dating A technique in which the decay of an isotope of potassium into the gas argon is measured

Potsherd, sherd A fragment of broken pottery

Prehistory The period before written history begins in a given area; the term Protohistory is occasionally applied to the archaeology of an area during the period when adjacent cultures were using written records but before its own began.

Processual archaeology The study of processes of cultural change, usually in a manner characteristic of the exponents of the 'new' archaeology

Pueblo A form of Indian settlement found in the south west of the United States

Radiocarbon dating A technique based on the counting of decays of isotopes of carbon 14 in samples of charcoal or other organic materials

Recalibration A correction process carried out on radiocarbon dates to adjust them to calendar years, using results gained from dated tree-rings

Relative date A date which can be said to be earlier than, later than, or contemporary with an event but which (unlike an absolute date) cannot be measured in calendar years

Rendsina A soil type characteristic of chalk or limestone subsoils

Resistivity The resistance of soil or buried features to the passage of an electrical current, measured during geophysical surveying

Ridge and furrow A pattern of parallel ridges resulting from the ploughing of strip fields in medieval and later open field systems

Robber trench A trench left by the removal of foundations of buildings for re-use in other structures

Sampling The selection of part of a site for excavation or an area for fieldwork, preferably according to a strategy which allows statistical estimates of the relation of the sample to the unexplored parts of the whole site or area

Section A vertical record of the stratification of a site or feature, either left standing for study during excavation or drawn cumulatively

Sequence dating A technique by which Petrie arranged undated graves into a hypothetical (relative) chronological order according to the typology and association of the artefacts found in them

Seriation A technique of relative dating by which the proportions of particular artefacts or types are compared on a site or between several sites, and arranged in a series so that individual types appear, flourish, and decline in an orderly manner

Shadow sites Traces of sites in low relief on the surface of the ground, highlighted by low sunlight

Site catchment analysis The measurement of the availability of different resources within an arbitrary circle centred upon an individual site, in order to study its possible economic system and to compare it with other sites

Sleeper beam A large horizontal timber into which uprights are socketed to construct the frame of a building

Soil marks Traces of buried sites on the surface of ploughed or otherwise disturbed ground

Sondage A trial excavation trench, also known as a test pit; the term is often associated with the investigation of the deep stratigraphic record of 'tells' in the Near East

Spatial archaeology The study of the interrelationship of sites with each other and their environments, or the distribution patterns of artefacts, using analytical methods derived from geography

Spectrometry The analysis of the constituent elements of metals, stone, or other materials by the measurement of the wave-lengths of light or radiation emitted from them

Strata Layers: the term has been adopted from geology

Stratification The accumulated sequence of strata on a site

Stratigraphy The study and interpretation of stratification

Terminus ante quem/terminus post quem A fixed date or stratigraphical point in relation to which an artefact or stratum can be said to be respectively earlier or later

Tell A man-made mound, often found in the Near East, resulting from the repeated construction, occupation and demolition of buildings on the same site

Thermoluminescence A dating technique in which energy derived from radioactive impurities trapped in minerals is released in the laboratory and measured: it is of considerable importance in the dating of pottery

Three Age System The division of prehistory into three successive technological stages characterized by the use of stone, bronze and iron. At first entirely hypothetical, these divisions were confirmed by archaeological observations

Trace elements Rare but sometimes significant elements revealed by spectrometry, which may help to define the origins of metal ores, obsidian, minerals in pottery, etc.

Type series The arrangement of a particular form of artefact into a logical series, usually according to a progression of changes in its shape, which sometimes reflect its efficiency in use. In the latter circumstances it provides a form of relative dating for objects, as well as a means of subdivision for the purposes of classification

Typology The study of changes in the form of classes of artefacts

Unit of stratification A neutral term which can be applied to any layers, interfaces, or structures encountered in the recording of the stratification of an excavation

Varves Annual deposits found in river and lake beds near glaciers, reflecting the fluctuation of the flow of water during periods of freezing and melting

Index